HENRY
CLAY
FRICK

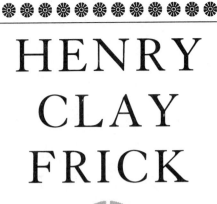

HENRY CLAY FRICK

The Gospel of Greed

Samuel A. Schreiner, Jr.

ST. MARTIN'S PRESS   *New York*

Design by Sara Stemen

Library of Congress Cataloging-in-Publication Data

Schreiner, Samuel Agnew.
    Henry Clay Frick : the gospel of greed / Samuel A. Schreiner, Jr.
        p.   cm.
    ISBN 0-312-11821-X
    1. Frick, Henry Clay, 1849–1919.   2. Businessmen—United States—Biography.   3. Capitalists and financiers—United States—Biography.
I. Title.
HC102.5.F75S34   1995
338.092—dc20
[B]
                                                                94-46628
                                                                CIP

First Edition: April 1995

10   9   8   7   6   5   4   3   2   1

To my wife, Dorrie, who long ago planted the seed that grew into this work when she suggested writing about the fabulous moneymakers of my native Pittsburgh area.

Contents

PREFACE

"See Him in Hell . . ."

ANDREW Carnegie, the penniless Scotch immigrant who turned steel into gold in 1901 to become the richest man in America, couldn't stand to be disliked. For years he was troubled by the fact that the man most responsible for his great wealth hated him. He could almost feel the heat of that hatred drifting up New York's fashionable Fifth Avenue, where he and Henry Clay Frick lived in palatial homes within walking distance of each other. From the day of their parting in Pittsburgh, Carnegie never saw nor heard a word from his former partner despite the fact that they still moved in the same financial circles and shared front-page coverage in the newspapers for their philanthropic and political activities and their frequent trans-Atlantic crossings. Finally, when his health was failing fast, Mr. Carnegie sent word to Mr. Frick that he would like to arrange a friendly meeting during which old grievances would be set aside.

The response, delivered verbally through Carnegie's messenger, must have been a shock to a man of Carnegie's ebullient and sunny nature: "Tell Mr. Carnegie I'll see him in hell, where we both are going."

Although nobody has suggested that Frick's blunt words were responsible, Carnegie died in August 1919, soon after receiving them. If it happened at all, the meeting Frick foresaw was not long in coming. Before the year was out, Frick, a considerably younger man, died, too.

It may be that Frick, a man of few words and fewer illusions, intended to strike a note of grisly humor. Instead, he struck a note of grim truth. Unlike Carnegie, Frick never pretended that the business of business was earning the love of his fellow man. The business of business was making money, and few men in American history have been better at making money than Henry Clay Frick. In 1910, with Carnegie and John D. Rockefeller retired and Andrew Mellon still largely unknown, Henry Clay Frick was listed by *The New York Times* as one of the nation's seven leading financiers. Looking back eighty years, a modern historian described Frick as "the plenipotentiary of his age." In a tough, competitive world, a man didn't reach such heights by being loved. Frick knew it, and he expressed nothing but scorn for what he regarded as Carnegie's hypocritical posturings.

Frick's toughness, particularly in his stoic acceptance of the shedding of blood—even his own—to put labor in its place, made him a hero to peers with names like Rockefeller, Morgan, Harriman, Stillman, Vanderbilt, and Mellon, the wealthiest of the wealthy. In a tone of reluctant admiration, Matthew Josephson, the chronicler of the "robber barons," called Frick a "master of all honorable tricks." But Frick's arrogance and ruthlessness in financial matters caused him to be called many other things, among them "toad" and "tyrant." He was undoubtedly of that goodly company that an ungrateful President of Frick's own making called "malefactors of great wealth."

Henry Clay Frick was the quintessential capitalist, a truly representative figure of America's Gilded Age. The span of his adult years corresponded almost exactly with that of the fantastic period of explosive growth in material wealth that made the United States of America the richest, most powerful nation on earth. Everything was up for grabs, and the spoils were plucked by those with the greediest grasp. Moneymaking was the national sport. Men of business were the admired celebrities of the age, as politicians and soldiers had been before them and as athletes and actors would be in an age to come. What Frick and his fellow architects of corporate America did and said was readily accepted as the ethic of the business world, the dominant ethic of American society then and again, nearly a century later, in the time of Ronald Reagan. In a popular book, Andrew Carnegie proudly proclaimed a happy "Gospel of Wealth," but, as Frick revealed in his bitter joke, the moneymakers lived by a gospel of greed.

The sharp edges of the portraits of these early men of money have been softened by time and the benevolences that have made their names synonymous with benign institutions. In New York, they would be known on first thought for the Frick Collection, Carnegie Hall, the Morgan Library, Rockefeller Center; in Pittsburgh, it would be Carnegie Mellon University (an odd combination in the eyes of history), Carnegie Library, Frick Park, Clayton (the Frick home) and its associated museum. Just as they established the ethic of acquiring unspendable personal wealth, they set an example of its distribution for public purposes that the rich still follow to this day. One shared passion among the very rich, then and now, was collecting antiques and works of fine art from around the world. In this, as in business, Frick occupied the position of *primus inter pares*. His collection of paintings and objects, housed in the Fifth Avenue home where he died and now open to the public, is a glittering gem—a tribute to his self-educated taste and evidence that he knew "all the honorable tricks" of collecting as well as doing business.

Despite his prominence, Henry Clay Frick was—and remains—something of an enigma. He was a silent man, a private man. He didn't make speeches or write articles and books. As a sworn witness in court or at legislative hearings, he was reticent and evasive to the point of contempt. He did grant interviews when absolutely necessary or unavoidable, as when he was cornered by shipboard reporters on one of his European voyages. Although polite and articulate on these occasions, he conveyed little in the way of hard information or personal opinion. A behind-the-scenes man in both business and politics, he quite literally took the cash and let the credit go. A firm family man, Frick was not obliged by scandal to open the door to his private affairs as were boisterous Charlie Schwab, his colleague in steel, and shy Andrew Mellon.

As of this writing, only one biography of Henry Clay Frick has been published. It was a worshipful book printed by Scribner's in 1928, and privately reprinted in 1936. Although there are reports of other books in the works, scholars and biographers have been discouraged through the years by the watchdog attitude of Frick's long-lived daughter, Helen Clay Frick. Not only did Miss Frick stand guard over the family archives, but she sallied forth to sue a distinguished historian who included some unflattering adjectives about her father in one of his books. To a lesser degree family reticence and a desire to control whatever is written about their fortune's founder remains. But Frick's part was so large on the stage of the Gilded Age that he is lighted up by spots shining from the public prints of his day and the memoirs of his peers. As an effective plenipotentiary, or ambassador among them, his works and personality were necessarily recorded.

To take a long look at what we can see of Henry Clay Frick is to gain more understanding of the whole era in American history that his life so well epitomizes. Such an understanding is valuable because the ethic he represents is very much alive and well in the conservative side of our ongoing national debate about how to allocate our national resources. Frick's times are the supposedly good old days to which conservatives allude when they deplore high taxes, government regulation of business, and the loss of piety and family values. But how good were those days? What was there about them that would make one of the winners in the great moneymaking game brood about hell? Just studying photographs and portraits of Frick in his last years makes you doubt that he was joking with Carnegie. There is strength in his handsome face but little joy. The eyes are downcast or inward-looking. You wouldn't bet that the meeting those eyes foresaw hasn't taken place.

CHAPTER I

Introducing Mister *Frick*

FAME does wonders for memories. Whenever a person arrives at celebrity status, those who knew him or her "when" come forward with amazingly prophetic anecdotes. In the case of Henry Clay Frick, the man with an astounding memory was a country schoolmaster named Voight. Long years after the event, an aged Mr. Voight recalled for Colonel George Harvey, Frick's biographer, young Frick's arrival at the one-room schoolhouse in West Overton, Pennsylvania, over which he presided.

Although he was a barefooted farm boy most of the year, the handsome eight-year-old was dressed for the important occasion in a store suit. His thick shock of dark hair with red overtones was neatly brushed; his pink cheeks were scrubbed to a shine. Moved by what he later described to Harvey as "purely intuitive recognition of one who was to become his most illustrious pupil," Voight took the boy by the hand, led him up onto the teaching platform, bowed to him and said to the other boys and girls, "I present to you *Mister* Henry Clay Frick."

While his schoolmates laughed, young Frick responded gravely and graciously with a bow of his own and silently took his seat. Apocryphal as this story might be, it reflects the quiet, icy dignity that would become Frick's public persona throughout a controversial life. Beginning in very young manhood, he was always addressed as Mister Frick, even by his intimates and equals. Since Voight couldn't have known that, his knowledge of just who the boy was then probably accounted for his deference rather than his intuition. Clay, as boyhood friends still had the nerve to call him, was the grandson of one of Westmoreland County's wealthiest and most prominent citizens.

Frick's mother was a daughter of Abraham Overholt, a third-generation American of German descent. By the time Clay was born, Abraham Overholt was settled in a stately Georgian mansion on 150 acres of land where he ran a mill to grind his neighbors' grain and a still to make whiskey. Although he was a strict and upright Mennonite, Overholt was following a hallowed practice of Pennsylvania farmers since revolutionary times by turning grain into a more portable and profitable form. So popular was Abraham's Old Overholt brand that he was never able to keep up with demand. Its reputation and reach outlasted not only Abraham but his grandson, and nearly a century later brought a touch of political embarrassment to Secretary of the Treasury Andrew W. Mellon.

Elizabeth Overholt's family thought that she had married down when she became the wife of John W. Frick from over in Ohio. He was also a third-generation American, but of Swiss origin, an amiable man with no "prospects." The Overholts let the Fricks set up housekeeping in a two-room, stone springhouse hard by the mansion, and it was in these cramped quarters that their second child and first son was born on December 19, 1849. Picking a name for the baby was easy. Both the Fricks and the Overholts were Whigs, and the leader of that party was very much in the news and on their minds. At the time of Clay Frick's birth, the eloquent and persuasive senator from Kentucky was pushing for what would become the Compromise of 1850 to settle the debate on how slavery should be handled during the nation's expansion toward the West Coast. The compromise became the basis of a decade of uneasy peace and stood as Senator Clay's last achievement.

Frick was a thin, small, delicate boy. When his father took him at the age of six to visit his grandfather Frick in Van Buren, Ohio, he developed a fever that lasted for two months. The state of medicine being what it was in those days, no definite diagnosis was made. Vague terms—chronic indigestion, inflammatory rheumatism—were used by different doctors to cover the condition that would persist throughout Frick's life. But he was making up for whatever he may have lacked in physical size and strength with spirit by the time he got to school. With a hindsight perhaps colored, as was Mr. Voight's, by what Frick became, schoolmates reminisced for a reporter from the *Pittsburgh Leader* at the time of the industrialist's death.

The school they described was a simple brick building where pupils sat at their desks on backless benches. The place was heated by a centrally located stove that was fed with wood or coal by the pupils themselves. In back of the desk on the teaching platform was a blackboard and the inevitable hickory stick. The books used to convey the three Rs were McGuffey's reader, Pinneo's grammar, Mitchell's geography, and Ray's arithmetic. Because all of the children, including Frick, whose family had moved to a farm of their own, were needed to work the land, school didn't start until after harvest in October and was suspended when plowing began in the spring.

Mister Frick or no, Clay wasn't spared the rod of discipline in school or hard work outside of it. Classmates recall his getting several doses of "hickory oil," as a whipping by the teacher was called. As for work, listen to the voice of Chester Bocher, whose testimony has to be judged in light of the fact that he later worked for Frick as superintendent of a coke plant:

> Clay Frick was impetuous like his father and his grandfather, but he was always good-hearted and generous. He was a fighter when he thought his rights were being trampled upon and there was not a cowardly bone in his body.
>
> After school hours and during vacation Clay and I used to feed the hogs and cattle at his grandfather's distillery and they would be fattened with mash from the grain after the juice had been taken out. Clay and I looked after raising the gates that held the mash which would allow it to run into troughs. Clay also helped his father and his grandfather by carrying wheat sheaves during harvest.
>
> What impressed me most about Clay Frick was his desire to get on. As a boy he was always wanting to get into business and make money. He was strong willed—more so than most boys—and when he set himself to do anything he did it.

Study was one of the things that young Frick didn't set himself to do, according to his contemporaries, although he was good in math and penmanship, which could be of use in business. A characteristic they all recalled was Frick's readiness to fight with little provocation. It may have surprised them in view of his size and the pacifist doctrine of his grandparents' Mennonite faith. Although he was willing to swallow his own doses of hickory oil, Frick saved a girl cousin from taking the same medicine by threatening to whip the teacher.

A less noble but more prophetic purpose provoked one well-remembered fight that took place between Frick and Robert Goodman. While the boys were playing in the backyard of Goodman's uncle, Frick saw two ripe apples hanging from a bough above them and said, "I must have those apples." Goodman, who considered the apples his uncle's property, said, "Not on your life." Ignoring his friend, Frick picked up a stone to dislodge the apples, and the fight started. The fight didn't end their friendship, according to Goodman, but the apples were still on the tree when it was over.

Bocher's recollection of Frick's burning desire to make money was shared by all the others. Frick told schoolmates, "I propose to be worth a million dollars before I die." It is the only statement of ambition, of purpose in life, ever attributed to him.

Whether he was aware of it or not, young Frick's piping voice was in perfect tune with the times. Ambitious young men everywhere were beginning to sense and seize the opportunities for making money in a country inexhaustibly rich in natural resources and in desperate need of everything that could be made from them. About the time that Frick started school, twenty-two-year-old Andrew Carnegie in nearby Pittsburgh found what he would gleefully call the goose that lays the golden eggs. At thirteen, Carnegie had arrived in the Pittsburgh area with his totally impoverished parents and younger brother and gone to work as a bobbin boy in a cotton factory at $1.20 a week. Working hard and moving from job to job as fast as he could, Carnegie finally landed in a telegraph office where his engaging personality charmed Thomas A. Scott, superintendent of the Pittsburgh division of the Pennsylvania Railroad, into hiring him as personal clerk and operator at thirty-five dollars a month.

Very fond of his little "white haired Scotch devil," Scott told Carnegie one day that a man owning ten shares of Adams Express Company stock had just died, and he advised Carnegie to buy it at fifty dollars a share. Scott even offered to loan his clerk all or part of the money, but Carnegie was too proud to take it. Instead, he talked it over with his parents, who agreed to mortgage the little house they had managed to buy for eight hundred dollars in Allegheny, across the river from Pittsburgh. The effect on his life of buying the stock was recounted in Carnegie's autobiography:

> Adams Express stock then paid monthly dividends of one
> percent, and the first check for five dollars arrived. I can see

it now, and I well remember the signature of "J.C. Babcock, Cashier," who wrote in a big "John Hancock" hand.

The next day being Sunday, we boys—myself and my ever-constant companions—took our usual Sunday afternoon stroll in the country, and sitting down in the woods, I showed them this check saying, "Eureeka! We have found it."

Here was something new to all of us, for none of us had ever received anything but from toil. A return from capital was something strange and new.

How money could make money, how, without any attention from me, this mysterious golden visitor should come, led to much speculation upon the part of the young fellows, and I was for the first time hailed as a "capitalist."

In New York at the same time, a young man who knew all about making money from money—twenty-year-old John Pierpont Morgan—was just entering the American business world. Born in Hartford, Connecticut, grandson of a wealthy hotelier and insurance executive, son of a banker, he had enjoyed a good education at English High in Boston and the University of Göttingen in Germany. After a brief apprenticeship under his father, who was with the American firm of George Peabody & Co. in London, Pierpont—or J.P., as he would be called—was assigned to work for Peabody's New York representatives, Duncan, Sherman & Co., where presumably his close relationship with his father would prove to be an asset. Although like Frick he had had mysterious problems with his health, Morgan was a large, attractive young man, full of the self-confidence of the well born and a burning ambition to shine in the eyes of his father.

That year of 1857 found a somber, lanky eighteen-year-old named John Davison Rockefeller clerking at $3.50 a week in a firm of commission merchants in Cleveland, Ohio. He had wanted to go on to college after graduating from Cleveland High School, but his father, a not very successful commission trader with six children to feed, insisted that he go into business. Reserved and pious like his mother, John didn't seem suited to a commercial career, but he brought the kind of determination that had made him a good scholar to bear on his situation. If he couldn't do what he wanted to do, he would do what he had to do in a big way, and he sought work only in the largest of concerns. As he later said, "I did not guess what it would be, but I was after something big."

It's to be presumed that Andrew William Mellon, only two years old that year, was blissfully unaware of even the need for something called ambition. In the home of his father, Thomas, a real-estate speculator and lawyer about to be elected a judge, he was coddled in comfort and spoiled by older brothers. Andrew would never have to worry about acquiring ambition; it was imbedded in his genes, and the very air around him was thick with it. Thomas Mellon had been brought over from Ireland at the age of five by Scotch-Irish Presbyterian parents down on their luck. By dint of extreme economies and relentlessly hard work, the Mellons made a go of a small farm outside Pittsburgh, and Thomas was destined to follow in the footsteps of his farmer father until a reading of Benjamin Franklin's autobiography gave him a broader perspective and raised higher hopes. He fled the farm for the city, earned an A.B. at Western University (now the University of Pittsburgh), passed the bar examinations, and entered into a lively legal practice and an even livelier practice of acquiring real estate by buying and foreclosing on mortgages. Shrewd and sharp in looks and mind, Thomas Mellon was determined to endow his sons with the acquisitive techniques that were working so well for him.

Like Rockefeller, none of the young people in pursuit of something big in the middle fifties could really guess what it would be. Theirs was still largely a rural America, moving at the pace of foot and horse. The steamship, the train, the telegraph, were relatively new phenomena. Most of the means they would use to satisfy their ambitions were undiscovered, unknown, or undeveloped. It wasn't until 1859, for instance, that petroleum was found when Edwin L. Drake blindly sank a well near Titusville, Pennsylvania. Iron was plentiful, but it wasn't until 1870 that a commercially feasible method of manufacturing steel became available. Baking coke was a small cottage industry. No national bank had yet opened its doors, and nobody had thought of a trust. Great stretches of the continent were without roads or railroads. In 1860, the Pony Express was organized from St. Joesph, Missouri, to Sacramento, California, to provide reasonably rapid communication—a ten-day link—until coast-to-coast telegraph lines were connected a year later. Nobody could guess that such a thing as a telephone could exist until 1876 or an electric light until 1879. The Otis brothers wouldn't install the first electric elevator, which, married to steel, gave birth to the skyscraper until 1889. Yet the Frick boy's determination to make a million somehow wasn't considered an impossible dream by his schoolmates or his elders. They had already seen so much growth and change that they had no doubt that more was in store.

What most of them could not have anticipated was the up side of the Civil War, which broke upon the country in the spring of 1861. Although it brought tragedy to the whole South and into the individual homes of men who died in battle for the North, the war acted as a force-feeder to the industrialization already begun above the Mason-Dixon line. For the most part, the men who would manage and profit from this wartime boom stayed as far away from the front as possible. When necessary they would resort to the legal device of buying substitutes after the draft was inaugurated. Presiding over his own business, Clark & Rockefeller, dealing in grain, hay, meats, and the like, John Rockefeller saw his income rise like a chip on the high tide of wartime commerce. Tending to affairs in New York as head of his newly formed J. Pierpont Morgan & Co., young J.P. profited from two still controversial activities—underwriting the sale of obsolete carbines to the army and speculating in gold. Andrew Carnegie came closest to service, spending some time in Washington helping Thomas Scott run the railroads and set up the telegraph service. Felled by sunstroke that would bother him for the rest of his life, he went back to the job he had inherited from Scott as Pittsburgh superintendent of the Pennsylvania Railroad. Andrew Mellon was too young to be involved in the war, but Thomas Mellon used his greatest powers of persuasion to keep his older sons out of uniform and in the thriving businesses that he had helped them to start.

As any young boy would, Henry Clay Frick simply carried on with his growing up during the war years. Schooling did not play a big part in this process. He continued to attend various primary schools for the winter term in and around West Overton, but by the time he was fourteen he had persuaded his grandfather to get him a paying job at Overholt, Schallenberger & Co., a general store in Mt. Pleasant run by his uncle Christopher Overholt. While working there, he lived with his uncle and briefly attended Mt. Pleasant Institute, a private preparatory school. He also spent ten weeks at Otterbein College in Westerville, Ohio, giving him a grand total of some thirty months in a classroom.

With the war over in 1866, seventeen-year-old Clay Frick borrowed fifty dollars to buy a new suit and pay the train fare to Pittsburgh, where, if anywhere, a fortune could be found. Munitions maker to the Union, producer of coal and oil, entrepôt to the West and South, Pittsburgh was made incredibly prosperous by the war. As one historian of this period in Pittsburgh noted, "Business went on, not as usual, but in a perfect frenzy." By way of munitions alone, Pittsburgh iron men turned out three thousand cannon and ten million pounds of shot and shell. Between the time of Drake's first oil strike in 1859 and the end of the war, some sixty petroleum refineries sprouted in the Pittsburgh area. Within a dozen years after the Pennsylvania Railroad's first steam engine chuffed into the heart of Pittsburgh, thirteen other lines penetrated the city. Like some strange antlered beasts at a giant feeding trough, twin stern-wheelers nuzzled the river wharves in ever greater numbers to handle the flood of passengers and freight.

All this activity was turning Pittsburgh into a restless, clangorous, noxious place that was loud at midnight and dark at noon. In their eagerness to exploit its resources, men were disfiguring one of the most spectacularly beautiful settings of any city in the world. Located on an arrowhead of land between the swift Allegheny River on the north and the sluggish Monongahela River on the south, it is surrounded by high hills that provide breathtaking vistas. But these hills hold coal, the source of the energy that Pittsburghers needed for manufacturing, transportation, and heating their homes, and coal, burned as it was in those days, created black smoke that would lie like a pall over the whole area. Artists' renderings of the Pittsburgh scene unfailingly showed columns of smoke sprouting like strange plants from boats, trains, buildings, and factories across the entire breadth of the landscape. Visiting Pittsburgh during the Civil War, the English novelist Anthony Trollope described it as "the blackest place I ever saw" and told graphically how "on coming out of a tub of water my foot took an impress from the carpet exactly as it would have done had I trod barefooted on a path with soot." To another author, James Parton, writing at about the time that Clay Frick came to town, Pittsburgh by day was "smoke, smoke—everywhere smoke" and "hell with the lid taken off" by night. British philosopher Herbert Spencer said that a month in Pittsburgh would justify suicide.

To a young man from a small town with moneymaking in mind, the city had a very different aspect, as it did to most of its citizens. Smoke was a sign of healthy commercial activity, and inhaling it was simply the price you paid for being part of progress. However appalling they might find its environment, the great and near great of the age were fascinated by the industrial phenomenon that was Pittsburgh and took pains to experience it. They often spoke from lecture platforms or, if politicians, from hotel balconies and made Pittsburghers feel themselves at the center of things. In some instances, it was more than a feeling; the Republican Party held its first national convention in Pittsburgh, and the historic union between the Old School and New School of the Presbyterian Church to form a national religious body of five hundred thousand communicants took place in Pittsburgh's massive Third Presbyterian Church. Ten newspapers flourished in a city of fifty thousand inhabitants, attesting to their lively interest in events everywhere. Predictably, Pittsburgh workers played roles as large in the national labor drama as its businessmen did in industry. The whole city seemed driven by the Calvinistic belief that salvation—wealth, in its earthly phase—was earned by hard work, and miserable conditions only made work a harder and therefore a straighter path to heaven.

Trading on his experience in his uncle's store, young Frick found work at White & Co., a notions emporium on Sixth Street. He was a salesman of buttons and bows and other trimmings for ladies' apparel. Although taciturn by nature, Frick could force himself to rise to any occasion when it was to his advantage. He became the store's leading salesman—at all of seven dollars a week—by beguiling female customers. In this, he was undoubtedly helped by his good looks and his care in dressing, which had manifested itself at the little West Overton schoolhouse. Not content with what he was earning and learning at work, Frick enrolled in a business school at night to learn bookkeeping. Having rented an inexpensive room in Allegheny to save money for clothes and schooling, he had to trudge back and forth across the bridge four times every day.

Looking for the main chance, Clay must have decided early on that it wasn't to be found in ribbon clerking. The smoke he ingested on his long walks, and the talk of the day, would have been constant reminders of the city's continuous and growing need for coal, a product that had been lying literally under his bare feet when he ranged the fields of his father's and grandfather's farms. If he could get his hands on enough of that, the possibilities were limitless. With this thought in mind, Frick didn't find it hard to give up city life after a year and a half of it and go back home. He was a single-minded youth with no observable interest in idle amusements, other than reading and an occasional game of chess, and no vices, other than an addiction to cigars. Glad to see him back in the fold and impressed by his studies in Pittsburgh, Grandfather Abraham offered him a job as bookkeeper at the distillery, which he had moved to Broadford, a village near Connellsville, at a thousand dollars a year, three times what he had been making at the store in Pittsburgh. At nineteen, Mister Frick was in business for good.

CHAPTER 2

Young King Coke

NO element in all creation is more important to mankind than iron. As part of the blood, it is essential to life itself; as a component of artifacts ranging from needles to skyscrapers, it is the sine qua non of human civilization. Fortunately, nature is lavish with iron. It can be found almost everywhere on earth and in the heavens, from which it occasionally drops in the form of meteorites. However abundant, iron in a useful form is not a free gift. It has to be smelted, or cooked, to separate it from other substances in the ore and alloy it with another element, carbon. Men have long understood this. A five-thousand-year-old iron blade was discovered in an Egyptian pyramid; the making of iron and even steel is mentioned in the works of Homer and the Bible's Old Testament.

In the absence of any certain evidence as to how people first learned to make iron, at least one historian suggests that a residue of iron was found in the ashes of a fire built near paint rock. This led to experimentation with combining fire and iron-bearing substances until it became apparent that charcoal was the best fuel for smelting. An impure form of carbon, charcoal could be made easily by burning wood with the air supply artificially limited, usually by partially covering the fire with earth. For millenia whatever iron was made was made by burning it with charcoal since human beings were bafflingly slow to take advantage of another natural substance as prevalent and useful as iron—coal. Although coal is mentioned as early as iron in the annals of human history, its use was limited by the smoke and odor it gave off during burning. In the thirteenth century, King Edward I of England decreed the death penalty for anyone using coal as fuel. It would be another four hundred years before coal was used at all in producing iron. Learning quickly that raw coal resulted in poor iron, iron makers tried a process similar to that used in converting wood to charcoal and came up with a new substance they called coke, a carbonized form of coal that combined with iron ore as well as charcoal. But incredibly, it would be yet another century, in the time of Henry Clay Frick, before coke came into general use.

Indeed, the farmers and miners around Broadford, where Frick went to work at his grandfather's distillery in the late 1860s, considered the little coke being baked in the ovens of some twenty plants along the Youghiogheny River a drug on the market. The product was sneeringly called "cinders," and everybody remembered the time back in '42 when whole barge loads of the stuff had been sent down the Ohio River without ever finding a buyer. Charcoal was still preferred, and as long as there were frontier stands of forest near the smelting centers, ironmasters weren't about to change their ways. One man who was discouraged by the prospects for coke was Abraham Overholt Tinstman, Frick's first cousin. Because Frick's mother was the youngest child in the Overholt family, Tinstman was nearly a generation older than his cousin and had been given the responsibility of managing the distillery under old Abraham's watchful eye. Despite their differences in age, the cousins got along well together, sharing a passion for playing chess. During their regular games after work, Tinstman unburdened himself of his worries about the money he had invested in the unpromising coke business.

Back in 1859, Tinstman and a friend, Joseph Rist, had bought six hundred acres of coal land together. In an effort to make this investment pay off, they had plunged again in 1868 to buy into a coke manufacturing business organized by Colonel A.S.M. Morgan. Sales were so poor that Morgan had dropped out, but Tinstman was too deeply in debt to follow suit. How could he get out of this fix? The irony of his situation was that making coke here in the Connellsville region ought to be a good business. They were sitting right on top of a rich, thick vein of soft, bituminous coal, the best coking coal in the world, and the manufacturing process was a simple affair that required little in the way of complicated equipment or skilled labor.

At that time, coke was cooked in what were called beehive ovens. Built of brick and shaped like igloos, each oven had a hole at the top and a door at the bottom. By letting very little air into the oven, it was possible to burn out the volatile matter in the raw coal—tar, oil, gases—and leave a residue of nearly pure carbon that burned only in the presence of a lot of oxygen. The ovens were set close together and either ranged single file along an embankment to take advantage of the heat preserving capacity of the earth or faced each other in blocks. Plants consisted of a manageable number of ovens—about three hundred—with tracks for wagons to carry coal to feed into the top, or trunnel-head, and tracks along the bottom for railway cars to take away the coke. When coal was fed into the trunnel-head, the volatile matter would burst into roaring flames that shot up through the hole, creating a fury of smoke by day and fire by night. Judging by the quality of the smoke and flame, the oven tender would quench the fire with water before it could consume the carbon. Thus suddenly cooled, the carbon cake would splinter into silvery cinders that would be drawn out of the door and loaded into the waiting freight cars. Tending the ovens called for a strong back and a high level of tolerance for fierce heat and gritty grime.

Frick was excited by his cousin's talk of making coke. This could be the something big he was looking for. Having so recently spent time in Pittsburgh, he was more aware than Tinstman of developments in the business world there. One of the most talked about men in the city was Andrew Carnegie, only in his early thirties but a millionaire many times over. Right after the war, he left the railroad and began flitting from business to business, enriching himself at every turn. Although he made money in an early oil venture, he gave it up after a visit to the oil fields north of the city, where the stench reminded him of his days as a bobbin boy. Carnegie then drew on his railroad acquaintanceships to sell bridges through the Keystone Bridge Company. Finding that iron made better bridges than wood, he put together the Union Iron Mills to meet Keystone's requirements. Learning that Union was paying forty dollars a ton for pig iron, he built a huge blast furnace and named it Lucy for his brother Tom's wife. There seemed to be no end to Carnegie's energetic expansion in iron works, and nobody doubted that he would one day look into that Bessemer process that was allowing the British to make steel rails and capture the American market. Unless they picked up and moved their expensive metal-making installations, the metal makers like Carnegie would have to start using more coke than the few existing plants could supply.

Sure that he was right about this, Frick told cousin Abraham that the way out of his dilemma was to buy more coal lands and build more ovens, even if it meant going deeper into debt for the moment. To demonstrate the strength of his conviction, Clay offered to join his cousin in an expansion program. It was an audacious thing to do since Tinstman must have known that Frick couldn't have more than a few hundred dollars saved up from his clerking jobs. It's certain evidence of the young man's powers of persuasion that Tinstman agreed. They had their eyes on 123 acres of land right there in Broadford belonging to a Mr. John Rist, who was willing to sell for $52,995. With Tinstman in debt and Frick barely solvent, they decided that they would have to bring others into the scheme. Tinstman enlisted his old partner, Joseph Rist, and Frick recruited a distant cousin named John S. R. Overholt.

Possibly because Joseph Rist was in better financial shape, they divided the interests in the enterprise into fifths. Rist took two; the others each one. This meant that Clay had to raise $10,599 to participate. In later life Frick's memory was fuzzy as to just how he managed to raise such a sum. But the evidence points to a shrewd manipulation of a family fund created by the death of the patriarch, Abraham Overholt. At the time Frick and Tinstman were getting their venture under way, the bulk of old Abraham's estate of some $500,000 was in a trusteeship managed by his sons, Martin and Christopher, and his son-in-law, Jacob O. Tinstman. Frick's mother was due to inherit $58,000, and a sixth of that—more than $9,000—would eventually come to Frick himself. Doubtless the trustees could have been persuaded to advance some or all of that with his mother's consent. In addition, Frick's partner, John Overholt, was courting Frick's sister, Maria, and it is known that Frick borrowed a $2,000 legacy that she had from her grandfather.

Where twenty-one-year-old Clay Frick got the nerve and savvy to borrow as he did remains one of the mysteries about him. Certainly not from his farmer father. Likable, intelligent, steady, John Frick was simply not a moneymaker—or a borrower. Clay's own tribute to his father says it all: "He raised six children without ever being in debt." It might be thought that John Frick would have disapproved of his gambler son. Instead, he was fascinated by him, as were the rest of the clan. As a result, Clay even found a way of turning his father's thrift into money. In addition to borrowing from the estate and its heirs, Clay asked his father to sign notes that he floated around the countryside to get hold of the funds that farmers kept under the mattress.

How his father's good name worked for him is evident in an incident that Frick must have recounted for his biographer, Colonel Harvey. On the day before a note for ten thousand dollars was payable to a farmer named Joseph Myers, Clay realized that there was no way he could come up with the money. The note had been endorsed by Benjamin Overholt, Abraham Tinstman, and John Frick, none of whom had that kind of money either. When he went to bed that night, Frick couldn't sleep. Finally, he got up and went to Myers's house and banged on the door at one A.M. A window shot up, and Myers stuck his head out. "Who's there? What do you want?" the farmer asked. "It's Clay Frick. My note is due tomorrow, and I can't pay it." "Ain't it endorsed?" "Yes, but Overholt's busted, and Tinstman's busted, and . . ." Myers interrupted: "John Frick is still on the back of that note and he ain't busted; he'll pay some time. I won't close you out." Within two years Frick himself was able to pay.

Clay's mother was as solidly behind him as his father, as the negotiations to buy the Alexander Miller farm in East Huntington township from the executors of Abraham Overholt's estate would indicate. Clay wanted to make this purchase only months after his first plunge into acquiring coal lands, and he was still deep in debt. The price was $37,842.50. Although the executors agreed to accept notes signed by Clay and his father for two-thirds of the sum, they demanded $12,514 in cash. Undaunted, the Frick men talked it over with Elizabeth and came up with the ingenious solution contained in this note:

> $12514 16⁄100   Mt. Pleasant, Penna.
> One day after date we promise to pay M.S. Overholt, C.S. Overholt and J.O. Tinstman, Trustees of Elizabeth Frick's portion of A. Overholt's decd estate, or order, Twelve thousand five hundred and fourteen dollars and sixteen cents, without defalcation, value received with interest from December 1st, 1871.
>
>   John W. Frick
>   H. Clay Frick

Making loans and signing their names to notes were not the only ways by which members of the Frick and Overholt families displayed their faith in Clay. When it came to organizing a company to manage the lands they purchased, the partners suggested that it be called

Frick and Company. The older men were involved in other enterprises, and wanted to keep this one distinct from them. But there is a suggestion that they didn't want their good names connected with a still dubious business. Young Frick had no such qualms. The only condition he made to using his name was that he have full authority. Nobody balked at this, and Clay's first wise decision was to persuade his older cousin John to become nominal head of the firm. He evidently thought that outsiders would have more confidence in an older man than in a beardless youth. There was another reason, too. Not all gambler, Clay wanted to hold on to his solid, twenty-dollar-a-week bookkeeping job at the Old Overholt distillery. With none of the usual distractions of youth, Clay would have plenty of time to think about how to make money out of coke.

One thing that became clear to him during his thinking was that the company would need more than fifty ovens to thrive, and there was no money in the till to build them. To make matters worse, he had exhausted local sources of credit in order to buy land. The time had come to go to a Pittsburgh bank for a straight commercial loan. Frick's choice of a bank was almost foreordained. Declining to run for another term on the bench, Judge Thomas Mellon had recently gone into banking as T. Mellon & Sons. When Mellon's father came over from Ireland, he had begun farming in Westmoreland County and had struck up a friendship with Abraham Overholt. Even if he had never heard of a young man named Henry Clay Frick, the judge would be familiar with the Overholt name and reputation. As an investor in the coal business himself, the judge would also be familiar with at least the mining part of Frick's business. On a fateful day in 1871, Clay Frick again put on his best suit and took the train to Pittsburgh.

The meeting between the austere old judge and the cool, confident young man became legendary in both the Mellon and the Frick families. Unannounced, Clay appeared at the building on Smithfield Street that was still under construction and said that he had come to see Judge Mellon "on a matter of business." It was perhaps fortunate that Frick had taken his usual care with his dressing, because the judge was a stickler for formality in business attire—a long-skirted black frock coat, stiffly starched white shirt and collar. In the words of a grandson, sharp-featured Judge Mellon was as "formidable as an eagle." But he did not awe Frick. Taciturn as they were, neither man ever recounted what was said at that meeting. The known fact is that Frick came away with ten thousand dollars at 10 percent interest for six months to build fifty coke ovens. Around Broadford Frick admirers said that he got the loan "on his nerve," but more persuasive to Judge Mellon must have been the young man's report on his personal investigations into the new steel business in which coke would be an absolute necessity.

Until the Bessemer converter came into use, steel was manufactured slowly and laboriously by cooking bars of pig iron between layers of glowing charcoal for as long as two weeks. Its use was limited to items like knives, watch springs, and sword blades. Discovered almost simultaneously by William Kelly in the United States and Henry Bessemer in Britain but given the Englishman's name, the Bessemer process consisted of converting molten pig iron to steel by blowing air through it under pressure. What had taken two weeks before could be accomplished in an incredible twelve minutes. Instantly, steel—a more durable, malleable, and useful metal than iron—could be created in a quantity and at a price that made it available for almost any purpose that the mind of man could conceive. An immediate need was for better rails for the roads being built at breakneck speed across the North American continent. The blast furnaces in which the pig iron was cooked would be calling for coke in ever increasing amounts. Everybody in Pittsburgh knew that two of Carnegie's partners—his brother Tom and Henry Phipps, Jr.—had seen Bessemer converters working in Johnstown and Cleveland and were planning to build their own if they couldn't argue Andrew into doing it. The Pittsburgh area had to become the center of steel production since it was more economical to transport iron ore than coal or coke. This vision of a lucrative future for coal lands must have been appealing to the judge because of his own investments in them, and it wouldn't be a bad idea to have this levelheaded young man experimenting with making money from coke.

It's certain that Judge Mellon never loaned money on anybody's "nerve." That grandson who likened him to an eagle, William Larimer Mellon, wrote of the judge:

> Grandfather had a will with more metal in it than is the common heritage of mankind. When it came to investments that jaw of his did not relax any more than the doors of a locked iron safe until his mind had explored every possibility of losing some of his money. He almost never made mistakes

when he was paying out money and was habitually careful because he had been brought up in a school where everything was hard, where one had to be careful with money for the simple reason that money was scarce. On top of this ingrained quality of his character he had developed a superb judgment. No amount of talking or "selling" influenced him. He made up his mind deliberately, soundly. In consequence, he rarely failed to make money out of his investments.

From his very beginning as a young lawyer, Thomas Mellon made sure of his investments by requiring a judgment on mortgages and a judgment note on personal security loans. Called DSBs, from the Latin *debitum sine brevi,* or "debt without a writ," these documents allowed an attorney or court officer to confess judgment and seize the debtor's property without the fuss of a trial. Over the years, the DSB mortgage books of Allegheny County grew fat with the Mellon name. Proud of what he would have called sound business practices, Judge Mellon wrote in his memoirs: "My nature and early training protected me from the folly of earning money and throwing it away. In pursuance of the wise advice of a favorite poet, I was disposed 'To gather gear by every wile/ That's justified by honor.' Accordingly when I obtained money I used it to the best advantage in the safest and most profitable investments I could find."

For twenty-one-year-old Clay Frick to get what was then a substantial sum of money out of such a man was clearly a feat and testimony to the kind of impression he made on his elders. Frick himself apparently regarded it as a piece of cake, for he was back for another ten thousand dollars before the first was paid off or the ovens built. This time Judge Mellon was a little more cautious. He sent a partner in some of his mining ventures, James B. Corey, out to Westmoreland County to investigate. Corey's terse report was: "Lands good, ovens well built; manager on job all days, keeps books evenings, may be a little too enthusiastic about pictures but not enough to hurt; knows business down to the ground; advise making the loan."

These days it is hard to understand why young Frick's enthusiasm for "pictures" was worthy of mention. But any diversion from business was suspect to men in Judge Mellon's favor, and anything connected with the arts would have seemed peculiar to a man like Corey, who had worked his way up as a river pilot and coal dealer. But as a counterweight, Corey was impressed to find Frick boarding in one room of a coal miner's home to save money and be near the office. The fact that the office was in a distillery may have given him pause since he was a Methodist and prohibitionist. Knowing this, Frick hinted that the distillery would be closed down and its warehouse used as a Methodist church. Why he wasn't similarly clever about his pictures—a few inexpensive prints—is hard to fathom except that it was an interest acquired from the man he most admired, his grandfather Overholt.

A favorite grandson, Frick was often in the company of Abraham Overholt, usually driving his grandfather's elegant team of one bay and one gray. It is likely that he was present when the old man picked up pictures that appealed to him. In one instance of record Abraham Overholt went into Martin Stauffer's photographic studio in Mt. Pleasant and saw a picture of a young woman reclining in dishabille and reading a book. Stauffer was rather shocked when the supposedly strict old Mennonite showed an interest by asking the price. Trying to put him off, Stauffer named a high figure—fifteen dollars. "Wrap it up," said Abraham. Whether Clay witnessed this particular scene or not, his grandfather's disdain for popular opinion, disregard for costs, and decisiveness would soon be characteristic of his own behavior. During his brief attendance at Otterbein, Frick was introduced to a slightly higher level of art, which was certainly another factor in his enthusiasm.

Despite appearances, Frick had little time for pictures for the next few years. He was almost frantically busy building ovens, buying land, selling all the coke he could produce. Within two years, he was able to pay off his pressing debts, justifying Judge Mellon's trust in him and positioning himself for more expansion on borrowed funds. Carnegie had at last decided to build a steel mill on the fields outside Pittsburgh where Braddock had fought and died, and Frick wanted to be in a position to supply him with coke. As might be expected from an old railroader, the principal product would be steel rails. And as might be expected from a supersalesman, Carnegie named his plant Edgar Thomson in honor of the president of the Pennsylvania Railroad. In addition to building bridges for them, Carnegie had kept his association with the railroads fresh by peddling their bonds abroad, largely through Junius Morgan in London. It wasn't a favor; his commission on only one transaction in 1872 amounted to $150,000.

The railroads that provided Carnegie with the money to get into iron and steel generated much of the gold of the Gilded Age. Enormous amounts of money were involved in their construction and the wild speculation in their often heavily watered securities. Railroads played a significant part in the story of almost every American of great wealth, including Henry Clay Frick. In addition to the money of private speculators, the railroads were showered with public funds and land grants from the national government right down to the smallest village. A place that didn't manage to get itself on a railroad was out of the money, deprived of any chance to become part of the great surge in commerce and industry. The crying need for the best transportation available created a public tolerance for what became the wholesale plundering of the railroads for private gain.

A sure sign of this tolerance came in 1872 when Clay Frick was just getting on his feet in the coke business. Ulysses S. Grant was enthusiastically reelected President despite the worst railway scandal in history, only one of the many money scandals sullying his administration. It involved the Crédit Mobilier, a company formed to construct the Union Pacific in its race toward the West Coast. With ownership in the Crédit Mobilier, directors of the Union Pacific awarded Crédit Mobilier construction contracts with such fantastic profit margins that it paid dividends of 348 percent in a single year. To avert a possible congressional investigation, large blocks of Crédit Mobilier were placed in the right hands. Among those hands were those of Vice President Schuyler Colfax. Colfax was not renominated, but Massachusetts Senator Henry Wilson, who was also associated with Crédit Mobilier, ran with Grant. To the voters how it was done and how much it cost was far outweighed by the great event in 1869 when the rails of the Union Pacific were joined with a golden spike to those of the Central Pacific (also plundered by Collis Huntington and Leland Stanford), at Promontory Point, Utah.

Thrift may have been preached in those days, but it wasn't practiced by the movers and shakers. In borrowing all he could talk anyone into lending, Frick was right in step with his peers. In Cleveland, John Rockefeller gave up the commission business at the end of the war and bought out his partners, including their interest in an oil refinery. Concentrating on oil, he began to expand with the help of the banks. "I was always a great borrower in those days," he once recalled. By 1870, Rockefeller was in a position to found the Standard Oil Company of Ohio, a million-dollar corporation. In

New York, J. P. Morgan was making money by seeing to it that the people who needed money got it. His customers included railroads, of course, and he earned a measure of fame by ousting speculators Jay Gould and James Fisk from control of the Albany & Susquehanna. Morgan gained even more prominence when he broke the monopoly in handling federal treasury loans held by Philadelphia banker Jay Cooke, who almost single-handedly financed the Union in the Civil War.

Tolerant as most people seemed to be about any means of making money, there were some who were alarmed by what they saw happening to their country—and especially their countrymen. In collaboration with Charles Dudley Warner, Mark Twain poked bitter fun at the aspirations of money-mad men in the novel that would give the times a lasting name, *The Gilded Age.* Twain's boasting, bumbling Colonel Sellers thrives on impossible dreams of sudden riches while actually dining on turnips and water. Perhaps sensing that the situation called for something stronger than humor, Twain wrote "The Revised Catechism" for the *New York Tribune* in September 1871:

> What is the chief end of man?—to get rich. In what way?—dishonestly if we can; honestly if we must. Who is God, the one only and true? Money is God. Gold and greenbacks and stock—father, son, and the ghost of same—three persons in one; these are the true and only God, mighty and supreme. . . .

It's doubtful whether a twenty-two-year-old scheming to build more coke ovens and worrying about notes falling due in a backwater of Pennsylvania would have read that item. If he had, it would have meant little to him. He was a man of his age, and no amount of literary sour grapes would change his mind about what a man ought to be doing with his little time on earth.

CHAPTER 3

Turning Panic into Plenty

IT began in a remote, romantic European city, known, if at all, in Broadford, Pennsylvania, only for its waltzes and chocolates. In May 1873, panic struck the bourse in Vienna, and it spread like a virus through the exchanges of Europe that were overloaded with stocks and bonds in American ventures, mostly in railroads. The rapid and seemingly endless expansion in American transportation and associated industries, the opening of rich and fertile farmlands, the swelling population as their own people sought new opportunity in a new world, had proved very attractive to European investors until accidents on poorly constructed railroads, scandals in finance that revealed watered stock and outright thievery, as in the Crédit Mobilier affair, and agricultural overproduction raised doubts about the real value of American securities. They had already displayed these doubts by more cautionary buying in 1872, and this may have contributed to the virus from Vienna that put an end to reckless investment in America and plunged Europe into recession.

American bankers weren't worried at first, probably because banking was still looked upon as a local operation except for a few houses like Morgan's in New York and Jay Cooke's in Philadelphia. Compared to Morgan, Cooke was a Johnny-come-lately. A poor boy from the Midwest, Cooke had started out in Philadelphia as a clerk in a packet line, and moved over to work in a banking house until his retirement in 1857. Wearied of that, he formed his own partnership, Jay Cooke & Co., took advantage of a family relationship with Ohio's governor Salmon P. Chase, who became Lincoln's Secretary of the Treasury, to become the chief salesman of the government's wartime securities. In four years he persuaded the public to take more than a billion dollars' worth of these securities with, of course, rewarding commissions to his firm. Through his government connections, he urged the establishment of national banks, and he established a bank in Washington and another in Philadelphia as soon as they were authorized by Congress. By war's end, Cooke was in a position to open branches in New York and London, where a former U.S. Secretary of the Treasury, Hugh McCulloch, became his agent. No more immune to railroad fever than Morgan in New York and other bankers, Cooke involved himself in underwriting a Northern Pacific route, an undertaking that would require the assistance of the European markets. Because of his patriotism, piety, and abstemious personal habits, Cooke was regarded as completely safe and sound, and so it was a severe shock to the whole financial community when Jay Cooke & Co. failed on September 18, 1873.

There was instant panic in the East. Stocks fell so fast on the New York Stock Exchange that its doors were closed within two days. Runs began on banks, and prestigious institutions went out of business one after another. But in Pittsburgh, Judge Thomas Mellon, a relatively new banker who was smug about the value of his well-protected real-estate investments, took the news calmly. When he first heard of the Cooke failure on that September afternoon, he was not disturbed. "Indeed," he wrote in his memoirs, "it scarce attracted my attention, as we had no business relations with Cooke or his railroad projects; and I supposed the flurry caused by it would blow over without any serious effect, as it had done after similar failures of others." But it didn't take long for the judge to learn how wrong he was, and no account of that panic is more vivid than his:

> Money immediately disappeared from circulation and values of all kinds subsided rapidly. Credit was gone, payment in money imperative but no money for the purpose. Dealings and business transactions had been carried on so generally on credit that everybody was largely both debtor and creditor, and now that clearings could no longer be made by an exchange of mutual obligations, a deadlock and general collapse was the result. . . .
>
> At the same time deposits in all the banks were rapidly decreasing, not only on account of the distrust produced by the daily recurring suspension of banks and firms and individuals everywhere, but also on account of the stagnations of

trade and demands on depositors to pay their own debts. It seemed as if everyone was overtaken by a necessity for money, and an irresistible disposition to insist on the payment of what was due him. Almost every one of the numerous savings banks and trust companies established during the inflation went under and closed their doors. These recurring failures intensified alarm.

As to myself, the storm struck us at an exceedingly inopportune moment. We had been unusually flush of cash until a few days before Cooke's failure, when an offering was made of Pennsylvania Railroad paper so well endorsed as to be considered gilt edged. The temptation induced me to take so much of it that our cash on hand was reduced greatly below our custom or the point of prudence. Only sixty thousand dollars or so was left to meet the deposits in both our banks, amounting to about six hundred thousand dollars at the time. We had good balances in New York and Philadelphia, but unfortunately our depositories in both cities failed before we secured the funds; and to convert unmatured mortgages or other securities into money, or even to obtain payment of such as were due, or to sell and procure cash for real estate at any sacrifice, was simply impossible. Such was the unpleasant predicament in which we were placed; . . . the checks and drafts on us grew rapidly in excess of deposits, and our cash balance at the close of each day showed a steady decline. . . .

I did my best to collect in over dues from all sources; and my sons Thomas and James had enough due on their notes and accounts for building materials and lot sales to relieve us of difficulty if they could get it, and they sent out runners to collect. . . . Their success was only partial, but the funds which they secured in this way contributed largely to keep us afloat for several weeks. . . . After all our exertions, the cash balance for both banks fell to nearly twelve thousand dollars, and as our suspension was not to be a failure involving loss to any one, I considered it better to keep this much on hand, to meet necessitous cases of depositors likely to suffer from want of their funds; and at the close of banking hours on the 15th day of October, 1873, I directed the officers to stop payment the next day to all except special cases, but not to close the doors of either bank: I thought it more satisfactory to customers to keep them open and continue the officers in their places to explain the situation to those interested. And this did have a good effect in preventing alarm. . . .

Although Judge Mellon's depositors may have kept their cool, people elsewhere and everywhere panicked. Soon Pittsburgh's major metal and mining businesses were closing down and sending idle workers into the streets. By the spring of 1874, the aftermath of panic reached Broadford, where young Frick was facing the prospect of selling his coke, if he could sell it at all, at ninety cents a ton, well below the cost of producing it. "It was an awful time," he told his biographer, but it never occurred to him to quit. If he closed down, the damage disuse would cause to his facilities would be worse than what he would lose by selling under cost. Since most of his rivals in the business were giving up, H. C. Frick and Company would be left in a good competitive position when business picked up again, as it surely would. With his new steel mill under construction at Braddock, canny Andrew Carnegie was reorganizing Carnegie, McCandless and Company, capitalized at $750,000, into the Edgar Thomson Steel Company, Limited, capitalized at $1 million. Carnegie always insisted to anyone who would listen that the time to expand a business was during a depression, when labor and materials were cheap. If Carnegie, whose judgment was confirmed by his many millions, was building for the future, why shouldn't Frick? When it got going, that steel mill would need a lot of iron that, in turn, would need a lot of coke.

In the meantime, Frick faced a daily problem of selling the coke he continued to mine at a loss. Before the panic disrupted commerce, all he had to do was to ship his coke to dealers in Pittsburgh who would dispose of it for him. With their markets drying up, the dealers went out of business, and Frick had to set up a sales office of his own in the city. This meant killing days, even for a twenty-four-year-old. His rigid schedule: up at six A.M.; an hour inspecting the mines and ovens; three hours on the train to Pittsburgh; from ten A.M. to three P.M. "legging it" to call on customers; three hours back to Broadford; from six P.M. to bedtime working on the books. Frick had a good product to sell—the best coke coming out of the Connellsville area. Although he was not a charismatic salesman in the Carnegie manner, Frick's knowledge of the business and the fact that he, as head of the company, was personally taking care of their interests proved persuasive to the few people buying coke, and H. C. Frick and Company was soon the only concern shipping coke out of an otherwise devastated region.

The deepening depression presented Frick with challenging opportunities. Rival coke operators, and even his own partners, pressed for cash, wanted to sell out at distressed prices. Farmers whose fields covered rich coal deposits were equally in trouble over mortgages and notes falling due, and they were willing to trade land for cash in almost any amount. But, as Judge Mellon noted, both cash and credit were hard to come by. For a while, Frick was still able to cover his operating deficit by peddling his notes to the thriftiest of farmers with savings to spare, and he used his mother's inheritance to option land. He hesitated to go back to Judge Mellon, who had problems of his own, and he knew of no other bankers in better shape. It was frustrating—if only his business had been granted time to accumulate savings as Carnegie and his partners had done. To a man of Frick's ambition, the thought of having to pass up a chance to monopolize the coke industry was unbearable, and he devoted many of his idle hours on the train to searching his mind for a viable way of raising cash.

When it came to him, the solution was like a gift from his surroundings, a reflection of the clack of the wheels under him, the drift of smoke and cinders through the open window, the hoot of the whistle at crossings. He would sell the railroad that carried his coke-filled gondolas from Broadford to the junction with the main line of the Baltimore and Ohio at Mt. Pleasant. In order not to be left behind in the rush of progress, the people of Broadford had raised two million dollars in the good times two years before to build a ten-mile feeder line to the B. & O. It had been a boon to citizens wanting to shop or do business in Mt. Pleasant or Pittsburgh and an essential factor in getting H. C. Frick and Company under way. Now, however, the stockholders were faced with cash shortages, business failures, mortgage foreclosures. If Clay Frick could sell their stock for them, he would help his beleaguered neighbors, make sure the little railroad he needed for his coke shipments kept functioning, and earn a well-deserved commission for himself.

Frick already had the capacity for recognizing a sound idea as soon as it surfaced and the decisiveness to act on it at once. The very night of that fruitful train ride he managed to get a list of the stockholders and found that they were widely scattered across the countryside. Instead of going to Pittsburgh the next morning, he borrowed the fastest horse in town—a gray single-footer owned by one Captain Markle—and set out with options he had prepared for the stockholders' signatures. The ride in the open air was a healthy change for an overworked man who spent most of his days in the smoky streets of Pittsburgh, and he had no trouble getting all the signatures he needed.

As he had done with Judge Mellon, Frick presented himself unannounced at B. & O. headquarters. He sent in word to the executives that he had come to sell them a railroad at a bargain owing to the depressed business conditions. In trouble themselves, railroads were not buying other railroads, however small. Still, the B. & O. executives were willing to listen to this audacious young man who apparently thought that they were in better shape than they pretended. Frick presented the options he had collected and laid it on the line. The little railroad wasn't making money now, but it would from the shipments of H. C. Frick and Company alone in due time. Because the stockholders were distressed, B. & O. could buy it now for cost— and a $50,000 cash payment to him personally as intermediary. He would give them forty-eight hours to make up their minds. With that, Frick picked up the options and headed for home. Before his deadline arrived, B. & O. met his demands in full.

Frick threw the $50,000 immediately into the purchase of more lands and ovens. He was free to do this because he had developed an ingenious method of taking care of his operating expenses without using legal tender. Early in his business operation, it became evident that the laborers he was recruiting were in need of a handy store. Rather than let the profit from such an enterprise go to others, he opened a company store. While money was plentiful, running the store was a simple process of buying from Pittsburgh wholesale houses and reselling at retail prices for cash. By keeping up with his bills in the city, Frick had established himself as a valuable customer by the time the panic struck, and the wholesalers were willing to work with him on any terms. In the cash crunch, Frick started issuing his own scrip to pay his workers' wages. Designed to resemble government greenbacks (they were actually printed in the official shade), Frick's bills were accepted first at the company store and then by other establishments throughout the community. With labor costs taken care of in this fashion, the company was free to use the legal tender it received from the sale of its products as necessary to

deal in outside markets. Obviously, workers became captive customers for the company, but at a time when workers elsewhere were
being idled, there was little cause for complaint.

His own confidence restored by the B. & O. deal, Frick felt it was
right to approach Judge Mellon again. Frick's gutsy business practices
appealed to the judge. Although T. Mellon & Sons wasn't in the
market for mortgages in 1874, it took one from Henry Clay Frick
to provide $15,000 for the purchase of freight cars and a line of
discount not exceeding $25,000. By 1876, Frick's borrowing from
Mellon had risen to $100,000, but by then he was again making
money on his coke. In addition to his own plants, Frick acquired
those of his main rivals, and he owned some 60 percent of the coal
acreage and produced 80 percent of the coke from the region by the
time the steel companies were pulling out of the depression. Frick
was in a position to set his own prices, and they jumped in accor-
dance with demand from 90 cents a ton to $3.60 a ton, to $4.00, to
$5.00. He was soon earning 100 percent over costs.

More indicative of what he thought of Frick than the $100,000
line of credit he extended was another gesture Judge Mellon made
at the time of that deal in 1876. Before Frick left the bank, the judge
introduced him to his son Andrew. Short like Frick but much thin-
ner, and with a mustache to make him look older than his twenty-
one years, Mellon had already completed all but three months of a
college course at his father's alma mater, Western University, and
had successfully run a lumber business before becoming the first of
"& Sons" in Thomas Mellon's bank. Andrew had to be impressed
with the extent of credit his tight-fisted father had allowed Frick,
but in case he missed that point the judge told him as soon as Frick
closed the door behind him,

> That young man has great promise. He is very careful
> making statements, always exact and wholly reliable. He is
> also able, energetic, industrious, resourceful, self-confident,
> somewhat impetuous and inclined to be daring on his own
> account, but so cautious in his dealings with others disposed
> to take chances that I doubt if he would make a successful
> banker. If he continues along his own line as he has begun,
> he will go far unless he overreaches. That is his only danger.

Such high praise from the older generation is usually death to a
relationship between young people seeking independence. Not so in

this case. Andrew Mellon not only worked with his father but, living at home, spent most of his evenings reading to the older man, whose eyes were failing. He was a favorite son whose judgment and ruthlessness in matters financial matched his father's. If his father liked Frick, he probably would, too. So when Frick invited him to spend a weekend in Broadford, Andrew Mellon accepted with interest. Although both of these young men were closemouthed and antisocial in the usual sense of the word, the chemistry of attraction between them created a lifelong bond. Their friendship would have far-reaching consequences in the worlds of finance and art.

As Frick had anticipated, Carnegie's Edgar Thomson works, going into production in 1875, was largely responsible for the demand for coke that allowed him to keep raising his prices. The "E.T." wasn't the first Bessemer mill in America, as often claimed—Carnegie had dragged his feet on going into steel until he saw the process with his own eyes in England—but it was the newest and the best. Of almost equal importance was the man who ran it. Carnegie's talent for salesmanship was matched by his talent for finding the kind of men he needed to make the most of the enterprises he founded and financed. Despite having his investments in Pittsburgh, Carnegie lived in New York to be in touch with the financial markets and the cultural and literary scene he enjoyed, and he spent the hot half of the year abroad, where he mixed selling with just plain loafing. So it was imperative that he exercise good judgment in hiring subordinates. In the case of the E.T., the man was a Civil War veteran, Captain William R. (Bill) Jones.

Son of a poor patternmaker in Catasauqua, Pennsylvania, Jones got his first job in an iron works at the age of ten. Fortunately for his education, his Welsh father had the town's largest library in his home, and Bill browsed through a mixed bag of history and classics to become a Shakespeare fan. Full of high spirits and great physical courage, he became a hero in war and a leader of men in the factories, where he was soon given supervisory positions. He had advanced notions of labor management such as the eight-hour day and was an inventive genius in the use of machinery. Carnegie had the luck to be able to hire Jones away from the Cambria Works in Johnstown when the owner there promoted a soberer and duller supervisor, also named Jones, over Bill's head. Within fifteen months Jones had E.T. producing more steel in a week than the average plant did in six weeks. He was also able to bring costs down to undersell the British on steel rails. The result: a profit of $41,970.06 in 1875, $181,007.18 in 1876, $190,379.33 in 1877, and upward while the nation was still in the grip of depression. As the Jones production broke record after record, so did the carloads of coke rolling in from H. C. Frick and Company to feed it.

Others with accumulated cash or borrowing power were as quick to take advantage of hard times as Frick and Carnegie. John Rockefeller's Standard Oil went on gobbling up competing refineries and pipe lines, squeezing rebates out of hard-pressed railroads, increasing capitalization. Recovered from the taint of irregular wartime operations, J. P. Morgan made himself a force for order in the chaotic financing of railroads and was in a position to take advantage of Cooke's collapse to capture the lion's share of international financing. One result of the depression was that producers who stayed in business felt that it was not only necessary but proper to cut the wages of workingmen. In this they received support from the press. *The New York Times* expressed hope that the depression would "bring wages down for all time," and *The Chicago Times* thought that labor would learn "the folly and danger of trade organizations, strikes, and combinations against capital."

Labor took a different view of the matter. In the summer of 1877, railroad workers staged one of the worst strikes in history. Although trouble started on the B. & O. in Maryland, it soon spread to the Pennsylvania, where president Thomas Scott ordered a 10 percent wage cut and instituted the laborsaving practice of "double-headers"—two freight trains with two engines run by one crew. On the morning of July 19, a crew refused to take a double-header out of Pittsburgh, and for the next five days the city was a scene of riot, death, and destruction. In an exchange of gunfire between strikers and their citizen sympathizers and the militia and federal troops brought in to restore order, some twenty people were killed and countless more wounded. The Union Depot was set afire, and lines of freight cars were looted and burned. Disruptions and more deaths on a smaller scale occurred elsewhere in the country.

Fear of complete social disruption, fed by an alarmed press, gripped the country. Strikers and their supporters were called every bad name in the book plus some newly invented ones. An historian counted some forty synonyms for strikers used in *The New York Times* for that month of July, including roughs, hoodlums, thieves, rabble, communists, and tramps. When the strike almost literally burned itself out, the workers learned that they had gained nothing, that the power of law was on the side of property and capital. In the Pittsburgh area whatever claim labor had to public sympathy was lost to the fear of violence. Employers like Frick and Carnegie who had to forfeit a week's good profit while transportation was disrupted developed a respect and concern for the potential power of organized labor and determined to fight it on every front. The great railway strike forever polarized America between the antagonistic forces of capital and labor.

Whatever long-term consequences the strike may have had, it did not halt the economic recovery then under way in which H. C. Frick and Company enthusiastically participated. By the end of 1879, the company was employing a thousand people and shipping out a hundred cars full of coke every day. On December 19 of that year Clay Frick celebrated his thirtieth birthday by going over the books and discovering that he had already achieved his life's ambition: he was worth a million dollars. On his way to his frugal bachelor quarters in the Washabaugh Hotel, he dropped into the Mt. Pleasant store where he had started clerking sixteen years before and indulged his only vice by buying a five-cent Havana cigar.

Although Frick himself must have been the source of this story, he evidently did not share any thoughts or feelings about the occasion with the biographers close to him like Colonel Harvey and his daughter, Helen Clay Frick. The picture is one of cool, quiet acceptance of his just deserts. In view of their future relationship, it's interesting to consider how another young man reacted years earlier in a New York hotel room to the discovery that he was incredibly rich. After toting up his income for the year, Andrew Carnegie scratched out a memorandum on a paper datelined "St. Nicholas Hotel, New York, December 1868":

> Thirty three and an income of $50,000 per annum! By this time two years I can arrange all my business to secure at least $50,000 per annum. Beyond this never earn—make no effort to increase fortune, but spend the surplus each year for benevolent purposes. Cast aside business forever, except for others.
>
> Settle in Oxford and get a thorough education, making the acquaintance of literary men—this will take three years' active work—pay especial attention to speaking in public. Settle

then in London and purchase a controlling interest in some newspaper or live review and give the general management of it attention, taking a part in public matters, especially those connected with education and improvement of the poorer classes.

Man must have an idol—the amassing of wealth is one of the worst species of idolatry—no idol more debasing than the worship of money. Whatever I engage in I must push inordinately; therefore should I be careful to choose that life which will be the most elevating in its character. To continue much longer overwhelmed by business cares and with most of my thoughts wholly upon the way to make more money in the shortest time, must degrade me beyond hope of permanent recovery. I will resign business at thirty-five, but during the ensuing two years I wish to spend the afternoons receiving instruction and in reading systematically.

Quite obviously, Carnegie did not find himself able to live up to the idealistic sentiments expressed in this memo for a long, long time. Frick may have saved himself a lot of anguish by never entertaining such guilts about the pursuit of money. But, however they differed in attitude, both men devoted themselves to the accumulation of personal wealth with unparalleled zeal in the years after 1879 when steel became their guiding star.

CHAPTER 4

The "Predatory Animus"

AN interested, educated, and critical observer of the times through which he lived was Thorstein B. Veblen. Lecturer in economics at such prestigious institutions as the University of Chicago, Stanford, and the New School for Social Research, he was the author of many books, including his first and most noted, *The Theory of the Leisure Class*. Published in 1899, it contained his reflections on the Gilded Age, then still in full swing. Concluding that "the discipline of the pecuniary employments acts to conserve and to cultivate certain of the predatory aptitudes and the predatory animus," he wrote:

> The gifts of good-nature, equity, and indiscriminate sympathy do not appreciably further the life of the individual. Their possession may serve to protect the individual from hard usage at the hands of a majority that insists on a modicum of these ingredients in their idea of a normal man; but apart from their indirect and negative effect in this way, the individual fares better under the regime of competition in proportion as he has less of these gifts. Freedom from scruple, from sympathy, honesty and regard for life, may within fairly wide limits, be said to further the success of the individual in the pecuniary culture. The highly successful men of all times have commonly been of this type; except those whose success has not been scored in terms of either wealth or power. It is only within narrow limits, and then only in a Pickwickian sense, that honesty is the best policy.

In the process of making his first million by the age of thirty, Henry Clay Frick was already exhibiting some of the predatory traits that Veblen spotted as necessary to success in a decidedly pecuniary society. To expand his business to the point of a virtual monopoly in coke production, Frick for the most part bought out his partners and competitors or, as in the case of a rival he admired like E. M. Ferguson, persuaded them to take stock in his company. In one instance, however, an explosion that buried thirty miners alive frightened a partner into selling out to Frick, who took the casualties in stride as an unfortunate fact of life in the coke business. It wasn't a business for the fainthearted. Sending men into the bowels of the earth or exposing them to the heat of the furnaces was very nearly the equivalent of ordering men into battle; there would be daily injuries and frequent deaths. In what time remained to them after a dangerous, twelve-hour day on the job, the men lived with their families in small company houses within walking distance of the mines and ovens. The surroundings were bleak—blackened and polluted by smoke—although some thought them possessed of a terrible beauty in the fiery nights.

As a fledgling captain of industry, Frick realized that the kind of discipline required by a captain at war would be needed to keep labor on the line under these circumstances. One disciplinary device was simply to keep workers in perpetual hock to the company. Even after there was available cash in the economy, Frick continued using his scrip and payroll deductions for house rent and purchases at the company store. Since most of the labor was unskilled, Frick became one of the first employers in the area to import immigrants from Eastern Europe—"Huns" and "Slavs," as they were called. Already indebted for their passage, unable to speak or understand English, these people had little choice but to follow the rules laid down for them. Few, of course, had the daring or the means to articulate their misery. But in a letter published by the *Pittsburgh Post-Gazette* not long ago, a man named Ben Shedlock said it all for them:

> I lived under the regime of the Henry Frick clan. I lived in a little town called Trotter, Pa., near Connellsville and my Dad and brothers worked in the coal mines and coke ovens of the H.C. Frick Coal Co.
>
> The song "16 tons" was all true. That little town was under the control of the Coal Iron Police, hired by the company. They were like the Gestapo. As a youngster I had to be in

the house by 9 P.M., no more than five boys were allowed to gather together in one place.

One had to buy from the company store or lose his job. Nothing was bought with cash. Purchases were put on a slip and taken out of your paycheck. Prices in the company store were always very high. Like the song said, you owed your soul to the company store. They robbed the people blind in those stores.

The men in the coal mines were slaves. They worked 12 hours a day. I remember my Dad coming home in the winter, his clothes frozen to his body from working in the water in the mines. Of course, if you were killed in the mines, the company paid your family nothing.

A lot of people don't know the truth about a lot of rich families—how they got their money. They got it from the sweat and blood of good men who died working.

Since Frick was a man of deeds rather than words, his thinking about these matters has to be deduced from his actions. But from the record, it would appear that he had other things on his mind in the first year or so of the eighties. With his business well organized and money rolling into his personal account faster than he could spend it, Frick felt that he could afford to ease up on the austerity of his personal life. Their friendship having deepened, he asked Andrew Mellon to join him on a "Grand Tour" of Europe. Judge Mellon's willingness to let his favorite son and mainstay at the bank take off for four summer months is more evidence of his trust in Frick. Andrew could hardly fail to learn something by close association with a man who had achieved so much in so little time. In many ways, Frick was as much mentor as friend to Andrew, who acknowledged this aspect of the relationship by always calling his companion "Mr. Frick." Frick's seniority was physically emphasized by the trimmed beard he now wore in contrast to Mellon's youthful mustache. Well aware of their mutual shyness in social situations, they invited a young man-about-Pittsburgh who had a fund of small talk and jokes and a way with strangers to go along. Although Mellon was happy to have the company of this entertainer, he was less than thrilled when Frick insisted on including a stodgy, older man from Connellsville. The man was not known to be a Frick friend, and Mellon asked why they had to have him. "You'll see, Andrew," Frick said.

In New York while waiting to board their ship, Frick and Mellon hired a carriage to take them up Fifth Avenue, which was lined with the mansions of the wealthy. The newest and one of the grandest had just been built at Fifty-first Street by William H. Vanderbilt, the Commodore's son and principal owner of the New York Central. Gazing at it, Frick asked his friend, "What do you suppose the upkeep of that place would be? Would you say three hundred thousand dollars a year—about a thousand a day? You know, that's all I'd ever hope to possess." There was an eerie element of prophesy in that little speech, which may be why both men remembered it. In view of what it would take to produce an income adequate to Frick's estimate, he had raised his sights well beyond the mere million of his youthful dreams.

During the European phase of their trip, the rather odd quartet did all of the things expected of them, including kissing the Blarney stone. That event happened to take place on July 4, and Frick exhibited an unusual streak of playfulness by waving a little American flag over the heads of his companions as they did it. From Ireland they went on to England and Scotland. Helen Clay Frick, who must have heard it from her father, reported that "the high spot of the trip was undoubtedly their first glimpse of the Wallace collection in England"—their first encounter with a great private art collection. But the art they saw later in Paris and in Italy must have been equally exciting. Frick and his disciple Mellon carried out some modest experiments in buying paintings in the thousand-dollar range on their own. Their tour ended in Venice, where Frick finally revealed the reason he had brought the dull man from Connellsville along. The man had enjoyed what he had seen of the world so much that he wanted to have a look at the rest of it instead of going home, but he had run out of funds. There and then Frick offered him cash for his coal and coke holdings, and he accepted. While the young men headed west to America, the older man headed east to Asia with a fat wallet on his hip. Frick had given Andrew Mellon the kind of lesson that the judge had hoped for; it might even make up for getting him interested in the expensive hobby of collecting "pictures."

One affectation that both young men acquired that didn't last long back in sober, smoky Pittsburgh was wearing the latest in London fashion—beaver top hats. Judge Mellon himself probably advised them that such headgear wasn't appropriate to businessmen who wanted to be taken seriously. They did, however, begin to go out into Pittsburgh society together, and at one social function Frick's eye was caught by a young woman across the room. He pointed her out to Mellon, who knew her—Adelaide Childs, youngest daughter of a prominent Pittsburgher named Asa P. Childs. Whether because of his own shyness or the Victorian code of manners, Mellon sought out an older man to perform the honors when Frick asked for an introduction to Miss Childs. But once that formality was dispensed with, Frick moved in with his customary decisiveness and asked the young lady for permission to call on the next Sunday. In the way of those times, it took three months before Adelaide Childs agreed to become Mrs. Frick—three months of the kind of courtship that caused Frick to bring Mellon along to entertain Adelaide's watchdog sister so that he could have a few minutes alone with his lady love. In December 1881, a few days short of Frick's thirty-second birthday, they were married with Andrew Mellon standing in as best man.

It's symbolic of the acquisitive spirit of the age that the highlight of the Frick honeymoon, even in their daughter's accounts, was an historic piece of business. Frick and Tom Carnegie, Andrew's younger brother and hands-on manager of his interests in Pittsburgh, had naturally become well acquainted as Frick took over as sole supplier of coke to the Carnegie furnaces. When Tom learned that Frick would be taking his bride on a tour of Eastern cities, he arranged for his mother and Andrew, living together in New York's posh Windsor Hotel, to entertain them. It was a pleasant social occasion and throughout the meal the talkative little host entertained with anecdotes while Frick sat silent. Finally, Carnegie rose to his feet and lifted his glass.

"This brings to mind one more story before I make a toast," Carnegie said, gesturing with the glass.

It concerns a man newly arrived in a village in Scotland. His neighbors chose one of their number to call and determine what manner of man he was. Returning to report, the caller said, "He came to the door and when I went in he asked me to hae a drink o' whiskey and he gied me a glass, an' he took the bottle himse' and began to pour—an' he said say when, an' I said when, an' he *stopped*—that's the kind of mon he is." Well, I am not the kind of man to stop pouring in business and neither is the man I toast—my new partner, Mr. Frick!

Although Frick and Tom Carnegie had evidently discussed the matter in detail, the news came as a bomb blast to everybody else at the table. Nobody was more startled than Margaret Carnegie, her son's counselor and confidante ever since she had mortgaged the house in Allegheny for his first investment. As Carnegie sat down, she whispered loud enough for all the guests to hear: "Surely, Andrew, that will be a fine thing for Mr. Frick, but what will be the gain for us?"

It wouldn't have been difficult for Carnegie to explain the gain to somebody with as good a business head as his mother. The Carnegie interests got more than 10 percent of a reorganized business to be called H. C. Frick Coke Company. Capitalized at $2 million, the company issued forty thousand shares of stock at $50 a share. Among them Andrew and Tom Carnegie and Henry Phipps, Jr., a partner who had been a childhood playmate in Allegheny, took two thousand shares personally, and Carnegie Brothers & Co., Ltd., bought twenty-five hundred shares. Frick, E. M. Ferguson, and Walton Ferguson also had shares in their own names, and 33,500 shares were assigned to the purchase of H. C. Frick and Company, which the new business would replace. As a result of the whole reshuffle, Frick's interest dropped from 33⅓ to 29½ percent, but he was debt free with $325,000 in cash to put into improvements and expansion. Of even greater value was the fact that the Carnegie involvement constituted a virtual guarantee that Frick's company would retain its best customer. In the first fourteen months of operation, the new corporation made a net profit of $400,000, or 20 percent on its capital, on shipments of 946,065 tons of coke.

Recalling the deal years later with considerable inaccuracy as to some of the facts, Carnegie wrote:

> We found that we could not get on without a supply of the fuel essential to the smelting of pig iron; and a very thorough investigation of the question led us to the conclusion that the Frick Coke Company had not only the best coal and coke property, but that it had in Mr. Frick himself a man with a positive genius for management. He had proved his ability by starting as a poor railway clerk and succeeding. In 1882 we purchased one half of the stock of this company, and by subsequent purchases from other holders we became owners of the great bulk of the shares.

Whether either man was fully aware of it at the time, Carnegie and Frick were taking a great stride forward together in the direction of organizing America's rapid industrialization. They were not alone in their intuitive sense that supplying a vast continent and markets abroad would require operations on a scale undreamed of a decade earlier. In the same year that Carnegie and Frick became "partners," Samuel Calvin Tate Dodd, the attorney for John Rockefeller's Standard Oil of Ohio, invented the trust. By then Rockefeller had a finger in companies and installations all over the country that had nearly cornered the world market for kerosene. What he needed was a device to make them all work in the same harness, and Dodd proposed a board of nine trustees who would hold the stock of Standard Oil itself and all the subsidiary companies and issue some seven hundred thousand certificates of interest to guarantee a proportionate distribution of dividends to the stockholders. Despite ruthlessly driving competitors out until he controlled all but about 5 percent of the oil business, Rockefeller claimed that he was not seeking a monopoly but "order" in what had been a chaotic business. By stabilizing costs in order to ensure profits, he would be able to lower prices to the public. Also in pursuit of order was J. P. Morgan, who was trying to eliminate wasteful competition and wild speculation in the railroads in order to restore confidence in American securities abroad. He had discovered what that could mean to him personally when he sold a large block of New York Central stock directly to English investors in 1879 and earned the gratitude and confidence of William H. Vanderbilt.

In one respect, Carnegie, who had established his fortune by peddling railroad stocks to Europe, was not with the times. Having discovered the profitability of steel, Carnegie developed and articulated a new philosophy of business: "Put all your eggs in one basket and watch the basket." The basket he preferred was an old-fashioned one—a partnership of men directly involved with the conduct of the business. Improvements and expansion would be paid for by withholding profits instead of diluting ownership by marketing stocks and bonds. The reformed securities salesman spoke of Wall Street with the same note of disdain and horror that a dried-out drunk would use about saloons. Like his works manager Bill Jones, Carnegie was a Shakespeare fan who would echo Polonius's advice to "neither a borrower nor a lender be." At one point, he even refused to cosign notes for his old mentor and boss, Tom Scott, who got into trouble building a new western railroad. It was not always that way. In the beginning, the Carnegies borrowed as recklessly as Frick. This job often fell to Henry Phipps, the small, mousy, green-eyeshade partner. It was said around Pittsburgh that Phipps's horse would clomp along the city streets, crisscrossing and stopping before the door of every bank, without guidance from his master.

For most businessmen in the eighties, stocks and bonds were the way to go. They were not only the shortest route to millionaires' row but the only way to raise the kind of capital required for large, new enterprises. The market was more of a gamble then than now because there were no effective restraints on it until the Great Depression gave rise to the New Deal. But for those with the savvy and the power it was far easier then to manipulate the market. Stock watering—issuing securities far in excess of a company's capital assets—was a favorite device. The phrase came into the language long before the Civil War when people learned how Daniel Drew, a crafty market operator, got the money to invest in the first place. Starting out in business as a cattle merchant before railroads were functioning, Drew would drive his beasts from the countryside to New York City, letting them grow lean and thirsty. Just before reaching the market scales, he would let them bloat themselves with water. In some cases, manipulators would wring not only the water but a lot of the real juice out of a stock by ugly rumors, by mismanagement, by misuse of the law, or by any other means that would allow them to acquire stock for less than a company's real assets. This occurred frequently in the railroad wars in a style set by the old master, Commodore Cornelius Vanderbilt and his clumsy imitators, Jim Fisk and Jay Gould.

In a three-year period after the war, Vanderbilt made more money out of railroads than he had amassed in some sixty years in the shipping business. The "predatory animus" that made this great gain possible was never more clearly demonstrated than in Vanderbilt's capture of the New York Central. The Central's eastern terminus was at Albany, where passengers and freight were shifted to Vanderbilt's Hudson River Line. This appeared to be a workable arrangement until Vanderbilt suddenly ordered his trains to be stopped just short of the Hudson River Bridge at Albany. Passengers had to get out and walk with all of their baggage in all weathers, and freight was left to rot or rust in the open. It was an intolerable situation, and Vanderbilt was called before the Legislature to explain himself.

He cited a law that the Legislature had passed at the behest of the New York Central prohibiting Hudson River Line trains from crossing the river.

"Why didn't you run your trains to the river?" he was asked.

"I was not there."

"But what did you do when you heard of it?"

"I did not do anything."

"Why not? Where were you?"

"I was at home, gentlemen, playing a rubber of whist, and I never allow anything to interfere with me when I am playing that game. It requires, as you know, undivided attention."

Vanderbilt's disruption of service caused a drop in the New York Central stock that made it prudent and profitable for him to buy a controlling interest. His attitude before the Legislature was echoed some years later by his colorless but shrewd son, William Henry, who inherited the Central. During a rate war between the Central and the Pennsylvania, Vanderbilt was interviewed in his private car as it rolled along between Michigan City, Indiana, and Chicago. He explained to reporters that the only reason the Central maintained its fifteen-dollar fare from New York to Chicago was that the Pennsylvania was forcing it to do so. "But don't you run the train for the public benefit?" one newsman asked. "The public be damned!" said Vanderbilt, adding that the train was run for the benefit of the stockholders.

Andrew Carnegie's personal knowledge of such shenanigans might well have accounted for his righteous disdain for the stock markets. But he wasn't above using stock ownership to his own advantage. Not long after becoming Frick's "partner" in the coke business, Carnegie managed to buy up enough stock from other owners to get a controlling interest in H. C. Frick Coke Company. In effect, the partner was transformed into the boss. Frick showed no concern since the Carnegie connection was leading his company on from strength to strength. There was something of a scare in 1881 when a steelmaking plant more modern than Carnegie's E.T. went into operation in nearby Homestead with the backing of a few well-heeled Pittsburgh investors. Within months the new plant was turning out two hundred tons of steel rails a day and taking ever larger orders. Wanting to cash in on this bright future, the Amalgamated Association of Iron and Steel Workers plagued Homestead management with a series of labor disturbances that frightened the stockholders. Carnegie moved in, offered to pay off their investment in full and even invited them to become his partners. Only one was wise enough to accept the invitation; the rest took Carnegie's notes. They probably thought they had done the right thing when Carnegie immediately began pouring more money into troublesome Homestead to switch it from producing rails to structural steel. Within two years, a hard-running Homestead had paid off the whole Carnegie investment, and the man who had become a partner was on his way to millions.

With Homestead coming on line to demand ever more of his product, Frick was kept busy in the early eighties with the management of a going concern that promised gratification of his most extravagant wishes. He was also establishing a home. In the summer after their marriage, he and Adelaide bought a house at Homewood and Penn Avenues along what was then called millionaires' row in Pittsburgh. It was a relatively modest gray stone structure at least twenty-five years old with eleven rooms on two and a half stories. But to the young couple, it presented interesting possibilities, and turning it into an ornate, turreted Victorian structure of four stories and twenty-three rooms was a joint enterprise that they both enjoyed. By 1884, they began peopling it with children when a son, Childs, was born.

Life was good and would certainly get better. Whatever it took in the way of tough-minded decisions to make this domestic idyll possible was part of another life—out at the mines and ovens or downtown at the office. Two very different Henry Clay Fricks were emerging, and, as in so many other ways, he was becoming a perfect model of his peer group, the aggressive captains of American industry.

CHAPTER 5

"The Gospel of Wealth"

VIEWED from the porch swings and fine equipages of the middle and upper classes, the America of the 1880s was in splendid shape. Although it was still a gaslit time, a horse-and-buggy time, it wouldn't be for long. People were fooling around with electricity to provide brighter light and quicker transportation. For anybody with gumption, with a willingness to get up and go, there was no end to opportunity. The Horatio Alger stories were the rage because they could be believed. There were no wars or natural disasters to remind the ambitious that they might not be in charge of their own lives. There were no income taxes, and the federal government's biggest problem was what to do with a huge surplus in the treasury. Almost daily, news from the West told of another army victory over the Indians. Spanned now by telegraph and train, a whole continent of fertile farmlands and rich mines was not only easily reachable but safe for settlement. Even though it ran counter to the Bible as most people read it, Charles Darwin's new theory of evolution found ready acceptance in an America on the move toward some higher form of civilization.

More than ever this promising America was becoming a mecca for the disadvantaged of Europe. Immigration was running at the rate of five hundred thousand souls a year. Beautifully symbolic of America's attraction to the rest of the world was France's gift of the Statue of Liberty, which was being slowly assembled for installation in New York Harbor in 1886. But unfortunately, the America that most immigrants saw from the empty prairies, the mining and mill towns, the city ghettos for which they were destined, was not a pretty place. In those times when the rich were building palaces, only 45 percent of industrial laborers managed to stay above the poverty line of five hundred dollars a year; another 40 percent fell below what was considered a level of tolerable existence. To survive even on this scale meant hard work for twelve or more hours a day, often seven days a week and for wives and children, too. The one difference between their lives in the New World and the one they left behind was hope. Being adventurous enough to make the journey, they weren't the kind of people to accept their sorry plight in a land that was said to be free.

The labor troubles that gave Andrew Carnegie his golden opportunity to acquire the Homestead plant were characteristic of the whole of the turbulent eighties. In all, there were some ten thousand strikes and lockouts, many beyond the control of captains of either business or labor. The unions of the time, like the Amalgamated Association of Iron and Steel Workers and the American Federation of Labor, both formed in Pittsburgh, represented only the skilled workers, men who could command as much as eight hundred to twelve hundred dollars a year. The unions active in the Connellsville coke area were the Knights of Labor and the Miners' and Mine Laborers' Amalgamated Association. Although they were national in scope, the unions often negotiated contracts on a local catch-as-catch-can basis, a situation that infuriated Carnegie when the unions embarked on a concerted effort to establish the eight-hour day in every industry.

Thanks to his wizardry in other matters such as the invention of the Jones mixer, the manager at the Edgar Thomson works was allowed by Carnegie to have his quixotic way in putting his labor force on eight-hour shifts. In a paper read before the British Iron and Steel Institute in 1881, Jones cited the eight-hour day as one of the reasons that he was outproducing the British. "Flesh and blood cannot stand twelve hours' continuous work," he wrote. During a brief recession in 1884 to 1885, Carnegie discovered that the Chicago steel mills were working twelve-hour shifts and paying 6 percent less for labor with the approval of the Amalgamated. Since he was taking advantage of depressed prices to upgrade the plant's machinery, he ordered a lockout until the workers would agree to return to twelve-hour shifts on a nonunion basis. He won. Resuming work with fewer men at lower wages, Carnegie had a 19 percent advantage in costs over his Chicago rivals instead of a 6 percent deficit. It must have been a bitter pill for Bill Jones to swallow.

Not long after that—in January 1886—the Huns and Slavs in

Frick's coke works rebelled. According to Frick's explanation, the problem was cultural rather than economic although he had been steadily lowering wages as profits rose. Years later, Frick told a committee of the U.S. Senate:

> The principal cause [of the strike] was for the reason that we refused to allow the women, the wives of the foreigners then in our employment, to assist their husbands on the coke yards. In 1885, I think it was, the State of Pennsylvania passed a law prohibiting the employment of women. While we had never employed any women, never had a woman's name on our payroll, yet the wives of these foreigners would go to work with their husbands and assist them. As these men did piecework, we paid them for what piecework they did. On the State passing this law, which went into effect on the 1st of January 1886, we issued an order that women should not go with the men to work. This caused the strike—it was the start of the strike. After the strike was once started other questions arose. Finally, on or about the 22nd of February, 1886, we conceded an advance to the workmen of 10 percent. I think all resumed work.

Frick's memory may have faltered a bit, if an account of the strike published by *Harper's Weekly* in January 1886, while it was still continuing, can be believed. Pointing out that the strikers were largely nonunion Hungarians imported by Frick, who wanted to replace native laborers after an earlier strike, the magazine claimed that the cause of the strike was management's refusal to increase the piecework rate. Coal diggers were getting seventy-five cents per wagon, and coke drawers were getting between fifty-five and sixty cents per oven. Under these circumstances, the willingness of women—employees or not—to work alongside their men is quite understandable. Deprived of these helpers by law, the men were asking for five cents more on each wagon and oven, and they went on strike—a word derived from striking, or taking off, sail in the time of tall ships—to get it.

The *Harper's* piece was not written by a bleeding liberal. Indeed, it reflects the prevailing chauvinism and general fear of labor unrest brought on by the railway riots in '77. Some excerpts give a flavor of the occasion that was missing in Frick's dry testimony to the Senate:

> On January 18 many of the Hungarians stopped work, and the strikers were reenforced during the next three or four days, until 3600 ovens were shut down, and 5000 men were idle. They immediately began to do deeds of violence. On the 19th 200 Hungarians and Poles, led by Steff Stanex, a gigantic miner, who was the most daring spirit among the strikers, all armed and many intoxicated, marched with banners, to the music of a fiddle and of a wash boiler as a drum, made an attack on the Alice Coke-works near Connellsville, drove the workmen away, pulled open oven fronts, and did what damage to property they could.
>
> At the Morewood mines there was an encounter between 300 armed followers of Steff Stanex and a posse of special officers. The Hungarians, men and women, armed with revolvers, clubs, and knives, resisted arrest. A pitched battle ensued. As many as a hundred shots were fired. Several men were badly beaten, a number were wounded, and one was killed. The Hungarian women fought with their husbands and brothers, and after they were driven into their houses they continued to shoot.
>
> A company marched through the streets of Scottdale armed with fence rails, clubs, pick handles, crowbars, and such rude but dangerous weapons, and made raids on the dram-shops, many of the women as well as the men becoming drunk. At another place, the Donnelly and Diamond works, a riot occurred in which five Hungarians and three Americans were fatally wounded. These Hungarians are the most difficult class of laborers to manage when they are peaceful, or to pacify when they are enraged.

Lethal though it turned out to be, the confrontation in the coke region was a minor incident compared to the battle in Chicago a few months later in that year of 1886. The trouble began on May 1 when some 340,000 union members staged a nationwide work stoppage as part of the eight-hour-day campaign. At the McCormick reaper plant in Chicago, police fired on a group of picketers on May 3, killing one and injuring others. A mass meeting was called at the Haymarket on May 4 to protest the killings. It drew a large crowd of union members and sympathizers, including socialists and anarchists. When the two hundred policemen assigned to keep order moved in to break up the meeting, somebody threw a bomb, starting a shooting spree that resulted in seven deaths and more than sixty injuries. No bomb thrower was ever identified, but a jury, guided by Judge Joseph E. Gary of Cook County Criminal Court, found eight anarchists guilty of murder for inciting the deed by their oratory. Of these eight, one was sentenced to life imprisonment, one committed suicide, four were executed, and two had their sentences commuted to life imprisonment. The dead became instant martyrs to anarchists like Emma Goldman and her lover, Alexander Berkman, who would hold in mind for years the hope of revenge.

The men on millionaires' row stood far above this strife. Some like Henry Clay Frick maintained a dignified silence and let the law, which favored keeping the peace and protecting private property, work its will. But others felt called upon to comment. It can hardly be coincidental that Carnegie chose to begin writing—and editors of influential magazines chose to begin printing—the essays that would eventually comprise "The Gospel of Wealth" when the strike-filled agitation for the eight-hour day began in 1886. Having avoided a strike himself by means of a peaceful lockout to get even with the Amalgamated, Carnegie evidently felt free to pontificate.

It's not hard to imagine how Carnegie's words would have been greeted in the saloons of Braddock if anybody had bothered to read "An Employer's View of the Labor Question" in the April issue of *Forum* magazine. Some samples follow:

On unions from a man who had just forced the union out of the E.T. plant:

> My experience has been that trades-unions, upon the whole, are beneficial both to labor and to capital. ... The ablest and best workmen eventually come to the front in these organizations; and it may be laid down as a rule that the more intelligent the workman the fewer the contests with employers. It is not the intelligent workman, who knows that labor without his brother capital is helpless, but the blatant ignorant man, who regards capital as the natural enemy of labor, who does so much to embitter the relations between employer and employed; and the power of this ignorant demagogue arises

chiefly from the lack of proper organization among the men through which their real voice can be expressed. This voice will always be found in favor of the judicious and intelligent representative. Of course, as men become intelligent more deference must be paid to them personally and to their rights, and even to their opinions and prejudices; and, upon the whole, a greater share of profits must be paid in the day of prosperity to the intelligent than to the ignorant workman. He cannot be imposed upon so readily. On the other hand, he will be found much readier to accept reduced compensation when business is depressed; and it will be better in the long run for capital to be served by the highest intelligence, and to be made well aware of the fact that it is dealing with men who know what is due to them, both as to treatment and compensation.

On management from a man who lived in New York winters and in Scotland summers:

One great source of the trouble between employers and employed arises from the fact that the immense establishments of to-day, in which alone we find serious conflicts between capital and labor, are not managed by their owners, but by salaried officers, who cannot possibly have any permanent interest in the welfare of the working men. These officials are chiefly anxious to present a satisfactory balance-sheet at the end of the year, that their hundreds of shareholders may receive the usual dividends, and that they may therefore be secure in their positions, and be allowed to manage the business without unpleasant interference either by directors or shareholders. It is notable that bitter strikes seldom occur in small establishments where the owner comes into direct contact with his men, and knows their qualities, their struggles, and their aspirations. It is the chairman, situated hundreds of miles away from his men who only pays a flying visit to the works and perhaps finds time to walk through the mill or mine once or twice a year, that is chiefly responsible for the disputes which break out at intervals.

In August 1886, a few months after the Haymarket riots, *Forum* published another Carnegie article, entitled "Results of the Labor Struggle." It created quite a stir, mostly because of one passage. Although deploring violence, Carnegie suggested that it was justified when strike breakers—or scabs—were brought in by employers. "There is an unwritten law among the best workmen: 'Thou shalt not take thy neighbor's job,' " he wrote. Taken out of context as they soon were, these words from a leading capitalist became a battle cry for labor. But in the same paragraph Carnegie says that the way to solve a labor dispute is his way: shut down the works and await the result of the dispute, which must inevitably mean surrender by men in dire need of income.

Carnegie's views would, in fact, be endorsed by any fellow capitalist who read the article carefully—which is probably why it was printed by a leading journal. As to the issue in dispute at the time— the eight-hour day—he wrote: "I trust the time has gone by when corporations can hope to work men fifteen or sixteen hours a day. And the time approaches, I hope, when it will be impossible, in this country, to work men twelve hours a day continuously." His desire that unions be governed by intelligent men was repeated with a slight twist: "The results of the recent disturbances have given indubitable proof that trade-unions must, in their very nature, become more conservative than the mass of men they represent."

It wouldn't be long before Carnegie, with his controlling interest in the H. C. Frick Coke Company, would see how his last bit of advice worked out in practice. The Carnegie interests had undergone a major reorganization in 1886. Rather than increase the capitalization of Carnegie Brothers & Co., Ltd., to accommodate the addition of the Homestead mills, Carnegie, Phipps & Co. was created. In the process, Carnegie placed the Lucy Furnaces, which had been functioning independently, under the new company. Shortly after this reorganization Tom Carnegie, his brother's chief lieutenant in Pittsburgh and owner of blocks of stock equal to those of Henry Phipps in both companies, died. Since executives of both Carnegie companies comprised a majority of the H. C. Frick Coke Company board, it is likely that Tom Carnegie, a friend of Frick, would have been one of the directors when labor trouble again broke out in the coke fields in the spring of 1887, and he might have prevailed upon his brother to chart a different course.

The issue this time was clearly economics rather than culture.

Early in the year, the coke operators got together and proposed a wage scale that the workers would not accept. Both parties agreed to submit the matter to arbitration. "We selected three men to represent us, the labor union selected three to represent them, and those six selected Mr. John B. Jackson, of this city [Pittsburgh], as the seventh man," Frick told the Senate committee. "The case was of course submitted to him; he rendered a decision refusing the workmen the demand they made. They immediately struck against the award." Deciding to stand firmly together, the operators selected Frick, representing the largest concern in the business, as their leader.

Since the main bodies of the unions accepted the decision of the Arbitration Board, the Knights of Labor declared the strike illegal. With this kind of backing, the operators felt certain of prevailing even though the local lodges voted to strike. Ugly fights broke out between the men who were willing to follow the union leadership and go to work and the strikers. Mines were dynamited; machinery was destroyed; tons of coke were allowed to spoil in the ovens. The turbulence generated bad news, but the operators knew that giving in would destroy not only their authority but that of the union leadership, which was behaving in the conservative way Andrew Carnegie had recommended.

As usual at that time of the year, Carnegie was far away in Scotland. In this season of 1887, his preoccupation with pleasure was intense and doubtless justified. He had not only gone through the death of his brother, but his mother and constant companion had also died. While Tom lay dying in the fall of 1886, Carnegie himself was so ill that his partners were afraid that he, too, would die and bring the companies to bankruptcy as a result of paying off the Carnegie family interests. In this crisis one partner put heart into the others by predicting that Tom would die because of his heavy drinking but that Andrew's more abstemious habits would save him. When the prediction proved true, Carnegie seemed to be granted new vigor. The fifty-two-year-old bachelor married a young woman named Louise Whitfield, whom he had met riding in New York's Central Park, and spirited her off for a honeymoon in Scotland. It was while he was enjoying this state of bliss that Carnegie got the news of the Connellsville strikes and cabled orders for the H. C. Frick Coke Company to meet the strikers' demands.

Accordingly, the chairmen of the Carnegie steel companies, Henry Phipps, Jr., and John Walker, told Frick that he would have to go along with Carnegie's order and, in effect, double-cross his fellow operators. It was a very heavy blow to Frick's pride. More than just the leading employer in the area, Frick was the leading member of a large family that had been regarded with respect for generations. Frick was not deceived as to the motives of Carnegie and his minions. They had nothing to do with the apparently prounion sentiments Carnegie had expressed in his writings. The intent was to demand a sacrifice from the coke company for the sake of the steel companies. Frick's perception was fully confirmed later by James Howard Bridge, Carnegie's secretary, whose book was truly titled *The Inside History of the Carnegie Steel Company: A Romance of Millions.* Bridge wrote:

> The apparent act of bad faith on the part of the Carnegies received universal condemnation. It was ranked above that of the strikers who had repudiated their umpire. The breaking up of the combination was also deplored because it involved demoralization of prices on which the wages ultimately depended; so that in the long run the workmen would suffer by the act. But those who made these criticisms did not consider the risk which the Carnegies ran in banking up their blast-furnaces. The best furnace will not stand banking for more than three months; and during this time there is always a danger of its becoming chilled. When this happens it has to be blown out, and partially if not wholly relined at a cost of at least $35,000. At this date the Carnegies had seven furnaces banked; so that there was almost a quarter of a million dollars in hourly peril. In addition, there was a positive loss amounting to many thousands of dollars daily through stoppage of iron production, and further losses in the steel-mill through lack of material. On the other hand, the advantage which the Carnegies would have over competing iron manufacturers by getting a regular supply of coke and continuing work while others were idle, was one almost beyond compute. While this alone might not tempt the average manufacturer to a breach of faith, it would do much to console him for it if other conditions produced it.

A breach of faith it was for Frick, and he must have wondered whether he had made a terrible mistake in allowing the Carnegies to acquire so much interest in the company he had built from scratch, the company he loved. Mr. Frick reacted like the Clay Frick of the schoolyard who would fight when his own interests or reputation were in jeopardy. On May 13, Frick wrote a letter to Phipps, Walker, "and others" in which he offered to resign as president of the company but made a last pitch in defense of his position:

> Having temporized with our employes and made concession after concession to satisfy them and largely in your interest, and against the interest and judgment of all other coke producers, and finally prevailing on them to agree to arbitration and decision having been rendered in our favor, I think that, cost what it may, we should abide by it, and not start our works until our employes resume work at the old wages, but inasmuch as you have large interests depending on our works being operated I do not feel like standing in the way of you managing the property as your judgment and interests dictate.

Some weeks of unrecorded dialogue between the parties went by before Frick again put pen to paper, on June 7:

> Messrs. Henry Phipps, Jr., John Walker, et al.
> Gentlemen:
> As you hold a majority of the stock and are entitled to control in the Frick Coke Company, and in view of what has passed between us on the subject, I feel compelled to vacate my position as its President. I therefore enclose, herewith, my resignation.
> But I accompany it with this my serious protest against the course you propose to take regarding the pending strike. I am satisfied that it must occasion heavy loss to the Coke Company. Besides the loss occasioned by granting the men's present unreasonable demands, it will only lead to still more unreasonable demands in the near future. The loss to the Coke Company may be far more than made up, so far as you are concerned, by gains in your steel interests, but I object to so manifest a prostitution of the Coke Company's interests in order to promote your steel interests.

STAGES IN THE LIFE OF HENRY CLAY FRICK
Clockwise, from top left: Brash and confident in his twenties, he borrowed thousands of dollars to become King of Coke; cool and arrogant in his forties, he used his power as chairman of Carnegie Steel Company to crush the union in a bloody battle at Homestead; brooding and bitter in his sixties, Frick talked of meeting his old partner, Andrew Carnegie, in hell.
The Carnegie Library of Pittsburgh

Often cited to show how far he rose, Henry Clay Frick's modest birthplace was a cottage next to the mansion of his grandfather Abraham Overholt, a wealthy farmer and distiller in Westmoreland County, Pennsylvania. *The Carnegie Library of Pittsburgh*

Shortly after their marriage, the Fricks bought a Victorian house at Penn and Homewood Avenues in Pittsburgh, which they remodeled into this reflection of a château they had admired in France. *The Carnegie Library of Pittsburgh*

In 1881, en route to Europe, Andrew Mellon and Henry Clay Frick rode past the newly built Vanderbilt mansions on Fifth Avenue in New York. Frick expressed a desire to live there, and twenty-four years later, he leased the one on the corner of 51st Street for an annual rent of six figures. *The Collection of the New-York Historical Society*

Judge Thomas Mellon, the stern Pittsburgh judge turned banker, from whom Henry Clay Frick borrowed his first ten thousand dollars to build coke ovens. *The Carnegie Library of Pittsburgh*

The product from coke ovens like this, tended mostly by immigrant labor, made Frick a millionaire by the time he was thirty years old. *The Carnegie Library of Pittsburgh*

When Frick tried to land Pinkertons to break the strike at Homestead, a
pitched battle broke out, which resulted in dead and wounded on both
sides. Strikers won, and surrendering Pinkertons were beaten by the strikers and their wives and children as they were marched through the streets.
The abandoned barges were looted and burned by angry citizens. *The
Carnegie Library of Pittsburgh*

Whilst a majority of the stock entitles you to control, I deny that it confers the right to manage so as to benefit your interests in other concerns at the loss and injury of the Coke Company in which I am interested.

Very respectfully yours
H. C. Frick

Frick accompanied this letter with a memorandum to Carnegie Brothers & Co., Ltd., offering to sell his entire interests in the Coke Company on very reasonable terms—an offer to be accepted by June 15. Reminiscent of his dealings with the B. & O. Railroad, this deadline approach didn't work this time. Frick's resignation was accepted, Phipps replaced him as president, a labor contract on the strikers' terms was negotiated, and production begun. But when Frick, his wife and two children, his mother-in-law and sister-in-law boarded a ship for Europe on July 22, his ownership in the H. C. Frick Coke Company was still intact. When the Frick party arrived in London, they were greeted with an unexpected note:

August 2, 1887

Welcome to Britain's Isle,
Of course you will all come and spend a week with us.

It's superb—Come and see what one gets in Scotland these summer days.

Just off this morning, ten in all, for three days coaching tour. Blaine the happiest man you ever saw. Let me hear your movements. Can take you all any time.

Yours always
Andrew Carnegie

P.S. Kind regards to Mrs. Frick and sister in which Louise heartily joins.

A.C.

In assessing this note, Frick knew that Carnegie, like himself, had learned that on July 27, the strike was settled in favor of the operators who held out. This meant that the Carnegies would be paying 12½ percent more for their coke than their competitors. The "white haired devil" was clearly eating a little crow. Not about to disrupt his family's long-laid plans to go running to Scotland, Frick let Carnegie, Phipps, Walker, et al., follow him around with communications until, finally and just before they were all to return to America, the visit to Carnegie's rented Cluny Castle was made. It apparently went off well, because Frick was reinstated as president of the company bearing his name in January 1888. Although the settlement of the disagreement between them on labor policy was publicly peaceable, it caused the two men to take a different measure of each other. Cynical as to true human motivation, Frick decided that he would have to be ever alert for attacks on his coke interests. Shocked into admiration for a man who would stand up to him, Carnegie decided that he had a tiger by the tail, and he could use a tiger to guard all those eggs in his basket, now that Tom was gone.

Tom's death left a huge hole not only in the executive ranks of the Carnegie companies, but also in the shares available to partners. In January 1889, Carnegie offered to lend Frick enough money to acquire a 2 percent interest in Carnegie Brothers & Co. to be paid off out of the earnings if he would assume the office of chairman. Should all go well, Frick's holdings would be advanced to 11 percent, an amount equal to Tom's old shares and to those of Henry Phipps. Only Carnegie's 55½ percent would be greater. Frick accepted, but he gave fair warning in a letter dated August 9, 1889, that he would not be Carnegie's patsy:

> My dear Mr. Carnegie:
> I have read with interest yours from Christiana.
> It is very much pleasanter to agree than differ with you and in most things I would and will always defer to your judgment because there is no one whose attitude I hold in as high esteem, but I always hold to the opinion that your attack on P.R.R. [Pennsylvania Railroad] was wrong and I should deprecate its renewal—you cannot expect me to succeed in carrying everything through that is wished for or undertaken.
> I could not and would not remain the official head of any concern that was not well managed. If a concern is not to be mismanaged, the official head's policy must have due consideration.
> I cannot stand fault-finding and I must feel that I have the entire confidence of the power that put me where I am, in a place I did not seek.

With all that, I know I can manage both C.B. & Co., and
Frick Coke Co., successfully.

Sincerely yours
H. C. Frick

A first test of how this very close partnership between Frick and
Carnegie would work out came in early 1890. By then Frick had
demonstrated very dramatically that he did have, as Carnegie put
it, "a genius for management." In his first year as chairman, the
net profit of the Carnegie concerns rose to $3,540,000 from
$1,991,555 the year before. A pleased Carnegie was addressing his
communications to "My dear Pard." Carnegie decided not to interfere when the unfavorable contract with the coke workers came up
for renewal. Once again the operators, led by Frick, agreed to stick
together and offer the workers a general wage scale that would be
equal to all. Once again the workers refused to accept it and went
on strike. As manager of the steel companies as well as the coke
facilities, Frick had prepared for this resistance. He had stored up
enough coke to continue operations. In this he had assistance from
the market: prices for steel and rails were so low that he found
it advantageous actually to curtail production to a comfortable
level by raising prices. He didn't care how long the diggers
and oven drawers laid down their tools; in fact, the right time
had arrived to get rid of the unions and troublemakers once and
for all.

Frick used the tactic that had worked for him years earlier
when he first imported foreign labor. He started hiring strike
breakers. Having once experienced Carnegie's compliance with
their demands and having read his commandment against this very
tactic, the strikers were shocked. Then they were enraged. The
battle between strikers and scabs and their protectors turned into
fierce guerrilla warfare that lasted for some three months. Given
orders to shoot to kill, deputy sheriffs carried them out with grim
determination. Eight strikers died and many more suffered crippling wounds before a kind of peace was restored to the area, and
the mines and ovens were being operated by men willing to accept
the owners' terms.

No hint of the terror and tears, the bloodshed and disruption of
lives during those dreadful months, is present in Frick's cool recollection of the event for the Senate committee:

I think it was in March of that year after, as I say, repeated conferences, and being unable to agree with our workmen, we posted notices stating just what wages we would pay. Our employes refused to accept it, and we began to introduce new workmen. Our experience had been such with organized labor that we could place no reliance on the agreements they made with us, and we concluded that we would end the thing once for all, and determine whether we had a a right to employ whom we pleased and discharge whom we pleased. That strike lasted, I think, until the latter part of May that year, at which time we succeeded in starting our works with what is called "nonunion workers," and from that time until the present we have had no trouble. Our men have been contented and happy. We have not been bothered with the labor agitator and with committees asking all sorts of concessions.

Silent for a change, Carnegie was off in Scotland much of this time polishing up another essay soon to be published in the magazine *Nineteenth Century* under the improbable title "The Advantages of Poverty." Citing Jesus' parable of the talents in which the servant who increased the money his master gave him was commended and a sermon by John Wesley, founder of Methodism, in which his followers are urged to "gain all you can by honest industry," Carnegie argued that the only sinners with respect to moneymaking are "those who hoard realized capital, adding the interest obtained for its use to the principal, and dying with their treaures 'laid up,' which should have been used as they accrued through the life of the individual for public ends, as the gospel of wealth requires." To this, he added:

> Acting in accordance with this advice, it becomes the duty of the millionaire to increase his revenues. The struggle for more is completely freed from selfish or ambitious taint and becomes a noble pursuit. Then he labors not for self, but for others; not to hoard, but to spend. The more he makes, the more the public gets. His whole life is changed from the moment that he resolves to become a disciple of the gospel of wealth, and henceforth he labors to acquire that he may wisely administer for others' good. His daily labor is a daily virtue. Instead of destroying, impairing, or disposing of the tree which yields such golden fruit, it does not degrade his life

nor even his old age to continue guarding the capital from which alone he can obtain the means to do good. He may die leaving a sound business in which his capital remains, but beyond this die poor, possessed of no fortune which was free for him to distribute, and therefore, I submit, not justly chargeable with belonging to the class which "lay up their treasures upon earth."

Not one to separate deeds from words entirely, Carnegie had begun his much publicized philanthropic activities by establishing public libraries before he published this sort of thing. Yet it is evident how far removed he was from the young man who wanted only fifty thousand dollars a year so that he could devote himself to good works. His motive in putting Henry Clay Frick in charge of his "capital" was clearly to live up to the millionaire's duty of increasing his revenues, and it would soon become apparent that he could not have made a wiser move to that end. As to living by the rest of his gospel, Carnegie was only making it harder for himself.

CHAPTER 6

Having a Grand Old Party

AMERICA was never more Republican than during the half century after the Civil War. Except for the two nonconsecutive terms of the conservative Democrat Grover Cleveland, the White House was occupied by a member of the Grand Old Party. Republican strength came initially from victory in war, and the party's leaders were accused of "waving the bloody shirt" at every election to take advantage of this patriotic sentiment. General Grant's election in 1868 and reelection in 1872 despite a plethora of scandals attested to the power of the "bloody shirt." The youngest man ever elected to the presidency up to then and a total political innocent—he had voted only once in his life—Grant was no match for the men of money. Before his tenure was over, both the party and the country would be in the grip of business interests fronted by powerful senators. This grip would tighten until Thorstein Veblen, writing at the turn of the century, could claim that "representative government means, chiefly, representation of business interests."

The political issues of the times were pocketbook issues for business—taxes, tariffs, distribution of public lands, monetary and labor policy. It made all kinds of sense for the captains of industry to devote some of their tax-free profits to the manipulation of the political process to make sure that there would be more of the same. Take tariffs, for instance. It may be a chicken-or-egg question as to whether the Republican Party took a stand for high protective tariffs and then got the liberal financial backing of the manufacturers or whether businessmen used their wealth to woo Republicans already in power because of the war. Whatever the answer, the Republican stance on tariffs was an important factor in the marriage between

Republicanism and business. This was particularly true in iron and steel manufacturing, as Abram Hewitt, one-time Democratic leader of the House and ironmaster by trade, noted wryly:

> Steel rails were subject to a duty of $28 a ton. The price of foreign rails had advanced to a point where it would have paid [the manufacturer] to make rails without any duty, but of the duty of $28 a ton he added $27 to his price and transferred from the great mass of the people $50,000,000 in a few years to the pockets of a few owners who thus indemnified themselves in a very short time, nearly twice over, for the total outlay of their business.

Andrew Carnegie and his lieutenant, Henry Clay Frick, were Republicans. So were Judge Thomas Mellon and his son, Andrew; John D. Rockefeller and his brother William; J. P. Morgan and his entourage. But the Republican ranks were not filled solely by the newly rich. Largely because of its bloody shirt banner in all of its connotations, the party enlisted the loyalty of the old rich from New England and New York, of the educated middle classes in the professions, and of veterans everywhere. On the local level where Republican politicians were the "bosses" handing out favors to the disadvantaged, as in Pittsburgh, even labor could be found in the ranks of the GOP. With a few unifying themes like patriotism and protectionism, the Republicans seemed to be pulling together to achieve progress through ever bigger and better businesses.

By contrast, the Democrats even then justified Will Rogers's remark, "I don't belong to an organized party; I'm a Democrat." Under the Democratic tent gathered conservative Southern whites who were Republican in every instinct but couldn't bring themselves to salute the bloody shirt; immigrant labor recruited by organizations like New York's Tammany Hall in the North and East; western farmers ever squeezed by the tight money policies of eastern banks. On the national level, the Democrats represented a collection of locally powerful constituencies willing to compromise their differences. In general, they favored policies that would decentralize the power and give wider distribution to the wealth of big business. They opposed tariffs that artificially raised the prices on the manufactured goods farmers had to buy, and they favored bimetalism—the free coinage of silver—for the inflationary effect that would ease the repayment of their debts.

There were actually more Democrats than Republicans scattered across the country. Several of the Republican occupants of the White House squeezed through the door with less than a plurality of the popular vote; after the election of 1876, Congress had to create a special Electoral Commission to sort out the contested electoral vote and designate Republican Rutherford B. Hayes the winner. Throughout the period control of Congress tended to seesaw back and forth. This being the case, Republican dominance was not bought easily or cheaply. The smallest slip could sometimes be fatal. An important factor in Cleveland's Democratic breakthrough in 1884 was the remark of a Protestant preacher who said that the Democrats were "the party whose antecedents are rum, Romanism and rebellion." When the Republican candidate, James Blaine, refused to repudiate the statement the Roman Catholics—and no doubt a great number of saloon keepers—turned against him. As one of those Republican senators in debt to big business, Blaine may have thought he was doing the right thing. Publicly at least, puritanism and Protestantism were almost as popular with business leaders as patriotism and protectionism.

Except for Mark Hanna, a large-scale dealer in coal, iron, and shipping in Ohio who became chairman of the Republican Party and served in the Senate, the big moneymakers preferred to stay behind the scenes in politics. Flush with his first million, thirty-year-old Clay Frick almost made the mistake of going the other way when he was offered the Republican nomination for Congress from the Connellsville district. Hearing about it, Judge Mellon, disillusioned by his own service on the bench and the City Council, told him that he would be "foolish to take it." The judge's persuasive argument was that a smart man could make more money by sticking to business. By staying out of politics himself the wealthy man would be free to use his money for pragmatic rather than partisan purposes. In his plain-speaking book, *The Passing of the Idle Rich,* Frederick Townsend Martin, a banker's son and socialite born in the same year as Frick, described the real politics of wealth in this way:

> The class I represent care nothing for politics. Among my people I seldom hear purely political discussions. When we are discussing pro and con the relative merits of candidates

or the relative importance of political policies, the discussion almost invariably comes down to a question of business efficiency. We care absolutely nothing about statehood bills, pension agitation, waterway appropriations, "pork barrels," state rights or any other political question, save inasmuch as it threatens or fortifies existing conditions. Touch the question of tariff, touch the issue of the income tax, touch the problem of railroad regulation, or touch the most vital of all business matters, the question of general federal regulation of industrial corporations, and the people amongst whom I live my life become immediately rabid partisans. It matters not one iota what political party is in power or what President holds the reins of office. We are not politicians or public thinkers; we are the rich; we own America; we got it, God knows how, but we intend to keep it if we can by throwing all the tremendous weight of our support, our influence, our money, our political connections, our purchased senators, our hungry congressmen, our public-speaking demagogues into the scale against any legislature, any political platform, any presidential campaign that threatens the integrity of our estate. The class I represent cares nothing for politics. In a single season a plutocratic leader hurled his influence and his money into the scale to elect a Republican governor on the Pacific Coast and a Democratic governor on the Atlantic Coast."

When Henry Clay Frick, at the age of forty, took over management of the nation's largest steel manufacturer and the nation's largest coke business, he found that Pittsburgh and surrounding Allegheny County were in safe Republican hands. Local government there was, in fact, the very model of the political "boss" system to be found in most urban areas. The rulers of Pittsburgh were two Scotch-Irish Presbyterians named Christopher Magee and William Flinn. Since they each had different financial interests, they could pull together comfortably in the same harness. Magee's reward for services rendered consisted of favorable franchises for street railways; Flinn was paid off in contracts for supplying materials on public building projects. They worked their wiles through having people beholden to them in the right jobs. Their power was so great that it could exasperate even a fellow Republican like Judge Mellon, who said of his experience on the city council:

> We all know that when Mr. Magee comes in here and indicates his desires, he generally gets what he wants. Anything he wants must succeed, it always succeeds. This is a coincidence, a phenomenal fact that always does occur. Did you ever see, did any man ever see an ordinance that he advocated that did not go through? Any man who has the faintest political aspirations in city, state or nation always votes as Mr. Magee desires.

An admirer of power efficiently applied, Frick apparently found it useful to have the right kind of bosses running the political show. By the time he was grumbling about Magee, Judge Mellon had long since turned his business over to Andrew and a younger brother, Dick. Out of the office, Frick spent a good deal of time with "the Mellon boys," as he called them, and was involved in a number of enterprises with them. A Mellon biographer, David E. Koskoff, wrote of the relationship: "Besides the Judge, Frick was the other great teacher in A.W.'s life. He taught A.W. about art, how to buy it and perhaps to some extent to appreciate it; about politics, how to live in the same world and make peace with the Magees and Flinns that the Judge abhorred and denounced for the mutual advantage of both the bosses and the businessmen; about business, how to think and work in bigger arenas than those of his mercantile-banker father."

Although the role that Frick was playing at the steel companies was his visible one, his offstage participation in the ventures that were cooked up on Sunday mornings in Frick's study at home when the Mellon boys dropped in ostensibly to talk pictures may have been as important and enriching. Among other things they would invest in downtown real estate, which they would enrich by prevailing upon Magee and Flinn to enlarge streets and put in utilities. Frick would become a major investor in the various banks the Mellons organized, and as the result of one deal Andrew Mellon acquired $25,000 worth of shares in the Old Overholt distillery. In addition to hosting the Mellon boys at home, Frick would see them almost daily at the exclusive Duquesne Club, where a group of congenial business leaders would gather for lunch in a private, third-floor room. They would discuss the state of the world in general and Pittsburgh in particular and have a little fun at the end by rolling poker dice to see which one would dig into his deep pockets to pay for the meal.

Undoubtedly much of the conversation turned around what Frick was doing with the Carnegie companies. He had been little more than a year in his new position before he arranged the greatest bargain in steel industry history. A few miles up the Monongahela River from Homestead, a group of investors had built a facility to go into competition with Carnegie in the manufacture of steel rails. Called the Duquesne Steel Works, it included a new process that eliminated a second heating of the ingots before they went into the rollers to make billets and rails. This would enable them to undersell Carnegie products, and it was not to be tolerated. Carnegie himself spread the rumor that rails from Duquesne would be unsafe since they lacked a second heating. The distrust that unfounded rumor caused, together with labor troubles and bickering among the investors, caused financial problems for the new enterprise, and Frick pounced. He offered to buy the facility for $600,000. Since this was only half the investment, the offer was rejected, but Frick kept negotiating and finally came up with an offer of $1 million in five-year Carnegie bonds. Although this meant that the Carnegie interests wouldn't have to put up a cent, the offer was accepted. Miraculously, under Carnegie management it appeared that rails only needed one heating after all. By the time the bonds came due, Duquesne had paid for itself six times over, and Carnegie crowed, "F is a marvel. Let's get all F's."

Another early step Frick took to bring order out of what he perceived as administrative chaos in the Carnegie companies was to create the Union Railway. This would connect the plants and carry freight inside the plants thus eliminating the inefficiency and bickering that had been going on with outside railroads competing for rights. With savings on switching charges and increased efficiency, the Union Railway paid for itself within months. More importantly, it was a physical symbol of the coordinating principle that would be the gift of Frick management to industry. In addition to tying the facilities together with rails, Frick worked with Carnegie and all the other partners to promote a single company in place of all the separate units that often got in each other's way.

Frick found his work thoroughly engrossing. From the beginning he set an example to the whole organization by working harder and longer than anyone except the mill hands on their twelve-hour shifts. Rising every morning at six, he would breakfast and walk to his downtown office to be at his desk by eight. He would seldom leave before six or seven in the evening, when he would go home for a romp with his three small children and a family dinner, after which he might take up his work again if there wasn't a bridge or poker game to divert him. For some six years while he was reshaping the Carnegie organization, Frick never took what could be called a vacation.

In the same year that Frick became chairman, there was another very significant change in the executive ranks at the Carnegie companies. Captain Bill Jones, the wizard of E.T. and a hands-on manager, was killed when a furnace exploded. To replace him, Charlie Schwab, a Jones protégé who was equally popular with the workers, was transferred back to the Braddock works from Homestead, where he had recently been installed as manager. Neither Jones, by his own choice, nor Schwab, by reason of youth, were partners, but they were the men who made the steel. An outgoing, cheerful, powerfully built young man, Schwab had grown up in a large Catholic family in Loretto, Pennsylvania, where his father ran a livery stable. By what would later seem a strange coincidence, Schwab occasionally drove Andrew Carnegie from the station in nearby Cresson to his summer home and charmed the older man with his high spirits and the sweet tenor voice he used to entertain his passengers. But as soon as he graduated from high school, Schwab took off for Braddock, where he was offered a job clerking in the store of a family friend from Loretto. Captain Jones, who frequented the store, liked the looks and attitude of the young clerk and hired him away as a stake driver at E.T. Within six months, Schwab was Jones's assistant and within five years he was managing Homestead. Despite his liking for good times, Schwab spent evenings doing the books for Jones and studying the chemistry of steel to keep up with the college-educated engineers that were beginning to filter into the industry. Schwab was creating an enviable production record at Homestead with the help of men who liked and respected him; his continued presence there might well have averted a terrible tragedy that began unfolding in that summer of 1889.

Even under Carnegie auspices, the Amalgamated Association of Iron and Steel Workers had kept six strong lodges going. With all of the improvements in machinery and methods that men like Jones and Schwab were introducing, production per man-hour was rising rapidly. Since wages were geared to production, it meant that skilled workers represented by the Amalgamated were making what people in the front office like insider Bridge considered earnings "beyond all reason." As Bridge, a presumable eyewitness, reported, "During this time some of the men earned from $12 to $15 a day; and Homestead became familiar with the sight of steel workers being driven to the mill in their carriages." With new contracts coming up in the summer of 1889, Carnegie, through his representative on the spot, William L. Abbott, chairman of Carnegie, Phipps & Co., tried to remedy it by a general reduction of 25 percent and an automatic sliding scale to keep future wages in line with steel prices like the one at nonunion E.T. Rejoicing in their benefits from being paid by tonnage, the Amalgamated men refused to go along and went on strike instead.

By this time, Andrew Carnegie was off on his usual summer visit to Scotland and Europe. Although he may have outranked Abbott as chairman of Carnegie Brothers, Frick evidently didn't feel empowered to interfere directly at Homestead. Nevertheless, Abbott's next move would strongly suggest that he took advice from Frick rather than relying on Carnegie's much publicized views on how to handle labor. Abbott tried to bring in strike breakers with near disastrous results. The strikers pounced on these scabs, hauling them off the trains as they arrived and beating them. The sheriff tried to come to their rescue with 120 deputies, but they were driven away by the angry mob. The Amalgamated celebrated this defiance of the law as a victory—and a victory it turned out to be.

Without consulting Carnegie—or "using the cable," as he put it—Abbott sat down with the union leaders and reached an agreement. "Both sides are victors, and both sides are probably vanquished in minute details," he said. The union agreed to a sliding scale but with the rate to be based on an average of six months' and then three months' prices rather than changed from month to month as the company demanded. Abbott's major concession—the one that would horrify Frick with his passion for absolute control of any enterprise, the one that would cause the union to claim complete victory—was to allow for workmen's committees in every department to advise on such matters as filling an empty position, apportioning work, and changing machinery. When news of the settlement reached him in Germany, Carnegie was not pleased, as a letter he wrote to Abbott from Berlin attests:

The great objection to the compromise is of course that it was made under intimidation. Our men in other works now know that we will "confer" with law breakers. At this distance one can be very brave no doubt; I don't like this feature at all, at all! It seems to me that a curt refusal to have anything to do with these men would have brought matters right in less time than to you seems possible. Whenever we are compelled to make a stand, we shall just have to shut down and wait, as at Edgar Thompson, until part of the men vote to work. Then it is easy. I am glad, however, that we shall have three years' peace under the sliding scale.

Carnegie's optimism was not justified, according to Bridge. With their demands and grievances, the workers' committees turned the three years into a period of incessant wrangling. Frick, who was laboring to put the pieces of the Carnegie enterprise together, was certainly aware of this, but his first priority was to get full control into his own hands. In order to convince Carnegie, who was happy with things as they were, he had to get the agreement of twenty-two other partners and especially Abbott, whose important position as chairman of Carnegie, Phipps & Co. would be eliminated in the process. He also had to come up with an alternative to the convenient practice they had fallen into of borrowing back and forth between the two companies. As early as February 1890, Frick was able to sit down and write a letter to Carnegie in his own hand that his confidant and biographer Harvey quoted as the clincher:

> My dear Mr. Carnegie:
> Referring to the condition of our finances, and looking towards consolidating C.B. & C.P. & Co., I find there is outstanding $1,185,000.00 of paper made by Carnegie Phipps & Co., to the order of Carnegie Bros. & Co., $860,000.00 of paper made by Carnegie Bros. & Co., to the order of Frick Coke Co., for the accommodation of the Frick Coke Co.
> So you see a few months of such earning as we are now having will enable us to get along without the necessity of taking paper form C.P. & Co. If anything of that kind is

needed, the Frick Coke Co. can be used. Had a talk with
Abbott who favors making one company.

> Yours very truly
> H. C. Frick

From that point on, it was a matter of getting the lawyers to dot the
i's and cross the *t*'s, a lengthy process that would result in the legal
birth of Carnegie Steel Company, Limited, on July 1, 1892. Capitalization was increased from $5 million to $25 million by giving a 400
percent dividend per share. This increased Andrew Carnegie's share
from $2,766,666.67 to $13,833,333.33. Henry Phipps, Jr., and Henry
Clay Frick, on an equal footing, had shares advanced from $550,000 to
$2,750,000. The next large share—$1 million—was assigned to a Carnegie cousin, George Lauder. The rest went down through $250,000
for Abbott to $27,777.78 for one Henry B. Bope. Only Carnegie,
Phipps, and Frick owned their shares outright. The others were
"debtor partners" who would owe the company for their holdings until they were paid for out of earnings. As of the formation of the new
company Carnegie and Phipps resigned from the board of managers,
and the partners agreed upon a new executive structure with Henry
Clay Frick as chairman. Other principal officers were Henry M.
Curry, treasurer, and Francis T. F. Lovejoy, secretary. In addition to
these three, the board of managers was comprised of George Lauder,
William H. Singer, John G. A. Leishman, and Lawrence C. Phipps.

Nobody could question the high evaluation put on the new company. It was the leading steel producer in the world, and the net
profit of $5,350,000 in 1890 alone amounted to more than 20 percent
of its new capitalization. But for Carnegie's ownership, the King of
Coke had become the King of Steel just before his leadership would
be put to its severest test.

At a little over forty, Frick was surpassing all of his youthful
dreams of business success. But all the power and wealth at his disposal proved useless when his six-year-old daughter Martha fell ill
and died in 1891. Although the death of children was a recurring
event in the best-protected of families in those days, Frick could not
take this loss of an adored little girl in stride. To keep the memory
of her alive, he had special checks printed with her picture to use
for special purposes such as his quiet giving to help families and
particularly children in distress.

At this time of his personal troubles, Frick was one of the loyal supporters being called upon for extra effort in the form of cash to keep the Grand Old Party going. It had managed to put Cleveland out of the White House and install Benjamin Harrison in 1888 even though the Democrat polled a plurality. With a do-nothing president who was willing to sign anything they passed, the Republican-dominated Congress tried to please everybody. Their gift to industrial backers like Frick and Carnegie was the highest tariff ever, named for William McKinley, an Ohio congressman. Another Ohio Republican legislator, Senator John Sherman, put his name to an antitrust act meant to quiet fears that businesses were getting too big, an act that would turn out in practice to be a weapon against unions instead. They even threw a bone to the farmers yearning for cheap money with the Silver Purchase Act. But all of this was to no avail. In 1890, a Democratic Congress was elected, and in 1891 the Populist Party came into being to field a candidate in 1892 who would represent the disaffected farmers and laborers. Worried Republican managers like Mark Hanna were passing the hat to collect a four-million-dollar war chest to back Harrison.

By the time the parties gathered in convention in June 1892, to nominate Harrison and Whitelaw Reid, editor of the *New York Tribune,* for the Republicans and Cleveland and Adlai Stevenson, a former congressman from Illinois, for the Democrats, nobody could have foreseen that the election would swing in large part on the actions of Henry Clay Frick, the new chief of Carnegie Steel Company, Limited. Frick himself was innocent of much interest in the election apart from his usual support for any Republican candidate. In fact, he and Carnegie agreed in correspondence that Cleveland was a sound man—for a Democrat, that is. From a practical point of view, which was the only point of view Frick had, they were still safe in the hands of Magee and Flinn in the Pittsburgh area and Senator Matthew Stanley Quay, whose Republican machine controlled the state of Pennsylvania. The party wasn't over where he was.

CHAPTER 7

The Fight for Fort Frick

IN the late winter and early spring of 1892, Henry Clay Frick spent many a night of uncertain sleep on the train between Pittsburgh and New York. An important piece of business was in process that required frequent personal consultations with the controlling partner, Andrew Carnegie, at his Manhattan home. The unfavorable contract that Abbott had negotiated with the Amalgamated Association of Iron and Steel Workers at Homestead in 1889 was due to expire on June 30, the day before Carnegie Steel Company, Limited, officially would come into being, and both men were determined that the new company would never suffer such a defeat again. The matter under discussion was how to achieve this end. Although they agreed that the only way to establish control over labor was to get rid of the union, as Carnegie had done at Edgar Thomson and Frick had done in the coke fields, they differed as to the means they should employ. As he had stated publicly in his articles, Carnegie favored a peaceable lockout; Frick wanted to provoke a strike.

No record was kept of what Frick and Carnegie said to each other, but it is to be doubted from what actually happened that Frick was completely honest in defending his point of view. What did come out of the talks was Frick's evident conviction that the end was more important to Carnegie than the means. He needed to be sure of this since Carnegie would be taking off in April to spend nine months or more abroad, leaving Frick, like Abbott, to handle matters alone. There was a difference this time, however. Under the reorganization, Carnegie had no office in the organization; he was only a stockholder. Frick reigned supreme, and he had already made it clear to

Carnegie that he wouldn't tolerate unwarranted meddling or criticism.

At their last meeting, Carnegie handed Frick a written memorandum of his views, a document that has disappeared. But its contents might be judged from another document that he instructed Frick to post in the Homestead works:

ANDREW CARNEGIE
5 West 51st St.

New York, April 4, 1892
NOTICE
TO THE EMPLOYEES AT HOMESTEAD WORKS
These Works having been consolidated with the Edgar Thomson and Duquesne, and other mills, there has been forced upon this Firm the question Whether its Works are to be run "Union" or "Non-Union." As the vast majority of our employees are Non-Union, the Firm has decided that the minority must give place to the majority. These works therefore will be necessarily Non-Union after the expiration of the present agreement.

This does not imply that the men will make lower wages. On the contrary, most of the men at Edgar Thomson and Duquesne Works, both Non-Union, have made and are making higher wages than those at Homestead, which has hitherto been Union.

The facilities and modes of working at Homestead Works differ so much from those of steel mills generally in Pittsburgh that a scale suitable for these is inapplicable to Homestead.

A scale will be arranged which will compare favorably with that at the other works named; that is to say, the Firm intends that the men at Homestead shall make as much as the men at either Duquesne or Edgar Thomson. Owing to the great changes and improvements made in the Converting Works, Beam Mills, Open Hearth Furnaces, etc., and the intended running of hot metal in the latter, the products of the works will be greatly increased, so that at the rates per ton paid at Braddock and Duquesne, the monthly earnings of the men may be greater than hitherto.

While the number of men required will, of course, be reduced, the extensions at Duquesne and Edgar Thomson as well as at Homestead will, it is hoped, enable the firm to give profitable employment to such of its desirable employees as may temporarily be displaced. The firm will in all cases give the preferences to such satisfactory employees.

This action is not taken in any spirit of hostility to labor organizations, but every man will see that the firm cannot run Union and Non-Union. It must be either one or the other.

When he got back to Pittsburgh, Frick quietly filed away Carnegie's proclamation to the workers. It was quite true that the Amalgamated represented a small minority of Carnegie workers. Out of a workforce of 3,800, at Homestead only 800 of the most skilled were admitted to Amalgamated membership, and the scale under negotiation applied to only 325 of these. But under the terms of the 1889 contract, union committees had a great deal to say—much more than Frick would ever tolerate—about personnel management and working conditions in the mill. Well aware of the union's power and position, the unskilled workers felt that the better the terms for Amalgamated men, the better they would be for them all. They wouldn't buy Carnegie's sophistry about having a nonunion policy forced upon the company; they would see his proclamation for exactly what it was—a direct attack on the union and as such the opening gun in a fight for survival. This was not at all in keeping with Frick's subtler strategy. He wanted to have the union fire the first shot. If the company appeared to be in the right, it would be far easier to summon support from the public and the law if necessary.

Frick already knew by April that the union would never accept the company's terms. There were three important changes from the current contract. The minimum of the sliding wage scale, based upon the price of four-by-four Bessemer billets, was twenty-five dollars—that is, on a falling market, wages could be reduced until the price hit twenty-five dollars but would remain constant thereafter. Since billets were selling at twenty-two dollars in early 1892, the company demanded that the minimum be dropped to that figure. In addition, the company wanted a reduction in the tonnage rate paid to workers at the open hearth furnaces and mills where new machinery had increased production per man-hour. The third demand was that the termination date be changed from June 30 to December 31, usually a low point in the annual business cycle.

Bridge, a Frick admirer writing from the vantage point of a scribe inside the executive offices, argued that the company's position was a proper product of Frick's logical mind. Considering the price of billets, the drop in scale spoke for itself. A million-dollar machine that permitted the 119-inch plate mill to roll plates from slabs instead of ingots doubled production. Yet, according to Bridge, "with the sweet unreason of the toiler" the men at the 119-inch plate mill insisted on receiving all of the benefit of the investment in the machinery. As for changing the date, the Amalgamated Association had agreed to a similar date at competing establishments, so why not at Homestead? Herbert N. Casson, another Frick admirer and author of a lyrical book full of poetic license called *The Romance of Steel,* saw Frick's demands as arising out of the inevitable thrust of history—the replacement of man by the machine. Casson's sources included interviews with Frick, whose hard logic involved the assumption that, since capital was required for physical improvements, the return on them belonged to capital.

Undoubtedly, both sides in the controversy were caught up in historical movements that they couldn't absolutely control. It was a case crying for compromise, and compromise was clearly possible. In general, the Amalgamated people had gone along with technological improvements even when workers were replaced by machines. Relations with the union were good in Carnegie's Union Iron Mills, which was one reason why Frick didn't want to draw the line where Carnegie's notice placed it. Nevertheless, Frick refused to compromise. He gave the union until June 24 to meet his terms—or else. The "else" was not spelled out, and it left union leadership in some confusion. Carnegie's intervention in the first coke strike was recalled, and it seemed even more likely now that he had gone on record with articles that appeared to be prounion. Frick's tough repression of the second coke strike, which included using the dreaded Pinkertons, was also recalled. Since his notice wasn't posted, the union men were in the dark about Carnegie's position. Not so Frick.

Along with the typewritten notice to be posted at the works, Carnegie had given Frick a handwritten note: "Should this be determined upon, Mr. Potter (John A. Potter, Homestead superintendent) should roll a large lot of plates ahead, which can be finished should the works be stopped for a time." Fortunately for the company, business was off, and the only sure market was for armor plate that the Navy had ordered. This evidence that Carnegie was willing to accept a work stoppage was reinforced by a letter from England, dated June 10:

> As I understand matters at Homestead, it is not only wages paid, but the number of men required by Amalgamated rules which makes our labor rates so much higher than those in the East.
>
> Of course, you will be asked to confer, and I know you will decline all conferences, as you have taken your stand and have nothing more to say.
>
> It is fortunate that only a part of the Works are concerned. Provided you have plenty of plates rolled, I suppose you can keep on with armor. Potter will, no doubt intimate to the men that refusal of scale means running only as Non-Union. This may cause acceptance, but I do not think so. The chances are, you will have to prepare for a struggle, in which case the notice (i.e. that the works are henceforth to be non-union) should go up promptly on the morning of the 25th. Of course you will win, and win easier than you suppose, owing to the present condition of markets.

The one command in that letter that Frick was obeying before it arrived was to prepare for a fight. He had ordered an unusually large number of plates to be rolled, a sure sign of coming trouble to the workmen involved. But if that left any doubts in the minds of the laborers, they were dispelled when Frick instructed Potter to have a wooden fence, topped by barbed wire and punctuated by watchtowers with searchlights, built around the entire periphery of the plant, leaving it open only on the river side. Ominously, the fence contained holes of the right size and placement for rifles; lethal gunfire had been part of Frick's recent labor battles in the coke fields.

The view from Homestead, with the warlike fortifications rising before their eyes and nothing but stony silence coming from the Pittsburgh offices, was bleak. The men no longer believed that Frick was bargaining in good faith. If his stand on wages could be called logical, it was not a logic of the marketplace but of the company's own making. The story was around that Carnegie used influence bought by his gifts to the Republican party to have the duty on steel billets reduced in the otherwise high-tariff McKinley bill. In a pep talk to his fellow laborers, Homestead burgess John McLuckie, himself a Republican, gave credence to this story:

> The cause of this wage trouble is not generally understood. We were persuaded to vote the Republican ticket four years ago in order that our wages might be maintained. As soon as the election was over a widespread feeling on the part of manufacturers towards a reduction of wages was exhibited all over the land. As soon as the McKinley bill was passed, the article in the production of which we work was the only article that suffered a reduction. It is Sunday morning, and we ought to be in church, but we are here today to see if we are going to live as white men in the future. The Constitution of this country guarantees all men the right to live, but in order to live we must keep up a continuous struggle. This is the effect of legislation and nothing else. The McKinley bill reduced the tariff on the four-inch billet, and the reduction of our wages is the result. You men who voted the Republican ticket voted for high tariff and you get high fences, Pinkerton detectives, thugs and militia!

At that point, McLuckie was only guessing that the fences would be followed by Pinkertons or militia. It was a believable guess to his fellow citizens of Homestead, because it had become a familiar pattern in labor disputes all over the country. The Pinkertons were especially despised and feared because of their willingness to shoot to protect property or establish order. Established in 1852 by Allan Pinkerton, a Scotch immigrant with a background of poverty and liberal political activity like Carnegie's, the Pinkerton's National Detective Agency earned an enviable reputation by uncovering a plot to assassinate Lincoln in Baltimore on his way to the inaugural and by its intelligence work in the South during the war. But after the war and under the direction of Pinkerton's sons, the agency became the strong arm of management in labor disputes. It was a very lucrative operation since local sheriffs often found it difficult to raise a posse of ordinary citizens who would, or could, move against their neighbors. Even as trouble in Homestead was brewing, there were movements afoot in the legislatures of many industrial states to ban the use of Pinkertons.

There was a brief flurry of hope on all sides when Frick suddenly announced that he would meet with union representatives in his offices in the *Chronicle-Telegraph* building in Pittsburgh on June 23. Indulging in a bit of bargaining duplicity, Frick had instructed Potter in the course of issuing his ultimatum that he didn't care whether the men were union or nonunion as long as they agreed to his terms. If that were truly the case, the union men stood ready to make compromises on all but one point—the termination date. To negotiate a new contract in mid-winter would be to put virtually all the power in management's hands. A strike in cold weather with the cost of living at its highest peak would be difficult to call or sustain. It was, in fact, this very point that proved most persuasive in recruiting the three thousand nonunion workers at Homestead to the union cause. Beginning at ten A.M., the crucial and difficult meeting lasted until four P.M. When the union indicated a willingness to accept twenty-four dollars as a minimum on the scale, Frick said that he might bring his demand figure up to twenty-three dollars, and that was as far as compromise went. Neither side would yield on the other two issues, and Frick closed the proceedings by saying icily, "Gentlemen, this ends all conferences between you and this firm."

Frick had his fight. On the twenty-fifth, he posted notices at the mill to the effect that henceforth the company would deal only with individual workmen who wanted to stay on the job after June 30. On the same day, he sat down and wrote a letter to Robert A. Pinkerton in New York, a letter indicating prior discussions between them:

> I am in receipt of your favor of the 22nd.
>
> We will want 300 guards for service at our Homestead mills as a measure of precaution against interference with our plan to start operation of the works on July 6th, 1892.
>
> The only trouble we anticipate is that an attempt will be made to prevent such of our men with whom we will by that time have made satisfactory arrangements from going to work, and possibly some demonstration of violence upon the part of those whose places have been filled, or most likely an

element which usually is attracted to such scenes for the purpose of stirring up trouble.

We are not desirous that the men you send shall be armed unless the occasion properly calls for such a measure later on for the protection of our employés or property. We shall wish these guards to be placed upon our property and there to remain unless called into other service by the civil authorities to meet an emergency that is not likely to arise.

These guards should be assembled in Ashtabula, Ohio, not later than the morning of July 5th, when they may be taken by train to McKee's Rocks, or some other point upon the Ohio River below Pittsburgh, where they can be transferred to boats and landed within the inclosures of our premises at Homestead. We think absolute secrecy essential in the movement of these men so that no demonstration can be made while they are en route.

Specific arrangements for movement of trains and connection with boats will be made as soon as we hear from you as to the certainty of having the men at Ashtabula at the time indicated.

As soon as your men are upon the premises we will notify the Sheriff and ask that they be deputized either at once or immediately upon an outbreak of such a character as to render such a step desirable.

Frick was careful to keep Allegheny County Sheriff William McCleary advised of his every move through his and the company's attorney, Philander C. Knox, and his partner in private business, Christopher Magee, one of the Republican bosses. But, as he later told congressional investigators, Frick had no faith in sheriffs because of past experiences, which was why he had turned to Pinkerton for protection. It was nevertheless necessary to make a pretense of going through the proper public channels to have right—and ultimately the might of the state militia—on his side. His stated intention of using secrecy and surprise to avoid inciting the workers to riot during the operation was something of a pretense, too. Aside from that highly visible fence that the Homesteaders called Fort Frick, there were the barges that a Frick agent had bought and was having refitted at the Tide Coal Co. in Allegheny City. Identical vessels 125 feet long and 25 feet wide, they looked like Noah's ark with a flat roof. One—the *Iron Mountain*—was turned into a dormitory with tiered berths along the sides; the other—the *Monongahela*—was fitted out with tables and a kitchen. The local crew of some twenty waiters hired to handle food service undoubtedly spread the word as to the nature and size of these accommodations. If the Pinkertons were coming, as rumored, they were coming in force.

In keeping with his ultimatum, Frick ordered Potter on the same day he wrote to Pinkerton—Saturday, June 25—to post notices throughout the plant to the effect that the company would no longer negotiate with the Amalgamated Association but would sign contracts with individual workers. Three days later, the company shut down the 119-inch plate mill and an open hearth department and thus began a lockout. But later that day the rest of the labor force turned it into a strike by walking out in sympathy. That night hundreds of men gathered in the streets outside Fort Frick to hang Frick and Potter in effigy. When a company loyalist tried to take down these figures, he was driven off with a fire hose. On the twenty-ninth, while executive personnel closed down the rest of the plant, the workers gathered at the Opera House in Homestead and voted to reject Frick's ultimatum.

Knowing it would be a fight to the finish, the eight lodges of the Amalgamated Association appointed an Advisory Committee of five men from each lodge with Hugh O'Donnell, a skilled roller, as chairman. Working with Burgess McLuckie, this committee moved quickly to take charge of the whole community. Saloons were closed, police appointed, and a strategy worked out for defense in the event of scabs or Pinkertons appearing on the scene. This committee was made up of "the most intelligent and conservative members" of the union, according to the *Pittsburgh Commercial-Gazette,* a business paper. The order of the day was no violence, no destruction of property. This did not mean that an invasion of scabs or Pinkertons would be tolerated. The committee drew up an elaborate plan of defense. They created three divisions of about a thousand men each to mount a round-the-clock watch on all approaches to Homestead—roads, railroad, river. To cover the most likely of these, the committee comandeered a flotilla of small boats and chartered a steamer, the *Edna.* Special steam whistles were mounted on the *Edna* and atop the borough's Electric Light Works to sound a warning. When, and if, outsiders arrived, they were to be "very gently, but very firmly" pushed away by order of Hugh O'Donnell.

The first few days of July were quiet but tense in Homestead. There was one small incident. When smoke was seen coming from the furnaces in Open Hearth Department No. 2, the committee notified an assistant superintendent in writing that they could not be responsible for the consequences if the gas was not shut off. But confrontation was averted when company watchmen on their own initiative let committee members in to take care of the matter. Celebrations of Independence Day were low-keyed, and Burgess McLuckie said of the occasion that "we can't celebrate the Fourth until we know whether or not the Declaration of Independence is still in force in this country. You see, H. C. Frick wasn't consulted when that document was drawn, and he may think it necessary to revoke its provisions."

During this period, Frick stayed away from Homestead. He went regularly to his city office, kept up with the other affairs of the world's largest steel company. Evenings he retreated to the haven of his home on millionaires' row. Resembling in its altered form a French chateau that the Fricks had admired, the enclave at Clayton was the equal of any neighboring property. Besides the house itself, there was a domed glass greenhouse, a carriage house and stables with a dozen or more vehicles to suit any occasion, a child's dream of a playhouse. In that year of 1892, the Fricks were still adding interior refinements. In the breakfast room, where the master of the house held his frequent poker sessions, the walls were covered with intricate aluminum leaf tracery; burgundy silk draperies, made especially for Mrs. Frick at the Prelle mill in Lyons, France, were hung in her bedroom. Judging from daughter Helen's memories, Frick left matters of business like the Homestead negotiations at the office so that Clayton could be a place of "azure skies and green lawns," where she could drive around in her goat cart or play with her imported dolls. Dinners in the mahogany-paneled dining room were family affairs where the austere Mr. Frick and gentle Adelaide would amuse the children by teasing each other. If there were no guests for cards, Frick might spend the evening in the velvet-lined music room listening to the self-playing orchestrion or wandering around to contemplate the increasingly valuable paintings he was acquiring. In some ways, that July was an especially happy time at Clayton since a new baby who might help them all to forget Martha's death was due to arrive any day.

With the men Pinkerton recruited already assembling at the staging area downriver, Frick decided late on Monday, July 4, to shift responsibility for whatever might happen at Homestead to the county. Using the Advisory Committee's note about Open Hearth Department No. 2 as an excuse, he sent Sheriff McCleary a formal, written notice that the Carnegie Steel Company would hold Allegheny County responsible for protection of its property. The next morning, McCleary went alone to Homestead, where he was met at the station by members of the Advisory Committee. They took him around the periphery of the Fort Frick stockade, pointed out the guards they had posted, and suggested that the best way to secure the property would be to deputize the union men. Knowing from his talks with Philander Knox how that would go down with Frick and Magee, McCleary declined, returned to Pittsburgh, swore in a dozen deputies, and dispatched them to Homestead. They were not received as politely as the sheriff himself. The Advisory Committee hustled them—how gently nobody has recorded—aboard *Edna,* transported them across the river, and shoved them into trolley cars headed for Pittsburgh. With the deputies gone, the strikers tore down a sheriff's proclamation warning against unlawful acts and watched the coming on of night with apprehension. It was now only a question of precisely when the county or the company or both would counter their defiance with force.

They didn't have long to wait and worry. Shortly after midnight an Amalgamated lookout on the Smithfield Street bridge in Pittsburgh spotted the dark shapes of two barges being towed slowly up the Monongahela River by a tug named *Little Bill.* The man ran to the nearest telegraph and sent word to Hugh O'Donnell. Sound asleep in *Iron Mountain* were 266 men dressed in the blue, brass-buttoned Pinkerton uniforms designed to evoke shades of the victorious GAR. But this was no army. For the most part, Pinkertons were recruited from the ranks of the shiftless and unemployed. They were desperate men who were willing to kill—ironically on behalf of society's wealthiest and most powerful citizens—for the sake of three square meals and a dollar a day. This night they could sleep because they had been told that no trouble was anticipated. The cases of Winchester rifles and ammunition shipped from the factory to the Carnegie Steel Company by Adams Express were still nailed shut. Along with their own commander, Captain Heinde, Homestead's Superintendent Potter and Colonel Joseph H. Gray, a deputy sheriff, kept watch in the wheelhouse of *Little Bill.* At the time of that midnight sighting, the off-duty union men and their families were also sound asleep in their narrow frame houses clinging to the steep hillside. At Clayton, Frick, in an exercise of customary discipline, had gone to bed to be ready for what promised to be a hard day at the office. Far across the Atlantic, Andrew Carnegie was arising from a good night's sleep at Haddo House in Aberdeen, Scotland, where he had just dedicated a library he had given to the city; he had to be up early to get to Loch Rannoch in time for some fishing.

When the *Little Bill* and its tow reached a lock a few miles below Homestead, the union watchers activated the alarm system. Out on the river, the *Edna* blew its whistles, and the big whistle on the electric works screamed alarm into the night. Other horns and bells joined in to create a harsh chorus. Virtually all of Homestead's twelve thousand inhabitants turned out of bed, pulled on any clothes at hand, and headed for the waterfront. Those with weapons—shot-guns, rifles, pistols, swords, knives, whatever—took them along; those without pulled the palings off picket fences to act as clubs. The women and older children were as eager to clobber the invaders as the men. Huddled together on the riverbank, calling curses down upon Frick and his mercenaries, they were a formidable force. As if nature were conspiring with the stealth Frick wanted, a smoky mist shrouded the river and melted the riding lights of boats and the fires of furnaces on the far bank into dim, fuzzy blotches of red. The strikers who fired at the ghostly hulks they took to be barges mostly missed, but the crackle and pop of their weapons alerted the men aboard, now thoroughly awakened by the din, to their danger. Cap-tain Heinde ordered his men to break open the crates of rifles and arm themselves.

With the works abeam at four A.M., *Little Bill* headed in toward shore. The crowd running along the bank was momentarily stymied by Fort Frick's fence, but they soon ripped away enough boards to pour through the gap. By the time the barges had been nosed into the steep bank at the landing site, the Homesteaders were there to give them a hostile greeting. Dawn was breaking, and they could see one of the Pinkerton commanders step out on the deck of *Mo-nongahela*. He ordered some of his men to put out the gangplank and shouted to the gathering on the bank that they were armed and would be taking over the works by force if necessary. Hugh O'Don-nell pleaded, "In the name of God and humanity, don't attempt to land! Don't attempt to enter these works by force!" Joining his fellow officers on deck, Heinde yelled, "We were sent here to take possession of this property and to guard it for this company. If you men don't withdraw, we will mow every one of you down and enter in spite of you. You had better disperse, for land we will!"

A young striker ran down and threw his body across the gangplank. Heinde started hitting him with a club. Somebody fired. History has yet to settle the origin of the first shot, but there was another shot in quick succession. Both the striker and Heinde were wounded. More fire followed from both sides. Men on ship and shore fell dead and dying. The crowd ran back up the bank, and sharpshooters among the strikers hunkered down behind piles of steel billets ready to pick off any Pinkerton who showed his head. An eerie silence prevailed as a brass ball of sun broke through the mist. Only occasionally would a tense rifleman on one side or the other think he saw a target and open fire. Then at eight A.M. the Pinkertons tried once more to come ashore. In the exchange of fire, several workers were wounded, and four were killed. One of these, twenty-eight-year-old John Morris, sticking his head out of the pump house high above the barges, was hit between the eyes. He fell sixty feet into a ditch in full view of the crowd. As his body was carried home, rage swept through people lining the streets like a brush fire. The Pinkertons retreated in the face of this fury.

During a lull *Little Bill* took the dead and wounded among the Pinkertons across the river. When she returned she was met with such fire from shore that the pilot had to lie on the floor of the wheelhouse until she drifted out of harm's way. She never did return, leaving the barges stranded against the bank. The sun turned the barges into intolerable hot boxes, but increasingly accurate sniper fire kept the Pinkertons sweating under cover. They, in turn, drove off the strikers with fire from the windows. Frustrated, the union men began to devise schemes for forcing the Pinkertons into the open. If the intent hadn't been so deadly, many of them would have been a farce. A lighted stick of dynamite thrown onto the roof of one of the barges rolled off and fizzled out in a bucket of water on deck. The shot from a cannon mounted across the river missed the barges and beheaded a worker. A flat car loaded with burning debris sent rolling down a track to the dock jumped the rails. Oil spread on the waters refused to ignite. Into midday and beyond the battle remained a standoff.

News of it reached Pittsburgh almost with the first shot. In his downtown office, Sheriff McCleary paced the floor in frustration. He had not authorized Colonel Gray to deputize the Pinkertons, and he couldn't do it now with Gray driven away on *Little Bill.* If nearly three hundred armed Pinkertons were being held at bay, what could he possibly do with a citizen posse of deputies? Instead of being hustled out of town as they were the day before, they would probably be shot. Chris Magee, McCleary's political mentor, was in the office as the sheriff wrestled with his problem. At nine A.M., William Weihe, national president of the Amalgamated Association and a conservative labor leader who had been urging his followers to maintain peace at Homestead, arrived in a near panic. The only solution, he told McCleary and Magee, was for Frick to meet with O'Donnell and his group at once. When McCleary sent Frick a message to this effect, he refused to negotiate, and the company's secretary, Francis Lovejoy, issued a chilling statement: "Our works are in the hands of the sheriff, and it is his official duty to protect the property from destruction or damage. If it is necessary in his judgment to call out troops, he is the proper authority to do so. Everything is in his hands."

By ten A.M., McCleary, with the advice of Magee, who was Frick's partner in a number of business ventures, cabled Governor Robert E. Pattison to ask for instructions in view of the fact that the striking workers and followers "number at least 5,000, and the civil authorities are utterly unable to cope with them." The reply from Harrisburg was something of a shock to McCleary and Magee: "Local authorities must exhaust every means at their command for the preservation of peace." Although Pattison was a Democrat—a political "sport" in a state house as traditionally Republican as the White House—he owed his 1890 election in part to Magee, who had swung the Allegheny County vote in his favor. Republican Magee saw Pattison's election as a thumb in the eye of Senator Matthew Quay, whose position as Republican boss of the state he coveted. Despite Magee's acknowledged power, both McCleary, who had refused to deputize the Pinkertons, and Pattison were well aware of the extent to which their supporters at the voting booths hated these mercenaries. Around noon, McCleary and Magee, joined by the county's other Republican boss, William Flinn, tried again to collect on a political debt with a message telling the governor that the emergency required a force beyond the sheriff's command and urging him to act at once. And once again the governor ducked: "How many deputies have you sworn in and what means have you taken to enforce order and protect property?"

At his *Chronicle-Telegraph* building office, Frick stayed cool and calm. His demeanor throughout that deadly day was recorded by a *New York World* reporter who wrote that "while the men whom he had locked out and the men he had employed to force an entrance into the mill were killing each other at Homestead the steel king sat in his magnificently furnished office and smoked cigars, gave orders to subordinates or chatted with visitors. To some of the latter he was cool and stern." One of these "latter" must have been the reporter who passed along to his readers the substance of an interview during which Frick spoke "nonchalantly":

> "The matter is out of our hands now. We look to the sheriff to protect our property. The men upon our properties now are not strikers, they are law breakers. We are conveying to the Sheriff all the information in our possession regarding the situation and he must take responsibility of action."
>
> "How about the military?"
>
> "The matter of calling out the militia is also in the hands of the Sheriff. He alone can decide at what point the disorder passes beyond the control of the civil power."
>
> "Will you hold any conferences with representatives of the workmen?"
>
> "I will hold conferences with nobody. The matter, as I have said, is out of our hands and the supremacy of the law is the only question involved. The officers of the law are the proper persons to deal with that. I was very sorry to hear of the disturbances at Homestead. We are entirely out of the deal now so far as protecting our interests up there are concerned. The matter now rests entirely with the Sheriff, and to him we look for protection of our property."

At the time of this interview, Frick had evidently given up on his own "watchmen," as he called the Pinkertons. During the afternoon, they were, in fact, doing their best to surrender. But when they raised a white flag, union sharpshooters blew it away to the delight of the onlookers. In late afternoon, William Weihe and Hugh O'Donnell assembled an emergency meeting of the Advisory Committee in a building at the mill to decide how to end the impasse and bloodshed. While they were still talking, the Pinkertons again raised a white flag. Calling on their followers not to shoot, O'Donnell and members of the committee rushed down to the landing for a conference with the men in the barges. It was agreed that the Pinkertons would drop their arms and march up the hill under union escort to a refuge in the Eintracht Saenger Halle where they would await transportation to Pittsburgh. The thought and intentions were good, but the events of the day had fired emotions beyond control of any leadership.

As the Pinkertons came off the gangplank, they had to run a gauntlet of enraged men, women, and children six hundred yards long. They were hit with fists, clubs, stones. They lost clothing, money, watches. One man was shot, another clubbed to death. All of them were hurt in some manner before they reached the hall. And while this was going on, other Homesteaders boarded the barges, stripped them of weapons, food, and any other useful item, and set them afire. The bright flames held back the hot July dusk, and the people danced and cheered at the sight. It was truly a victory bonfire. When the last ember sizzled out in the waters of the Monongahela, the crowd dispersed, some to homes where the grim process of mourning was already under way. In the dark of midnight Sheriff McCleary arrived in a special train to haul the battered Pinkertons away. The fight for Fort Frick was over. The workers had won at a terrible cost—seven union men and three Pinkertons dead, and more than sixty people wounded, some of whom would later die.

Leaving his office that night about the time that the bonfire was extinguished, Henry Clay Frick displayed no emotion—nor any concern about that cost, according to the *World* reporter. He told the people around him that he was determined to win "at any cost," that Allegheny County would be charged for the damages (amazingly, there were none except for the barges) since the company had surrendered all responsibility to the county, that in the future the Homestead works would be run according to the company's wishes, and that no terms other than the company's would be considered. Although Frick shrugged off the possibility that he might be in personal danger, his associates saw to it that he was discreetly guarded at the office that day and at home that night. Rightly or wrongly, this cool and collected little man with the bright blue eyes, the soft voice, the neatly trimmed beard and impeccable dress, the logical mind, the dignified manner, had become the most hated man in America, and the number of people who would willingly see him dead was legion.

CHAPTER 8

"H. C. Frick Forever!"

BY the dawn of Thursday, July 7, 1892, Homestead had turned into a national media event. Each of Pittsburgh's ten newspapers had between two and twenty men on the spot; the major New York papers sent crews of four, and there were correspondents from Chicago, Philadelphia, Baltimore, Boston, St. Louis, Cincinnati, and many other points. They used up the town's limited hotel space and commandeered the telegraph facilities. Both the Postal Company and Western Union were quick to lease temporary additions to their quarters and to lay on extra help. Arthur G. Burgoyne, a veteran Pittsburgh newspaperman and eyewitness who later wrote a seminal book about the strike, said that the coverage was the kind that "makes American journalism a world's wonder."

Newspapermen were virtually the only outsiders allowed into the town by the Advisory Committee, which had tightened its control over the whole community after driving away the Pinkertons. Burgoyne credited Hugh O'Donnell, who had been a newspaper correspondent "in a small way" with the generally cooperative attitude toward the press. O'Donnell recognized the value of having the union's side of the story told, and he wasn't above going along with the rest of the committee in exercising a form of censorship by turning away reporters from papers that were clearly hostile to the strikers.

For the most part, men on the ground in Homestead sent sympathetic dispatches back to their papers. They would have needed hearts of stone to do otherwise on that July 7, when the main public events were the funerals for three slain strikers. The ceremony that received most attention was for John Morris, the young man whose sixty-foot fall had been watched with horror by nearly every citizen of Homestead the day before. Staged by the Order of Odd Fellows, of which he was a member, the funeral packed the Fourth Avenue Methodist Episcopal Church. The minister, the Reverend J. J. Mc-Ilyar, used the occasion to tell the world through the press his view of the tragic events. An unabashed partisan of the working men, McIlyar argued that the differences between the company and the union could have been settled by arbitration. "But," he said, "this town is bathed in tears today and it is all brought about by one man who is less respected by the laboring people than any other employer in the country. There is no more sensibility in that man than in a toad."

Everybody knew, of course, that the man was Henry Clay Frick, who was having his own innings with the press in Pittsburgh at about the same time that Homestead was burying its dead. Colleagues of the correspondents in Homestead were besieging the *Chronicle-Telegraph* building to have a word with the Carnegie chairman. Unwilling to face them en masse, Frick finally agreed to a one-on-one interview with George N. McCain, of the Philadelphia *Press,* who in turn engaged a stenographer to transcribe the proceedings so that he could share them with the other reporters. It was a lengthy interview in which Frick defended the company's position in every detail and particular. In the light of the bloody battle just concluded, Frick's discussion of the points at issue such as the sliding scale and the termination date of the contract seems irrelevant. But much of what he said is revealing in terms of his intransigence and his willingness to resort to force that were clearly the immediate causes of the battle. There was no hint of apology or remorse in the interview, and the following excerpts reflect an attitude that would be defined by congressional investigators, courts, and historians as arrogant:

> "The question at issue is a very grave one. It is whether the Carnegie Steel Company or the Amalgamated Association shall have absolute control of our plant and business at Homestead. We have decided after numerous fruitless conferences with the Amalgamated officials in the attempt to amicably adjust the existing difficulties, to operate the plant ourselves. I can say with greatest emphasis that under no circumstances will we have any further dealing with the Amalgamated As-

sociation as an organization. This is final. The Edgar Thompson works and our establishment at Duquesne are both operated by workmen who are not members of the Amalgamated Association with the greatest satisfaction to ourselves and to the unquestioned advantage of our employés. At both of these plants the work in every department goes on uninterrupted; the men are not harassed by the interference of trade union officials, and the best evidence that their wages are satisfactory is shown in the fact that we never had a strike there since they began working under our system of management. . . .

"The facts concerning the engagement of the Pinkerton men are these: From past experience, not only with the present sheriff but with all others, we have found that he has been unable to furnish us with a sufficient number of deputies to guard our property and protect the men who are anxious to work on our terms. As the Amalgamated men from the 1st of July had surrounded our works, placed guards at all avenues or roads leading to our establishment and for miles distant therefrom, we felt that for the safety of our property and in order to protect our workmen it was necessary for us to secure our own watchmen to assist the sheriff, and we know of no other sources from which to obtain them than from Pinkerton agencies, and to them we applied.

"We brought the watchmen here as quietly as possible; had them taken to Homestead at an hour of the night when we hoped to have them enter our works without any interference whatever and without meeting anybody. We proposed to land them on our own property and all our efforts were to prevent the possibilities of a collision between our former workmen and our watchmen. We are today barred out of our property at Homestead and have been since the 1st of July. There is nobody in the mills up there now; they are standing a silent mass of machinery, with nobody to look after them. They are in the hands of our former workmen."

"Have the men made overtures for a settlement of difficulties since this trouble commenced?"

"Yes, sir. A leading ex-official in the Amalgamated Association yesterday, when this riot was going on, called on the sheriff and I am informed asked him to come down to see me, stating that if he could get a promise that we would confer with the representatives of the Amalgamated Association looking toward an adjustment of this trouble, that he would go to Homestead and try to stop the rioting."

"Did you consider this proposal?"

"No, sir. I told the gentleman who called that we would not confer with the Amalgamated officials. That it was their followers who were rioting and destroying our property, and we would not accept his proposition. At the same time this representative of our former workmen said they were willing to accept the terms offered, and concede everything except the date of the termination of the scale, which they insisted should be June 30 in place of December 31."

"What of the future of this difficulty?"

"It is in the hands of the authorities of Allegheny County. If they are unable to cope with it, it certainly is the duty of the governor of the state to see that we are permitted to operate our establishment unmolested. The men engaged by us through the Pinkerton agencies were sent up to Homestead with the full knowledge of the sheriff and by him placed in charge of his chief deputy, Col. Gray, and, as we know, with instructions to deputize them in case it became necessary. We have made an impartial investigation and are satisfied beyond doubt that the watchmen employed by us were fired upon after they had reached our property. That they did not return the fire until after the boats had touched shore, and after three of the watchmen had been wounded, one fatally...."

"How do you regard the present trouble at Homestead from a political standpoint? What effect will it have as a tariff issue in the political campaign of the coming fall?"

"We have never given a thought as to what effect our affairs might have on either of the political parties. We cannot afford to run our business and run politics at the same time...."

In the reams of copy being published about the Homestead affair, there was one glaring omission—any reaction from the voluble Andrew Carnegie. There was good reason for this: nobody but a few intimates knew where he was. The place he had been renting for years—Cluny Castle—was undergoing repairs, and Carnegie had arranged to occupy Sir Robert Menzies's Rannoch Lodge in a remote area of the Scotch highlands. Since it was accessible only by private road and had no telephone, communication with the lodge from almost anywhere was necessarily slow. This was ideal for Frick and the other partners who didn't want to have Carnegie undermining them by spouting his theories of labor management to the press. Although Frick kept Carnegie dutifully informed, it was generally after the fact and tersely. On that same day that he talked so freely to the press, for instance, Frick cabled Carnegie in a kind of code via the Morgan offices in London: "Small plunge, our actions and position there unassailable and will work out satisfactorily."

Unfavorably slanted from Carnegie's point of view, the news from Homestead was given as much play in the British Isles as in Pittsburgh. Stung by it, Carnegie panicked and cabled that he was coming home. Frick responded that there was no need for such a trip and enlisted the aid of the senior partners—Henry Phipps and George Lauder, Carnegie's cousin, who were also vacationing in Britain—in a campaign to keep Carnegie isolated. Although he agreed to go along, Carnegie grumbled to Lauder in a letter: "Matters at home *bad*—such a fiasco trying to send guards by Boat and then leaving space between River & fences for the men to get opposite landing and fire. Still we must keep quiet & do all we can to support Frick & those at Seat of War. I have been besieged by interviewing Cables from N York but have not said a word. Silence is best. We shall win, of course, but may have to shut down for months."

It was naive of Carnegie to think that an enterprising press would let him keep silent on a story of such magnitude. Within two days, a reporter found him and cabled the following account datelined Kinloch Rannoch, Perthshire, Scotland, to the *St. Louis Post-Dispatch*:

> The *Sunday Post-Dispatch* correspondent today called at this magnificient [sic] shooting cottage occupied during the summer by Mr. Andrew Carnegie and requested an interview with that gentleman.
>
> For three days Mr. Carnegie has been coaching from Edinburgh via Braemar and Pitlochry, coming to this place. He drove through here today behind four superb grays in the most elaborate coach that Scotland has ever seen upon its

roads and which has figured in the guide books and the literature of this neighborhood.

This cottage for which Mr. Carnegie has found it desirable to reduce the wages of his workmen in order that he may pay $10,000 to occupy it for eight weeks, is situated ten miles from Kinloch and at the head of the Loch, a beautiful sheet of water, surrounded by broad grouse moor and dark green forests, both fat with game. It is a comfortable, rambling, two-story building of gray stone, fronting on the lake and surrounded by stone out-buildings with gardens and lawns running down to the edge of the water.

The correspondent drove this afternoon to the lodge where he was received by a dignified English servant in blue livery, white stripes on his trousers, giving him in this uniform quite a military or even Pinkerton air.

In response to the correspondent's request to see Mr. Carnegie he was ushered into a bare, sportsmanlike reception room whose walls are covered with antlers, twenty-eight pairs in all, each bearing the card of the gentleman who had killed the buck, the absence of a card being presumed to indicate that Mr. Carnegie had been the victor himself. On a table in the center of the room were two newspapers open and articles in them marked showing that Mr. Carnegie was perfectly au courant with the situation at Homestead. One of these papers was a *London Times* of Friday last containing the story of the riot and telling that six strikers had been killed outright and six fatally wounded and that nine Pinkerton men fell in the struggle. Around these figures Mr. Carnegie or someone else had drawn a ring with a lead pencil. The other paper was the *Pall Mall Gazette* and on its open page was the deadly parallel column, one showing Mr. Carnegie's philanthropic talk at the opening of the free library in Aberdeen, where the Earl and Countess of Aberdeen were flanking him, on the other side was the table of the reduction of wages at Homestead. In this room the correspondent sat for over an hour without any intimation being given that he was to be received. Finally, Mr. Carnegie came through the hall with a quick, energetic step and entered the room.

The correspondent asked him if he cared to say anything

in regard to the troubles at his mills, and Mr. Carnegie in the most contemptuous and insulting manner replied: "I have nothing whatever to say. I have given up all active control of the business, and I do not care to interfere in any way with the present management's conduct of this affair."

"But do you not still exercise a supervision of the affairs of the company?" he was asked.

"I have nothing whatever to say on that point. The business management is in the hands of those who are fully competent to deal with any question that may arise."

"But you must have some opinion in the matter that you are willing to express."

"No, sir. I am not willing to express any opinion. The men have chosen their course and I am powerless to change it. The handling of the case on the part of the company has my full approbation and sanction. Further than this, I have no disposition to say anything."

When Mr. Carnegie had thus delivered himself he turned abruptly and left the room. All that had been said was said standing. The correspondent was neither invited to take a seat nor was there any hesitancy on the part of Mr. Carnegie to indicate that the visit was an intrusion upon his ducal magnificance [sic], and it is not at all likely that had he known that it was a correspondent who awaited him that he would either have appeared at the end of an hour or spoken when he did appear.

As the correspondent stepped upon the stairs the dignified and uniformed servant who had so courteously born off his card an hour or so earlier ascended the steps, and with a suavity that any ten of the ironworkers at Homestead would willingly have sacrificed their entire wages to have seen, said: "Mr. Carnegie is in the garden. I have just found him, and he does not care to have anything to say to you."

"Thank you," your correspondent replied. "I found him myself five minutes ago."

In a small New York apartment, the news out of Homestead caused even more distress than in that sprawling hunting lodge in Scotland. The occupants of the apartment—a young woman and two young men, both of whom were her lovers—had, in fact, been so agitated by what they read of the negotiations prior to the battle that they had given up their ice cream parlor business in Worcester, Massachusetts, to move back to the city and prepare themselves for some sort of role in what they saw as a pivotal event in the great world class struggle. They were anarchists, immigrants from Russia, who considered all authority, whether in private business or government, oppressive. Their plan had been to print a manifesto for the workers, take it to Homestead and organize a mass meeting for the young woman, Emma Goldman, to address in her fiery style. But word of the deaths in the fight with the Pinkertons changed their minds. One of the young men, twenty-one-year-old Alexander Berkman, known to his friends as Sasha, would go alone to take a life for lives, to sacrifice himself if necessary by killing Henry Clay Frick.

It is well for most of us ultimately helpless human beings that we can't foresee the future. This was certainly true for the apparently fortunate Frick family in the hot and hectic days of that July. With boys screaming headlines along the streets, it was impossible for Frick to keep the Homestead troubles from penetrating the decorative walls of Clayton. Worry over her husband's safety and anger at the names he was being called caused Mrs. Frick to deliver the baby she was carrying prematurely on that Friday when Frick was downtown talking to the press. Granted she had a house full of servants, a doctor, and numerous Childs relatives in attendance, but she wanted Mr. Frick to be there for the arrival of the child who turned out, as they had hoped, to be a boy who would be named Henry Clay Frick, Jr. Caught in his business crisis, Frick could only make amends by sitting up most of the night with mother and child, both of whom were alarmingly weak and ill.

Weary and worried about what might happen at home any moment while he was gone, Frick was nevertheless back at his desk at eight A.M. on Saturday, July 9. Although all was quiet in Homestead, a situation in which the company could not enter its own multimillion-dollar facility was not to be tolerated. Frick had to be on hand to keep pressing the sheriff through his politically powerful envoys to keep pressing the governor to reestablish lawful authority in Homestead. But Pattison kept dragging his feet until his own personal emissary was twice thrown out of town by the strikers on Sunday, July 10. That evening, the governor issued an order to Major General George R. Snowden, commander of the state's national guard: "Put the division under arms and move at once, with ammunition, to the support of the sheriff of Allegheny County, at Homestead. Maintain the peace, protect all persons in their rights under the constitution and laws of the state. Communicate with me."

When word that the militia had been ordered out reached Homestead, it provoked debate. Some were for resisting even this form of authority, but cooler heads like O'Donnell's prevailed. Indeed, plans were made to greet the troops with flowers and marching bands, but General Snowden curtly put an end to them. He wanted his men to be aloof, impartial, a force to be respected and feared. Within twenty-four hours of the governor's order, General Snowden had eight thousand uniformed men neatly encamped in open fields above the Homestead works. There was peace on the streets of the town, and the Carnegie Steel Company was once more in possession of its property, where supervisory personnel and such scabs as they were able to recruit began preparations for refiring the furnaces.

But the strike was far from over. What Frick called his "former workmen" stuck together at Homestead, and the Amalgamated Association prevailed upon union members at the Upper and Lower Union Mills and Beaver Falls to break their contract and go out on a sympathy strike. It was a costly gesture. Carnegie Steel Company simply hired nonunion labor to replace them, as it was doing at Homestead from the day the militia made it possible. Frick had a notice posted setting July 21 as a deadline for individual applications from former workmen. "It is our desire," the notice said, "to retain in our service all of our old employés whose past records are satisfactory and who did not take part in attempts which had been made to interfere with our right to manage our business." There weren't many takers, and the plant was put back in operation with some seven hundred imported strike breakers, who were housed within its borders to protect them from the angry strikers.

Frick's lack of concern about the political ramifications of the Homestead affair was not shared by politicians. As early as July 14, a committee from the House of Representatives arrived in Pittsburgh and conducted hearings at the Monongahela Hotel. Frick was, of course, a major witness. Much of his testimony covered the same ground as his press interview a week before. When the committee's probing threatened to uncover any trade secrets such as the actual cost of producing billets, Frick simply refused to answer. Typical of his performance on the stand is the following exchange:

Q: Can you state independently of other costs the labor cost of producing a ton of steel billets?

A: I could get those figures for you, but I think I will have to decline to give them to you.

Q: You decline to give all the cost to you or your company, but upon what ground do you decline to give the labor cost separate from the other?

A: Well, I do not think we should be asked to give away those details of our business.

Q: You asked the Government for a duty to compensate between the difference in the American labor cost and the foreign labor cost; then upon what principle, receiving from the Government a protection which is ostensibly and avowedly for that purpose, do you decline to give information upon which that legislation is based?

A: We did not ask the Government for such protection.

Q: You did not?

A: No, this concern did not.

Q: You are greatly misrepresented then if you did not. The press misrepresents you very much.

After it returned to Washington, the committee could not agree on a joint statement. The chairman, W. C. Oates, of Alabama, nevertheless issued a report in which he found Mr. Frick to be "too stern, brusque and somewhat autocratic" and suggested that company officers had invited trouble by not exercising "patience, indulgence and solicitude." To be sure, Oates also condemned the workmen for turning away the sheriff, hanging Frick and Potter in effigy, trying to bar nonunion men from employment, and resisting the landing of the Pinkertons. No matter who was at fault, it was not an affair over which Congress had any jurisdiction in the opinion of Chairman Oates.

The congressional hand washing did not extend to the Republican managers of President Harrison's reelection campaign. With the press on both sides of the Atlantic lambasting Carnegie and Frick, both of whom were known to be close to the Republican throne, a quick and fair resolution of the Homestead strike was seen to be essential. Harrison's opponent would again be Grover Cleveland, whose popular vote had been larger in '88 than the President's. At the suggestion of Christopher Magee, a top emissary of the Repub-

lican National Committee, John E. Milholland, was sent to Homestead to confer with Hugh O'Donnell. Magee's intelligence indicated
that there was a rivalry and disagreement between O'Donnell and
Burgess McLuckie, that O'Donnell was eager for a settlement. Magee
was right. O'Donnell was eager to accompany Milholland to New
York on a secret mission to meet Whitelaw Reid, publisher of the
New York Tribune, who had been nominated to run as vice president
with Harrison. At Reid's suggestion, O'Donnell dictated a letter addressed to him and supposedly mailed from Homestead in which he
stated that the Amalgamated Association would agree to the company's demands if only Frick would recognize the union and reopen
negotiations.

O'Donnell's New York trip was cut short on July 18 by news
from home that a warrant for his arrest on a charge of murder had
been issued by Pittsburgh Alderman McMasters. The case against
him, McLuckie, and five others had been instituted by F.T.F. Lovejoy, secretary of Carnegie Steel Company, under the orders of Chairman Frick and with the aid and advice of Attorney Philander C.
Knox. On his way to jail, McLuckie told reporters that the union
would be filing a counter case against Carnegie, Frick, and Superintendent Potter and that "we will make this man Frick come down
on his knees so hard that the sound will be heard in the farthest
corner of civilization." After a night in jail, McLuckie was released
on $10,000 bail; O'Donnell, who gave himself up to authorities, spent
a little more time behind bars before he and the others were also
released on the same bail on Saturday, July 23, a day when the
Homestead drama took a dramatic turn that none of its actors could
have foreseen.

A week earlier, Alexander Berkman had arrived in Pittsburgh
with murder in his heart, a dollar in his pocket, and a scheme in his
mind. Hearing that Frick was hiring strikebreakers, Berkman invented an employment agency, had cards printed up, and presented
one at the Carnegie Steel Company's offices when he sought an interview with the chairman. An appointment was scheduled for July
23. During that first visit, Berkman was able to locate Frick's office,
get a glimpse of the man himself, and observe that Frick returned
from lunch earlier than his staff. During the week he waited for his
appointment, the fundless Berkman stayed with fellow anarchists
across the river in Allegheny. In New York, Emma Goldman raised
enough money for him to buy a gun and sent it to him.

Both of these young people were driven by an exceptional fervor for what they perceived as the cause of The People, a cause they had brought with them from their native Russia, where they had grown up in a community of impassioned, idealistic Jewish intellectuals. For them the Capitalist was as much an enemy of The People as the Czarist. Their heroes in America were what they considered the martyrs of the Haymarket riots in Chicago. From school days, young Berkman's ambition had been to carry out an *Attentat*—propaganda by deed—to celebrate the anarchists' cause. In his own mind, the killing of Frick would not be murder. He would not be taking the life of another human being out of personal hatred or for any selfish reasons, and he fully expected—even wanted—to suffer the consequences. Indeed, if he died in the process, his act would gain the power of martyrdom. Although Emma pleaded to go with him and share his fate, Berkman insisted that she stay behind not only to raise funds but to be free to explain the idealistic purpose of his mission through her crowd-pleasing oratory.

Berkman could trust his "sailor girl," as he called Emma, because she fully shared his motives and intensity. She showed this through her desperate fund-raising effort. Having no other means of raising quick cash, she decided to try streetwalking. If Sasha could give his life, she could give her "honor." Although Emma shocked her generation by preaching—and practicing—free love, the adjective was the key to her attitude. The thought of selling her body was so repugnant that she shied away from every man who approached her through a footsore day of teetering up and down New York's Fourteenth Street on high heels. Finally, near midnight, a white-haired man took her firmly by the arm and proposed buying her a drink. It was a now-or-never situation for her, and she agreed. Over a mug of beer, the man told her that he had spotted her as a novice, argued that she had no talent for the "profession," insisted that she accept ten dollars, and sent her home. Both relieved and defeated, Emma wired one of her sisters that she was ill and in need of fifteen dollars for medical attention. With twenty-five dollars in hand, Emma was able to send Sasha enough for both a gun and a suit of clothes.

The suit, she thought, would facilitate Berkman's getting through to Frick, and she was undoubtedly right. Short, lean, smooth-shaven, dressed conservatively in gray, the Berkman who presented himself at Frick's *Chronical-Telegraph* building offices overlooking Fifth Avenue at a little before two P.M. on that Saturday could easily pass for the businessman he claimed to be. His looks aroused no suspicions in the mind of the black messenger boy who took his card into Mr. Frick. As he had hoped, Berkman saw nobody else in the outer offices. Through the door the messenger opened, Berkman could see the black hair and beard of a man seated crosswise in his chair, a leg cocked over one arm, at a flat-topped desk or table. It was Frick himself. There was no time to lose, no time even to think. He brushed past the boy who was returning with a message from Frick. One hand clutching the .38 bulldog revolver in his pocket, Berkman shoved open the door.

As a surprised Frick tried to disentangle himself from the chair and rise, a surprised Berkman saw another man at the table. It was John G. A. Leishman, vice chairman of the Carnegie Steel Company, who had been lunching at the Duquesne Club with Frick and attorney Philander Knox and had lingered in the boss's office to conclude their conversation. The sight of Leishman only inspired Berkman to quicker action. He fired once, hitting Frick in the neck and knocking him to the floor. Aiming for Frick's head, he fired again, hitting him on the other side of the neck. Just as Berkman was firing a third time, Leishman got to him and knocked his right hand up. The bullet embedded itself in the room's high ceiling. Berkman tried to fire again, but the hammer clicked uselessly.

Leishman clung tenaciously to Berkman's right hand. Bleeding profusely but full of adrenaline, Frick rose from the floor and tackled his assailant. The three struggling men crashed against the low wall beneath a huge window looking out onto Fifth Avenue. Alerted by the gunfire, crowds passing through the street looked up and saw by the bright sunlight streaming through the window that there was some kind of fight going on. Fascinated and frightened, they hesitated for precious moments before crying alarm. In those moments, Berkman got his left arm free, pulled out a knife he had made from a file, and stabbed Frick in the back and both legs before Frick was able to grab that arm and pin it beneath his body. Before Berkman could do more damage, a number of clerks and a carpenter working in the outer offices arrived on the scene. As later calculated, the action up to that point had consumed sixty seconds from the time Berkman brushed past the messenger.

When the rescuers had wrestled Berkman into a chair with the aid of a tap from the carpenter's hammer, Leishman fainted dead away and was carried from the room. His beard and clothes covered with blood, Frick propped himself against the table, told the carpenter who was about to strike again that he wanted Berkman kept alive. He conveyed the same message to a deputy sheriff who arrived with drawn gun and every intention of using it. Berkman's head was hanging, and Frick asked his captors to raise it so that he could look at the man's face. Seeing Berkman's lips working, Frick said, "What's in his mouth? See what he's chewing." The men who pried open Berkman's jaws found a capsule of fulminate of mercury between his teeth, a charge strong enough to have blown the room and everybody in it to bits.

By the time police arrived to take Berkman away, Fifth Avenue was almost impassable for the crowds. Angry voices were calling out, "Hang him! Lynch him!" His new suit soaked in his victim's blood, Berkman looked half dead himself as the police hustled him through the hostile crowd to a patrol wagon. From eyewitnesses, everybody knew that Frick had been shot, and the news spread across Pittsburgh, out to Homestead, and along the wires to New York and the world beyond within minutes. What wasn't known immediately was whether Frick would live or die.

Several doctors, bidden and unbidden, came to Frick's aid within minutes. One of them was his personal physician, Dr. Litchfield, who had also been lunching at the Duquesne Club. They stretched him out on a couch in a nearby office and first attended to the knife wounds. When it came to probing for the bullets, the physicians proposed using chloroform, but Frick refused any kind of anesthesia. If he could feel the instruments, he could guide their hands—and he did, saying, "There, that feels like it, Doctor," in each case. Throughout the two hours that the doctors worked on him, Frick kept the others around him hopping. He dictated a cable to Carnegie and a telegram to his mother, hoping to reach them before the news. In each case he said that he had been shot but was not in serious condition, and in the message to Carnegie he emphasized that there was no need for him to come to Pittsburgh. He sent his Childs in-laws who had hastened to his side out to Clayton to break the news gently to his ailing wife. The minute the doctors were through with him, he demanded to be propped up at his desk, where he signed the letters he had dictated that morning and completed an important loan application.

To the astonishment and dismay of the doctors, Frick talked of going home in a carriage and returning to the office on Monday morning. Ignoring him, they ordered an ambulance from Mercy Hospital, but the vehicle could hardly reach the building through the still large and curious crowds milling around outside. Frick didn't want to face the crowds, and so he stayed at work until after seven. Even then, they needed a ruse to get him out. They took the ambulance to the back of the building with the crowd in pursuit and rushed it again to the front to pick him up. At home while he was being carried past the door to his wife's bedroom, Frick called out cheerfully, "Don't worry, Ada, I'm all right; I may come in to say good night; how is the baby?"

Frick was underestimating the extent of his wounds. By the next morning, he knew that he would have to spend some time in bed. But he was not going to let that inconvenience keep him from running the business or masterminding the fight with the Amalgamated Association. Even before he had left the office, he had dictated a statement for the press: "This incident will not change the attitude of the Carnegie Steel Company toward the Amalgamated Association. I do not think I shall die but whether I do or not the Company will pursue the same policy and it will win." On July 24, the morning after the assassination attempt, he dictated a notice to be posted at the Homestead Steel Works:

> To all men who entered our employ after July 1st, 1892: In no case and under no circumstances will a single one of you be discharged to make room for another man. You will keep your respective positions so long as you attend to your duties. Positive orders to this effect have been given to the general superintendent.

In order to keep on top of things, Frick had a telephone installed by his bed and secretaries in constant attendance. He kept reassuring Carnegie that he was all right and at one point enlisted the aid of other partners to scotch a Carnegie plan to send George Lauder back to Pittsburgh as a sort of personal emissary. Frick was afraid of any move that might indicate a weakening of the company's position. As the ongoing effort on the part of the Republican leadership soon revealed, Frick had reason for worry. With O'Donnell's letter in hand, Whitelaw Reid tried to contact Carnegie and urge him to sit down with the union. Frick refused to give Reid Carnegie's address in Scotland, and Reid enlisted the White House to have his message delivered by way of John C. New, the American Consul General in London. It reached Carnegie on July 28 while Frick was still lying abed, and two Carnegie cables in the peculiar company code tell the rest of the story:

> We have a telegram from Tribune Reid through high official London Amalgamated Association reference Homestead. The proposition is worthy of consideration. Replied "Nothing can be done. Send H. C. Frick document." You must decide without delay. Amalgamated Association evidently distressed.

The very next day, before he could hear from Frick but obviously after talking with Lauder and Phipps, Carnegie cabled again:

> After due consideration we have concluded Tribune too old. Probably proposition is not worthy of consideration. Useful showing distress of Amalgamated Association. Use your own discretion about terms and starting. George Lauder, Henry Phipps, Jr., Andrew Carnegie solid. H. C. Frick forever!"

Armed with this cable, Frick was in a good position to deal with Milholland of the Republican National Committee, who arrived at his bedside on July 30 per Carnegie's response to Reid. His written account of the visit provides a very vivid glimpse of Frick, the captain of industry, in action:

> Mr. Frick declared emphatically that he would never consent to settle the difficulties if President Harrison himself should personally request him to do so. Notwithstanding the fact that he was a Republican and a warm friend and admirer of the President, the whole Cabinet, the whole leadership of the party might demand it, but he would not yield. He was going to fight the strike out on the lines that he had laid down. I remarked, "If it takes all summer?" "Yes," he said, "if it takes all summer and all winter, and all next summer and all next winter. Yes, even my life itself. I will fight this thing to the bitter end. I will never recognize the Union, never, never! . . . It makes no difference to me what Mr. Car-

negie has said to General New or to anybody else. I won't settle this strike even if he should order me preemptorily to do so. If he interferes every manager that he has will resign and of course I will get out of the concern. But I do not think he will interfere."

Perhaps even more revealing of Frick's extraordinarily tough character were the events of the next few days. On Wednesday, August 3, he was present in the room when the baby, his namesake, died; on Thursday, he sat through a short funeral service at home and stayed up most of that night to console his sick and saddened wife. Virtually sleepless, he left Clayton at the usual hour on Friday morning, walked alone to the road, and stepped on an open streetcar that delivered him to the office by eight A.M. One of his first acts was to get rid of the detective assigned to guard the company offices. When he went home that night and found police stationed at Clayton, he asked that they be removed. Told that they were there for Mrs. Frick's peace of mind, he went into the house and returned with a message from Ada: "My wife asks me to thank you most kindly for your thoughtfulness but earnestly requests that you take the men away; she fears that their being here all the time might make the servants nervous." Frick told a newspaper reporter, "If an honest American cannot live in his own home without being surrounded by a bodyguard, it is time to quit."

From that moment on, it was once more business as usual for Frick. The *New York World* reporter who had found Frick so heartlessly calm on the day of the battle was moved to write that "those who hate him most admire the nerve and stamina of this man of steel whom nothing seems to be able to move." By then few, if any, observers of the struggle at Homestead had any doubts about its eventual outcome. Berkman's *Attentat* would turn into one of the most counterproductive acts of political martyrdom in history.

CHAPTER 9

Counting the Cost

IMMEDIATELY after the attempted assassination and the personal tragedy he went through in the privacy of his home, Henry Clay Frick became a sympathetic figure. Even the Advisory Committee of the Amalgamated Association passed a resolution deploring the act and extending its condolences to the wounded chairman. The workingmen of Homestead, most of whom had voted as Republicans, were as horrified by an anarchist's *Attentat* as anybody in a corporate boardroom. They had, in fact, driven sympathetic anarchists out of town before the fight with the Pinkertons. Politically savvy union leaders like Hugh O'Donnell were despairingly aware of the damage Berkman had done to their cause. The confusion created in the ranks of liberals by Berkman's act was most strikingly expressed in an editorial in Joseph Pulitzer's *St. Louis Post-Dispatch:*

Count no man happy until he is dead. Three months ago Andrew Carnegie was a man to be envied. Today he is an object of mingled pity and contempt. In the estimation of nine-tenths of the thinking people on both sides of the ocean, he had not only given the lie to all his antecedents, but confessed himself a moral coward. One would naturally suppose that if he had a grain of consistency, not to say decency, in his composition, he would favor rather than oppose the organization of trades unions among his own working people at Homestead. One would naturally suppose that if he had a grain of manhood, not to say courage, in his composition, he would at least have been willing to face the consequences of his inconsistency. But what does Carnegie do? Runs off to

Scotland out of harm's way to await the issue of the battle he was too pusillanimous to share. A single word from him might have saved the bloodshed—but the word was never spoken. Nor has he, from that bloody day until this, said anything except that he had "implicit confidence in the managers of the mills." The correspondent who finally obtained this valuable information expresses the opinion that "Mr. Carnegie has no intention of returning to America at present." He might have added that America can well spare Mr. Carnegie. Ten thousand "Carnegie Public Libraries" would not compensate the country for the direct and indirect evils resulting from the Homestead lockout. Say what you will of Frick, he is a brave man. Say what you will of Carnegie, he is a coward. And gods and men hate cowards.

The more conservative *New York Times* echoed the *Post-Dispatch* without going so far as to praise Frick:

But it would be well to keep sight of the fact that the chief source of unkind feelings toward Mr. Carnegie is the manner in which he accumulated his wealth rather than the manner of treating his employés. In availing himself of the purchased favor of Federal legislation he makes any profession of extraordinary benevolence a little absurd, and recalls the definition of a Scotchman which is too sweeping to be true, but which applies to certain specimens as "a man who believes in keeping the Sabbath and everything else he can lay his hands on."

This sort of attack inflicted wounds as deep in Carnegie's psyche as Berkman's bullets had in Frick's body. It was particularly galling in the light of his efforts to persuade Frick simply to close down the plant and outwait the workers instead of importing scabs. But with his senior partners all on Frick's side, Carnegie couldn't reveal this internal disagreement without seriously damaging the company, nor could he deny with even a shred of honesty his own desire and intention to break the union. The right words for Carnegie's dilemma would not be invented until many years later; it was a catch-22. Although he lived through it in silence, he never got over it. In later writings, he would inaccurately describe his part in the affair—

for instance, an imagined cable from the Homestead workers saying, "Kind master, tell us what you wish us to do and we will do it for you"—and confess that "nothing I have ever had to meet in all my life, before or since, wounded me so deeply. No pangs remain of any wound received in my business career save that of Homestead. It was so unnecessary."

Frick's role as heroic victim in the drama didn't last long. Within days, the Iams incident surfaced as a reminder to the strikers and the general public of how harshly power was being used on the company's behalf. When news of the attempt on Frick's life reached the National Guard camp at Homestead, a young private named W. L. Iams shouted, "Hurrah for the man who shot him!" The remark was overheard by an officer, who demanded to know why Iams had made it. "I did it because I hate Frick," the boy said. Given a drumhead trial, Iams was hung by his thumbs from a tent pole until his heartbeat grew so weak that the surgeon ordered him cut down. Because he refused to apologize during that ordeal, he was given a dishonorable discharge and drummed out of camp in rags with his head half-shaved.

The punishment was widely held to be excessive but typical of the way other instruments of law and order were reacting to the crisis. In the suits and countersuits charging murder, all of the union men spent some time in jail before being released on bail, but the judge made special arrangements for immediate bail in the cases of Carnegie Steel Company executives. Because of his wounds Frick himself was released on $10,000 bail without ever appearing in court. Only a few union men, including O'Donnell, were brought to trial. All were acquitted, and all murder charges against union and company people were then dropped at the instigation of Carnegie attorneys. Perhaps they felt that the trials were doing more harm than good by providing a platform for impassioned speeches such as the one that union attorney W. M. Erwin delivered to the jury on behalf of Sylvester Critchlow. Calling the prosecution's claim that the killings were caused by "a riot" a "doubly damned fiction," Erwin said:

> Is there another such hard-hearted, villainous man within the limits of the land as this man Frick, whom we find hob-nobbing with the leaders of the Republic? This man Frick, whose name will be more notorious than that of the man who fired the Ephesian dome, did not apply to your legislature,

but violated the agreement with his men, and assumed, like a tyrant, to act as arbiter; this most brutal tyrant of all tyrants tried to force his men to bow to his will by an armed force of invaders. Thus have these scoundrels defied the laws of the commonwealth. Carnegie bent the eternal laws of God and the poorer imitations by man. We will show the defendants only tried to straighten these laws. If there is no Judas Iscariot among you, gentlemen of the jury, you will plant the flag of independence on your hills.

It's likely that Erwin drew inspiration for his address from a poem entitled "Tyrant Frick" that was published in the *National Labor Tribune* in August of that year. Clearly the rosy blush of personal courage had faded from the image of a recovered Frick, who was relentlessly adding new scabs to the population of what was called Potterville—the makeshift living quarters inside the mill—under the protection of the militia. The force had grown so large that Frick made his first personal inspection of the Homestead works since the lockout cum strike began that month and told reporters that everything was in good working order and that, from his point of view, the strike was over. Not so from the union point of view, as the poem attests:

> *In days gone by before the war*
> *All freemen did agree*
> *The best of plans to handle slaves*
> *Was to let them all go free;*
> *But the slave drivers then, like now,*
> *Contrived to make a kick*
> *And keep the slaves in bondage tight,*
> *Just like our Tyrant Frick.*
>
> Chorus: *Of all slave drivers, for spite and kick,*
> *No one so cruel as Tyrant Frick.*
>
> *The brave Hungarians, sons of toil,*
> *When seeking which was right,*
> *Were killed like dogs by tyrant's hands*
> *In the coke district's fight*
> *Let labor heroes all be true—*

Avenge the bloody trick!
Be firm like steel, true to the cause,
  And conquer Tyrant Frick.

Chorus
The traitorous Pinkerton low tribe,
  In murdering attack,
Tried hard to take our lives and homes,
  But heroes drove them back.
O! sons of toil, o'er all the land,
  Now hasten and be quick
To aid us in our efforts grand,
  To down this Tyrant Frick.

Chorus
The battle of "Fort Frick" is stamped
  On page of history,
And marked with blood of freemen true,
  Against this tyranny!
The sons of toil, for ages to come,
  His curse will always bring;
The name of Frick will be well known —
  The Nigger driver King!

Chorus: *Of all slave drivers, for spite and kick,*
  No one so cruel as Tyrant Frick.

As the strike dragged on through August and September, the people of Homestead were finding it harder and harder to be "firm like steel." Lounging idle on their doorsteps and in the streets, they had to watch the smoke rising from the fires and hear the clank of the machinery from a working mill. Some couldn't hold out at all; there was an almost daily sight of meager belongings in the street as yet another family was evicted from a company house. Once in a while, the men relieved their frustration by beating up a scab— particularly a black one—who ventured outside of Potterville, but it was a risky business with troops still patrolling the town. The troops were a very visible and tangible symbol of the discouraging fact that the power of the state was at the command of the company.

If the strikers had any doubts about their powerlessness before the law, they were dispelled when Frick's legal strategist Philander Knox picked up on a proposal by General Snowden to charge twenty-three members of the Advisory Committee with treason. After consultation with Chief Justice Edward Paxson of the Pennsylvania Supreme Court, who was, like Knox and Frick, a friend of Christopher Magee, Knox filed a brief with the court claiming that the Advisory Committee members were in violation of a state Crimes Act of 1860, which had been passed to deal with people who might be found guilty of aiding the Confederacy. Paxson surprised even Knox, Frick, and Magee by bringing treason charges himself as a result of the brief. The Homestead workers were guilty of "war, insurrection, and rebellion against the Commonwealth of Pennsylvania" for usurping civil authority, organizing, violating the company's property rights, and engaging in unlawful violence by fighting the Pinkertons, according to Paxson. If found guilty they could be sentenced to twelve years in jail. Although cooler heads prevailed and no prosecution was instituted by state authorities, the indictment by the Chief Justice hung ominously over the heads of the Amalgamated Association's leaders during the last months of the strike.

In an effort to counteract these discouragements, national labor leaders descended upon Homestead. Samuel Gompers, the generally conservative president of the American Federation of Labor, with which the Amalgamated Association was affiliated, gave a fiery speech to an audience of fifteen hundred strikers gathered at the Homestead rink. If he had been a citizen of the state, Justice Paxson might have included him among the treasonous for proposing a boycott of the Carnegie Steel Company despite the fact that Pennsylvania courts had ruled that boycotts constituted conspiracy. The law would also have looked unkindly on Gompers's remarks about the attack on Frick:

> I have been asked for my opinion of the attack on the life of Mr. Frick. I don't know why I should be asked to go out of my way to give Berkman an additional kick. I never heard of him until after he made his attack. The laws of Pennsylvania will take care of him. I do know, however, that I have heard of thousands of men being shot down by day and by night, each and every one of whom was a better man than

this despot, Frick. Yet I have never been asked for my opinion
in any of these cases.

The laws of Pennsylvania did take care of Berkman in September,
and in this case there was no protest from workers who still regarded
his *Attentat* as an unwelcome intrusion into their affairs. Convicted
after an inept effort to defend himself and spread his anarchist convictions in the process, Berkman was sentenced to one year in the
county workhouse for carrying concealed weapons and twenty-one
years in the state penitentiary for assault with intent to kill. As he
related later in his memoirs, Berkman's greatest shock and disappointment in the whole experience came from encountering in jail
one of the strikers charged with murder. When he introduced himself as the man who shot Frick, the striker wanted to have nothing
to do with him. Although he admitted that it was too bad Berkman
hadn't killed Frick, the striker didn't want to have the act associated
in any way with his own effort to protect job, home, and family.

In mid-October the militia was withdrawn from Homestead, but
the strike was still officially in progress. Among the twenty-five hundred workers in the plant, only two hundred were former employees;
the rest were still loyal to the Amalgamated Association leadership.
With the troops gone, violence between the two groups of men es-
calated, but Frick remained firm. He did, however, make one important move in the direction of improving employee morale. He
promoted the by now hated Potter to a supervisory role in the Carnegie Steel Company and moved amiable Charlie Schwab from the
Edgar Thomson works to Homestead. "Tactful and conciliatory, he
at once set himself to win back the heads of departments and foremen," wrote insider Bridge, "and before many days had passed had
secured the best of them. The immediate consequence was that better
work was done inside the shops, and the foremen were soon followed
into the works by their favorites among the strikers."

Over in Scotland, Carnegie was running out of patience with the
strike and again talking of sending George Lauder back to Pittsburgh. Rejecting this idea, Frick said that Leishman and other partners on the spot thought that Lauder, Phipps, and Carnegie himself
should stay away "until this matter is over." He encouraged Carnegie
to carry on with his previous plan of going to Italy in November.
In response, Carnegie wrote:

My dear Pard:

H.P. and I are delighted with *tone* of your reply to Lauder. Altho we don't agree with your decision—Lauder is a *partner*—big word, inside Homestead Works, and not a small word anywhere—His presence there could only tell the strikers the firm was a unit—not a personal quarrel of any one member—If twenty of our young partners were inside Homestead encouraging new men so much the better.

This fight is too much against our *Chairman*—partakes of personal issue. It is very bad indeed for you—very and also bad for the interests of the firm.

There's another point which troubles me on your account—the danger that the public and hence all our men get the impression that is *all Frick*—Your influence for good would be permanently impaired—You don't deserve a bad name, but then one is sometimes wrongfully got—Your partners should be as much identified with the struggle as you— think over this counsel. It is from a very wise man as you know and a true friend.

A.C.

Frick did not share Carnegie's concern for his personal reputation. Having lived down the bitter things said about him during the bloody coke strikes, he was certain that he could survive the harsh reaction to Homestead, too. Among the people who mattered—the "Mellon boys," rival executives in the steel industry, leaders in New York financial circles—his fight was regarded as a gallant and necessary stand against the rampant unionism that was threatening profits and impeding progress. Especially after the Berkman incident, Frick was an authentic hero to his partners in the company and his peers in the business world. He did not feel in need of any advice from Carnegie, and he didn't take it, as evidenced by his letter of October 12:

I note the counsel you give, but I cannot see wherein I can profit by it, or what action could be taken by me that would change matters in respect to that which you mention.

As you understand, the only objection to Mr. Lauder's returning now, or when he proposed it, was the fear that it might prolong the strike. For no other reason, I assure you.

So far as the strike is concerned, you will recollect, in your library, before you left for Europe, during my next to the last visit with you, when you gave me a memorandum expressing your views about the labor situation at Homestead, I told you then that I did not like to think of the labor situation at Homestead, etc., etc. If we had adopted the policy of sitting down and waiting, we would still have been sitting, waiting, and the fight would yet have to be made, and then we would have been accused of trying to starve our men into submission. This is the way I think.

Of course I may be wrong, and if we had eventually been compelled to make a deal with the Amalgamated Association just think what effect that would have had on Edgar Thomson and Duquesne, and when this victory is won it will not take very long to show our men at Homestead how much better it is to deal with us direct, and anything we do for them will not be credited to the Amalgamated Association, or any other Association, but to the one that we are most deeply interested in.

After this letter, there were no more recorded arguments to the contrary from Carnegie, perhaps because he was on the road again dedicating libraries. On one aspect of the situation, Carnegie and Frick were in perfect accord—their resistance to all pleas from the Republican Party to end the strike before the November elections. Strangely, their indifference to politics on this occasion even extended to giving. The Carnegie interests had contributed handsomely to Harrison's campaign in 1888; the money that Pennsylvania's Republican boss, Senator Quay, raised from businesses in hopes of a high tariff was responsible for popular President Cleveland's losing his own state of New York and a squeaker of an election. Expecting gratitude for the McKinley tariff in 1892, the Republicans assigned their top fund-raisers—Secretary of War Stephen B. Elkins and Postmaster General John Wanamaker, the Philadelphia merchant prince—to the Carnegie people. Although Wanamaker intimated to Frick that Carnegie had expressed a willingness to give $50,000, Frick knew better. Now that the tariff issue was settled, Carnegie had expressed a desire to cut the company's contribution considerably. No amount had been agreed upon when Frick, on business in New York, met with Secretary Elkins and drew a check to the

party's treasurer, Thomas Dolan, for $25,000. On his return to Pitts-
burgh, he found a letter waiting from Carnegie suggesting only
$10,000. In explaining what he had done, Frick wrote that "Mr.
Elkins told me that Quay, Carter, Dolan and Clarkson felt very
confident, to which I said I thought it a waste of money, but we
wanted to do our duty and I hoped Mr. Harrison would be elected."

Frick's mission did not go unnoticed, and *The New York Times*
editorialized:

> The appearance of Mr. Frick, the General Manager and a
> partner of Mr. Carnegie, at the Republican Headquarters here
> in connection with a committee that notoriously relies on
> money and money only to carry the election next week was
> to say the least, in very bad taste. . . . Mr. Frick and his su-
> perior, Mr. Carnegie, have so large and direct a money interest
> in a Republican victory that they cannot free themselves from
> the suspicion of very low motives in cooperating with the
> Republican managers, and since those managers have been
> detected in efforts at the corrupt use of money, the nature of
> the aid given by wealthy tariff pets is only too plain.

The contribution was indeed a waste of money. Not only did
Cleveland return to the White House in triumph, but the Democrats
carried both houses of Congress. In letters written on the same day,
November 9, and crossing each other on the Atlantic, Carnegie and
Frick echoed Frederick Townsend Martin's rather cynical view of
political loyalty among the very rich. Frick: "I am very sorry for
President Harrison, but I cannot see that our interests are going to
be affected one way or the other by the change in administration."
Carnegie: "Cleveland! Landslide!! Well, we have nothing to fear and
perhaps it is best. People will now think the Protected Manfrs. will
be attended to and quit agitating. Cleveland is pretty good fellow.
Off for Venice tomorrow."

If the Republican leadership could have seen this private correspondence, they would have been even more incensed than they
were. Reid flatly blamed their loss on Homestead, as did Ohio Congressman Charles Grosvenor, who called Carnegie "the arch-sneak
of this age." Chauncey M. Depew said that the Homestead strike
"injured us irremediably," and President Harrison himself attributed

his defeat to "the discontent and passion of the workingmen growing out of wages or other labor disturbances." Virtually every historian has agreed that the ugly circumstances of the Homestead struggle were an important factor in that 1992 election. Historians would also agree that, as Carnegie and Frick foresaw, an administration headed by the fiscally conservative Cleveland would in no way prove counterproductive to the advantages they gained by getting rid of the union.

This was at last accomplished shortly after the election as signaled by two cables from Frick to Carnegie in Italy:

Nov. 18:—Victory!—EARLY (H.C.F.)

Nov. 21—Stike officially declared off yesterday. Our victory is now complete and most gratifying. Do not think we will ever have any serious labor trouble again, and should now soon have Homestead and all the works formerly managed by Carnegie, Phipps & Company, in as good shape as Edgar Thomson and Duquesne. Let the Amalgamated still exist and hold full sway at other people's mills. That is no concern of ours.

The strike was called off after meetings in the Homestead Opera House, where the voting went against the Amalgamated leadership. The next day Frick himself was on hand at the works to help screen the "former workmen" who wanted to get back into the fold. As it turned out, only four hundred of the twenty-two hundred strikers who applied were hired. The rest were left to shift for themselves, and those in any position of leadership were blacklisted throughout the steel industry at the request of the Carnegie company. Burgess John McLuckie resigned his office and drifted off to Mexcio, where, years later, he kept his pride intact by refusing an offer of money from Andrew Carnegie. Hugh O'Donnell wound up on a blacklist by both company and union because of his secret mission to Whitelaw Reid. When last heard from he told a scholar researching Homestead that "I am now shunned by both labor and capital, a modern Ishmael, doomed to wander in the desert of ingratitude." Homestead, once a proud town of well-paid workers and home owners voting Republican, became a place of despair. Visiting it a few months later, novelist Hamlin Garland called the town "as squalid and unlovely as could well be imagined, and the people were mainly of the discouraged and sullen type to be found everywhere where labor passes into the brutalizing stage of severity."

Counting the costs, the veteran Pittsburgh journalist, who was sympathetic to the workers, wrote:

> The outlay on the side of the Carnegie Company has never been made known, but it cannot have fallen short of $250,000. The workmen, in the course of twenty weeks of idleness, lost $850,000 in wages, and the expense to the state of maintaining the militia at Homestead was about $500,000. In round numbers then, the total cost of the strike to all parties involved, allowing for the pay of deputy sheriffs, the expense of court trials and relief funds, may be set down to *two million dollars,* an enormous sum to be paid for the gratification of Mr. Frick's desire to get rid of unions and unionism. Inasmuch, however, as but a small portion of this amount came out of the coffers of the Carnegie Company, Mr. Frick had no reason to feel dissatisfied. His victory was, in reality, a cheap one. Had he not precipitated a bloody conflict by shipping Pinkertons to Homestead and in this way secured the support of the entire military force of Pennsylvania, there is no telling how long the strike might have been continued and how heavy the loss that might have been inflicted on the firm by the stoppage of operations.

Whatever the cost to others, Homestead was an immediate monetary boon to the Carnegie partners. In the recession of 1893, Frick was able to cut wages at Homestead by 60 percent and stay in production. Shifts remained at twelve hours, seven days a week. By the time Carnegie returned to the United States and visited the Homestead Works in February of that year, the Carnegie Steel Company was in a position to outproduce and underprice its competitors during hard times. In a speech he read to the Homestead workers on that occasion, Carnegie was gracious enough to give credit where it was cleary due by saying of Frick:

> I am not mistaken in the man as the future will show. Of his ability, fairness and pluck no one has the slightest question.

His four years' management stamps him as one of the foremost managers of the world—I would not exchange him for any manager I know. His are the qualities that wear; he never disappoints; what he promises he more than fulfills."

CHAPTER 10

Business Triumphant

HENRY Clay Frick's victory at Homestead ushered in a decade of unbridled capitalism in the United States of America. According to a theory that wouldn't find a proper name for more than a century— "trickle down economics"—it should have been an enriching period for the whole society. But was it? Certainly it was a period during which the illusion of ever greater wealth raining down on everybody in this still half-unexplored, half-undeveloped continent was created by the rich getting richer. It was an illusion that would be repeated in the 1920s and again in the 1980s, a decade that was ushered in with an eerie echo of Homestead by Ronald Reagan's firing of the air-traffic controllers. These later manifestations of the illusion were, however, only pale reflections of the real thing—the "Gay Nineties." Never before or since has there been a time when the ingenious, the industrious, the lucky, the daring, the unprincipled, could make as much money as fast as they could in that decade, and, at least in the eyes of those looking upward, their lives did appear to be gay.

Frick, the great emancipator of capital, soon gave the lead to his fellow captains of industry by cutting wages at Homestead. He had an excuse of sorts in the form of a recession that began in May 1893 and deepened throughout the rest of that year and the next. By mid-1894 more than a thousand banks failed, a quarter of American industry was idled, and some twenty thousand miles of railroad went into receivership. The sorry state of affairs among the farming and laboring classes in society was symbolized in the spring of 1894 by a ragged army of unemployed, five hundred strong, that marched behind Jacob S. Coxey from Massillon, Ohio, to Washington, D.C., to petition Congress for relief. The attitude of authority with respect to mass grievances throughout the decade was symbolized by the prompt arrest of Coxey and two followers on the steps of the Capitol for the misdemeanor of trespassing on government property.

Only two months later, in July, there was an even more dramatic—and nearly as tragic—demonstration of the government's support of business interests as that at Homestead. Ironically, the trouble began in the supposedly ideal community of Pullman, Illinois, a model village provided for workers at the Pullman Palace Car Company plant as part of an enlightened personnel policy. In response to the recession, a third of the workforce was laid off and wages for the remainder were cut by 25 percent. Possibly encouraged by the outcome of Frick's intransigence, George Pullman refused to negotiate with his employees, who then went on strike. The 150,000-man American Railway Union, led by Eugene V. Debs, voted to boycott the use of Pullman cars on all railroads as a gesture of sympathy. A General Managers' Association of Railroads backed the Pullman company, and transportation throughout the North was virtually paralyzed.

The railroad managers had no hesitation in asking for intervention from President Cleveland, whose response to the economic crisis in general was vindicating the lack of concern that Carnegie and Frick had shared with each other after his election. Much to the dismay of many Democrats, for instance, Cleveland proved to be what they called a "gold bug" by heeding the advice of financiers like J. P. Morgan and August Belmont and using his influence to get repeal of the Sherman Silver Purchase Act of 1890. In this instance, he used the excuse that the strike was interfering with delivery of the mails to have his Attorney General, Richard Olney, and Special Counsel Edwin Walker, both former railroad attorneys, get an injunction against the strikers from the federal court. When rowdy strikers responded by ditching a mail train, Cleveland ordered a regiment of the regular army into Chicago on July 4. A few days later seven strikers were killed in a clash with the troops. Governor John P. Altgeld, of Illinois, who had been maintaining peace with his militia, was incensed by the federal intervention. But conservatives like Cleveland and his lawyers didn't trust Altgeld, who had established his liberal credentials by pardoning the three anarchists from the Haymarket riots who had managed to escape the noose. Debs was arrested on charges of criminal conspiracy and contempt of court on July 10, eventually convicted, and sent to jail for six months. The federal troops were withdrawn on July 20, and by August 6 the strikers ran out of funds and gave up. Pullman rehired only those who would sign a nonunion pledge and had the rest blackballed throughout the industry in yet another imitation of Frick.

"The dramatic events of this Pullman strike," wrote historians Samuel Eliot Morison and Henry Steele Commager, "placed the Federal Government in direct antagonism to union labor. The President simply saw the issue of law and order, but through permitting Olney to appoint a railroad attorney special counsel of the government, he played into the hands of those who wanted federal troops to break a strike, and not state militia to preserve order."

Disillusioned by the attitude of government and courts, Debs, a charismatic leader, spent his prison time studying and emerged as the leader of American Socialists. In doing so he was committing political suicide. Socialism was anathema to most Americans, especially those immigrant laborers who thought of it, if at all, as another of those "isms" from the Europe they had fled. Although not as abhorrent as the anarchism of a Berkman, socialism was understandably confused in many minds with communism and the doctrines of Karl Marx. What American workers wanted was a fair share of the wealth they were helping to create and an opportunity to move upward to the extent of their abilities. Samuel Gompers thought it was futile to fight against "the legitimate development or natural concentration of industry." He proposed instead that labor, through its unions, become a second and equal force in the economy to protect its own interests. As for the capitalist's view of socialism, old Judge Mellon reflected it well when he wrote, "Nothing has appeared in my time which threatens more serious consequences than socialism. . . . In all its forms it springs from the same root, the desire of him who has nothing to share with him who has: the desire of the idler, the worthless and good for nothing, to place himself on a footing of equality with the careful, industrious and thrifty."

In the struggle between labor and capital, the prevailing and popular thought of the times was quite definitely on the side of Frick and his fellow captains of industry. The politicians were not just hirelings of the rich; many were rich themselves. The Senate then, as now, was a "millionaires' club." In taking a stand for the primary rights of property and capital and the authority that ownership of either or both of these conferred, the representatives of the people were listening as much to preachers, professors, and publishers as to business managers. An authoritative spokesman for the dominant economic thinking of the 1890s was William Graham Sumner, most fittingly an Episcopalian priest turned Yale professor. A defender of big business, Sumner believed that government should keep its hands off industry. He wrote articles with lively titles like "That It Is Not Wicked to Be Rich; Nay Even, That It Is Not Wicked to Be Richer Than One's Neighbor," and he endeared himself to the middle class by writing: "I affirm that there is always somebody who pays, and that it is always the sober, honest, industrious, economical men or women, who attend no meetings, pass no resolutions, never go to the lobby, are never mentioned in the newspapers, but must work and save and pay."

There is an echo of Judge Mellon in that statement, an echo of Calvinism, which was then the predominant religious strain in the Pittsburgh area, the engine room of big business. Until Calvin came along in the mid-sixteenth century, trade and finance were regarded with suspicion in Christian circles. They relied upon credit and the consequent collection of interest—a dubious practice at best and an immoral one that went by the name of usury at worst. Only income from land rents or labor was held to be compatible with spirituality. Living and preaching in Geneva, a commercial center, Calvin recognized essential business practices as legitimate. "What reason is there why the income from business should not be larger than that from land-owning?" he once wrote. "Whence do the merchant's profits come, except from his own diligence and industry?" In Calvin's view, those profits would be sinful without the "diligence and industry"; hence the Calvinistic work ethic. By the same token, interest would become usury if it were not kept within strict limits and if free loans were not granted to the poor. Undoubtedly, Calvin would be askance at the Pandora's box his tolerance for the fruits of finance unlocked.

Calvinism came to America largely through John Knox, a Scotch divine who lived and worked with Calvin in Geneva for a while and passed the doctrine on to the Presbyterian Church, to which the Scotch-Irish immigrants like the Mellons belonged. But in fact, all of American Protestantism was imbued with the concept that the ability to accumulate wealth, however much, was a sign of God's favor. To be sure, a Calvinistic sense of the responsibility for the proper use of wealth was also preached. It has to be assumed that much of this was absorbed through osmosis by the Scotch-bred Carnegie, who belonged to no church, and ingested directly by the pious John D. Rockefeller, the twin pioneers of massive giving. What seems to have been filtered out of Calvinism by the time it reached America was any condemnation of the means of acquiring wealth. A curb on interest or free loans to the poor would have raised a hue and cry of communism from boardroom and pulpit alike.

In this climate of opinion, it isn't surprising that the captains of industry, few of whom devoted themselves to religious or philosophical speculation, felt justified in their labor policies. Obeying a divine mandate to prosper personally and a mandate from stockholders to provide the highest possible profits, they looked upon labor mainly as a factor—and one of the few factors that they could control, if the unions and government stayed out of it—in the equation that ended in the bottom line. Impersonalizing labor in this manner was made easier by the nature of the labor force. The "native" American population—that is, immigrants and descendants of immigrants from Britain and northern Europe, white Anglo-Saxon Protestants, or WASPs—wasn't adequate to staff the rapidly expanding mines and mills and railroads, as Frick was one of the first to discover. The people imported to do the jobs from Ireland and eastern and southern Europe were usually Catholic or Jewish and often illiterate in English; those from Asia were "heathen" and yellow; those from the South, black and untutored. They were a people apart. Even unions like the Amalgamated did not admit them to their lodges. The WASPs who manned the executive offices, the courts, the schools, the churches, the legislative halls, did not have to associate with them in the daily rounds of their lives. To demean and depersonalize and in some case demonize them, they were given names such as Hunkies, Micks, dagos, kikes, and niggers. If they got kicked around by the bosses and the law, it wasn't like hurting real people.

The extent and depth of chauvinism, racism, and prejudice among the higher orders of American society is difficult to understand today. There's a possibly apocryphal story about Judge Mellon that rings too true to be ignored. One day when he was on the bench, he was looking through some papers and missed the drift of a petition being brought before him. "What did you say that petition was for?" he asked an attorney. "For a charity, your honor, for a Jewish burial ground." "For a place to bury Jews?" Mellon asked. "Yes, sir." Reaching for the petition, the judge signed it, saying, "With pleasure." As for the supposedly more sophisticated financial circles of New York, the humorist Finley Peter Dunne, sensitive no doubt because of his own Irish background, has this to say in his memoirs, *Mr. Dooley Remembers:*

> The extent of this Jew-searching and Jew-baiting in New York is amazing. I know scores of otherwise sane men who attribute all that is perverse in public or private morals to them. . . . J. P. Morgan would have no dealings whatever with a Jew. Only the other day the president of one of the banks that are called "Morgan banks" boasted that not one Jew was employed in his institution. Henry Cannon, who in other respects was one of the most fair-minded of men, would not even take the account of a Jew in his old bank, the Chase. "If you let one of them in," he said, "he'll bring others and the first thing you know your cashier and your loan clerks are corrupted." "Did it ever happen to you?" he was asked. "No," he said, "but it might." "Did you ever know it to happen in any other bank?" "No, but it might. Anyhow, that's the way I feel about it."
>
> Few Jews have been able to get into a good New York club. I have seen E. H. Harriman, during the Northern Pacific panic, leave Jacob Schiff at the door of the Metropolitan Club because even he did not dare to take a Jew into this not-too-exclusive club. There was no rule against taking him in. In fact, there was a by-law permitting a member to introduce a resident of New York. And at the time Schiff's firm, Kuhn, Loeb and Company, was lending millions of dollars to Harriman in his fight with Morgan. Yet even the audacious Harriman did not dare face the hostility of his fellow members by taking a great Jewish financier in for a cocktail.

The WASP attitude toward people apart was based as much on fear as snobbery. In the freewheeling economic competition of the times, there was the fear of losing out to people who were willing to work harder for less. There was a more generalized fear of riot and revolution on the part of people who had nothing to lose, and a more subtle fear of dilution and adulteration of the culture and even bloodlines of white Christian civilization. Distressed by developments in industrializing America, a Unitarian minister named Jonathan Baxter Harrison went among the workers in a New England mill town to make a firsthand study of their lives and thinking. He came away alarmed. Ironically, he found "distrust, suspicion and hostility regarding all who do not belong to their class" and therefore feared a "war on property, and upon everything that satisfied the higher wants of life." Although the younger men and women sought diversion in the town's saloons and music halls, the minister detected little in the way of sexual immorality. Concluding that "toil represses passion," his solution to labor troubles and the threat of revolution was more of it. Workers needed more than eight hours of labor a day "in order to keep down and utilize the forces of the animal nature and passions."

There were, of course, other voices, other sensibilities. One of the most popular books of the time was *Looking Backward,* by Edward Bellamy. Son of a Baptist minister, Bellamy was born a year after Henry Frick in Chicopee Falls, Massachusetts, a town very like the one the Reverend Harrison examined. Instead of arousing fear in young Bellamy, the hard life around him—low wages, unemployment, child labor, tenement house living, long hours, deadly illnesses—aroused sympathy. Bellamy became a lawyer but quit after his first case—eviction of a widow behind in her rent. He learned newspapering on William Cullen Bryant's *New York Evening Post* and then returned to New England, where he would have an uneven career as a free-lance writer of everything from light romances to economic tomes. In the novel *Looking Backward,* Bellamy imagined a wealthy young Bostonian, Julian West, who is hypnotized to cure his insomnia on a night in 1887 and sleeps so deeply that he doesn't awake for 113 years. Julian finds himself in a new house on the same spot as his had been and in the company of a congenial Dr. Leete and his family. During explorations of the city with one of the Leete daughters and long conversations with the doctor, Julian discovers that twentieth-century America has become a utopia. The nation has become one large cooperative society in which there is no poverty, in which each individual does his or her own thing and is rewarded accordingly. It is socialism writ large, and it was arrived at, as Dr. Leete explains, not by revolution but by the force of enlightened public opinion. Bellamy had Dr. Leete tell it this way:

> Early in the last century the evolution was completed by the final consolidation of the entire capital of the nation. The

industry and commerce of the country, ceasing to be conducted by a set of irresponsible corporations and syndicates of private persons at their caprice and for their profit, were intrusted to a single syndicate representing the people, to be conducted in the common interest for the common profit. The nation, that is to say, organized as the one great business corporation in which all other corporations were absorbed: it became the one capitalist in the place of all other capitalists, the sole employer, the final monopoly in which all previous and lesser monopolies were swallowed up, a monopoly in the profits and economics of which all citizens shared. The epoch of trusts had ended in the Great Trust. In a word, the people of the United States concluded to assume the conduct of their own business, just as one hundred odd years before they had assumed the conduct of their own government, organizing now for industrial purposes on precisely the same grounds on which they had then organized for political ends. At last, strangely late in the world's history, the obvious fact was perceived that no business is so essentially the public business as the industry and commerce on which the people's livelihood depends, and that to entrust it to private persons to be managed for private profit, is a folly similar in kind, though vastly greater in magnitude, to that of surrendering the functions of political government to kings and nobles to be conducted for personal glorification.

Needless to say, there are no very rich people in Bellamy's utopia, but the general availability of all creature comforts, the magnificence of public facilities, the social tranquility, do away with the need for personal wealth. It's interesting to speculate on why this book was so popular in a society that hated and feared socialism and communism, that supported and admired unlimited personal success and acquisitiveness. One reason may have been that a vision of peace on any basis may have been appealing during a period of bloody economic and ethnic confrontations. Another may have been that Bellamy made his utopia an outgrowth and extension of the trend toward industrial concentration. Instead of being the villains of the piece, captains of industry were depicted as enthusiastic leaders in the direction of the ultimate corporation, the perfect rationalization of economic activity to achieve the most efficiency. The leading literary critic of the day, William Dean Howells, gave the book a smashing review and said that it "revived throughout Christendom the faith in a millennium."

Howells himself was a convert to socialism who somehow managed to stay in the mainstream of American literary life. His novel, *The Rise of Silas Lapham,* was a realistic, apolitical depiction of an honest businessman struggling with the moral problems and economic uncertainties of the Gilded Age. Howells was a close professional and personal friend of Mark Twain. By the nineties Twain had given up his humorous and acerbic attacks on the economic system. He had, in fact, become a wealthy man himself by writing the likes of *Tom Sawyer* and *The Adventures of Huckleberry Finn* and dominating the lecture platform. The publishing company he formed to bring out the memoirs that rescued ex-President Grant from bankruptcy made a fortune but, ironically, ended up putting Mark Twain himself into bankruptcy. The help Twain got in meeting this crisis—he paid off his debts by making a world lecture tour—from H. H. Rogers, a ruthless mastermind of the Rockefeller financial interests, influenced the author's thinking. Nevertheless and in private, according to Howells, Mark Twain never lost his sympathy for the underdog of society and felt that the only way to arrive at a more equitable distribution of wealth would be to strengthen the labor unions.

In terms of practical politics, the banner for economic reform was carried by the Populists and the liberal wing of the Democrats. They were for free silver, a cause that would propel the charismatic William Jennings Bryan into the Democratic nomination for president in 1896 after his famous speech in which he charged that Americans were being crucified on a cross of gold. Dominating together the Congress elected with Cleveland in 1892, these liberal forces threw a scare into the wealthy by including a small income tax on people making more than four thousand dollars a year to compensate for loss of revenue in the Wilson-Gorman tariff bill they passed. The conservatives breathed a heavy sigh of relief in 1895 when the Supreme Court, muttering about communism, declared the income tax unconstitutional.

One of the few real radicals who made any progress at all in politics was Henry George, the single taxer, who once ran for mayor of New York. George's economic theory was as contrary to classic capitalism as Karl Marx's. The capitalist's view is that capital is the engine of the moneymaking machine—trickle down, again—and that, therefore, the cure to economic ills is to create more capital. Marx held that labor was the fundamental source of wealth and should take precedence over capital in the ordering of a proper economic society. Disagreeing with both, George concluded that land was the key to the economic equation. Although labor, capital, and land unite in any form of production, George argued that only the wealth left over from the rent of land can be divided between labor and capital. Hence a single tax on the rent of land would fall fairly on all elements of society. At a time when the phenomenon of the rich getting richer and the poor getting poorer was especially noticeable, George's explanation was appealing:

> It is the general fact, observable everywhere, that as the value of land increases, so does the contrast between wealth and want appear. It is the universal fact, that where the value of land is highest, civilization exhibits the greatest luxury side by side with the most piteous destitution. To see human beings in the most abject, the most helpless and hopeless condition, you must go, not to the unfenced prairies and the log cabins of new clearings in the backwoods, where man single-handed is commencing the struggle with nature, and land is yet worth nothing, but to the great cities, where the ownership of a little patch of ground is a fortune.

The very fact that George's ideas, like Bellamy's, had a wide circulation and sympathetic reception is indicative of a growing concern throughout society about the excesses of runaway capitalism. This concern was not yet great enough, however, to make much headway against the better organized, better financed forces of conservatism. Republicans recaptured the Congress in 1894, and in 1896 William McKinley, author of the tariff bill beloved of industrialists, was swept into the White House on a high tide of money raised by Mark Hanna, a wealthy Ohio businessman turned politician. In gratitude for past favors, Frick and Carnegie were among the contributors to the McKinley fund. They were to be rewarded by the appointment of their lawyer, Philander C. Knox, as Attorney General. Business was very firmly in the saddle, and the end of the recession in 1897 made it likely that it would remain there indefinitely.

The growth and power of business was accepted as inevitable even by the critics of its consequences. "To resist it successfully, we must throttle steam and discharge electricity from human service," said Henry George. Thorstein Veblen, observing the ascendancy of business, dispassionately if rather cynically as a social scientist wrote:

> Representative government means, chiefly, representation of business interests. The government commonly works in the interest of the business men with a fairly consistent singleness of purpose. And in its solicitude for the business men's interests it is borne out by current public sentiment, for there is a naive, unquestioning persuasion abroad among the body of the people to the effect that, in some occult way, the material interests of the populace coincide with the pecuniary interests of those business men who live within the scope of the same set of governmental contrivances. This persuasion is an article of popular metaphysics, in that it rests on an uncritically assumed solidarity of interests, rather than on an insight into the relation of business enterprise to the material welfare of those classes who are not primarily business men. This persuasion is particularly secure among the more conservative portion of the community, the business men, superior and subordinate, together with the professional classes, as contrasted with those vulgar portions of the community who are tainted with socialistic or anarchistic notions. But since the conservative element comprises the citizens of substance and weight, and indeed the effective majority of law-abiding citizens, it follows that, with the sanction of the great body of the people, even including those who have no pecuniary interests to serve in the matter, constitutional government has, in the main, become a department of the business organization and is guided by the advice of business men.

This accurately described state of affairs was, of course, very welcome to Henry Clay Frick as he literally capitalized on his defeat of the Amalgamated by using the management talents Carnegie attributed to him. Just as he had no union to worry about, he had no government, either. Most of what teeth there were in the only antibusiness legislation of the decade—the Sherman Anti-Trust Act— were removed in 1895 by that same Supreme Court that threw out the income tax when they ruled that the act did not cover monopolistic intrastate business. Frick could safely ignore the carpers and critics and go on making as much money as possible for himself and his colleagues in the comfort of knowing that the law and prevailing public opinion was on his side. Since he was capable of caustic humor himself, it's to be hoped that Frick enjoyed the conversations between Finley Peter Dunne's fictional Mr. Dooley and his bartender friend Hinnissy. In one of these Dunne addressed himself to business in politics in a manner that must have delighted ordinary citizens in that era of business triumphant:

Whin a rayformer is ilicted he promises ye a business ad-ministhration. Some people want that but I don't. Th'American business man is too fly. He's all right, d'ye mind. I don't say anything again' him. He is what Hogan calls th' boolwarks iv pro-gress, an' we cudden't get on without him even if his scales are a little too quick on th'dhrop. But he ought to be left to dale with his akels. 'Tis a shame to give him a place where he can put th' comether on millions iv people that has had no business thrainin' beyond occasionally handin' a piece iv debased money to a car conductor on a cold day. A reg'lar pollytician can't give away an alley without blushin', but a business man who is in pollytics jus' to see that th' civil sarvice law gets thurly enfoorced, will give Lincoln Park an' th' public libr'y toth' beef thrust, charge admission to th' lake front an' make it a felony f'r annywan to buy stove polish outside iv his store, an' have it all put down to public improvemints with a pitcher iv him in th' corner stone.

Fortchnitly, Hinnissy, a rayformer is seldom a business man. He thinks he is, but business men know diff'rent. They know what he is. He thinks business an' honesty is the same thing. He does, indeed. He's got them mixed because they dhress alike. His idea is that all he has to do to make a business administhration is to have honest men ar-round him. Wrong. I'm not sayin', mind ye, that a man can't do good work an' be honest at th' same time. But whin I'm hirin' a la-ad I find out first whether he is onto his job, an' afther a few years I begin to suspect that he is honest, too. Manny a dishonest man can lay brick sthraight, an' manny a man that wudden't steal ye'er spoons will break ye'er furniture. I don't want Father Kelly to hear me, but I'd rather have a competint man who wud steal if I give him a chanst, but I won't, do me plumbin' thin a person that wud scorn to help himself but didn't know how to wipe a joint. Ivry man ought to be honest to start with, but to give a man an office jus' because he's honest is like ilictin' him to Congress because he's a path-rite, because he don't bate his wife or because he always wears a right boot on th' right foot. A man ought to be honest to start with an' afther that he ought to be crafty. A pollytician who's on'y honest is jus' th' same as bein' out in a winther storm without anny clothes on.

Whether a figure of admiration or ridicule, the businessman had taken a position at front and center stage of American life in the nineties. Nobody was more sensitive to his presence than members of the old elite. In a personal memoir, novelist Edith Wharton complained in her delicate way of the businessman's intrusion into New York society:

> It will probably seem unbelievable to present-day readers that only one of my own near relations, and not one of my husband's, was "in business." The group to which we belonged was composed of families to whom a middling prosperity had come, usually by the rapid rise in value of inherited real estate, and none of whom, apparently, aspired to be more than moderately well-off. I never in my early life came in contact with the gold-fever in any form, and when I hear that nowadays business life in New York is so strenuous that men and women never meet socially before the dinner hour, I remember the delightful week-day luncheons of my early married years, where the men were as numerous as the women, and where one of the first rules of conversation was the one early instilled in me by my mother, "Never talk about money, and think about it as little as possible."

Wharton would come to grip with the new phenomenon in novels where crude business types and the lust for money would be the undoing of her characters. Her fellow novelist and good friend Henry James could never bring himself to do that. A member of the Boston intelligentsia and an expatriate, James wrote after a tour of his native country that "no impression so promptly assaults the ar-

riving visitor of the United States as that of the overwhelming pre-
ponderance, wherever he turns and twists, of the unmitigated
'business man' face." James found America to be a "huge Rappacini-
garden, rank with each variety of poison-plant of the money passion," found its people immersed in a "foredoomed grope of wealth."
Because he had no personal acquaintance with business or businessmen, James decided he could not write an all-encompassing novel
about American society. In *The Rise of Silas Lapham,* Howells has a
character viewing the scene from the same intellectual heights in
Boston as the James family and saying:

> The suddenly rich are on the same level as any of us now-
> adays. Money buys position at once. I don't say that it isn't
> all right. The world generally knows what it's about, and
> knows how to drive a bargain. I dare say it makes the new
> rich pay too much. But there's no doubt that money is to the
> fore now. It is the romance, the poetry of your age. It's the
> thing that chiefly strikes the imagination. The Englishmen
> who come here are more curious about the great new mil-
> lionaires than about anyone else, and they respect them more.
> It's all very well. I don't complain of it.

Howells's fictional character was right on the mark. Given entrée
into the international society of wealth by his own inheritance, Frederick Townsend Martin met a woman in England whose family was
famous, powerful in politics, and "wealthy beyond all human need."
He was astounded by the turn their conversation took immediately
after they were introduced. As he reported it in *The Passing of the
Idle Rich,* it ran this way:

> "Oh, Mr. Martin, you are an American. You are a Wall
> Street man. You could help me get some of your American
> gold!"
> "Why, my dear lady, surely you have gold enough. If I am
> not mistaken, you rank amongst the wealthiest women of the
> nation. Why should you want more gold?"
> I can still see the haggard face, the quivering lips, the blaz-
> ing eyes of this great Society woman as she answered me.
> "Oh, Mr. Martin, you do not know me—I am almost
> ashamed to confess the truth. I dream night and day of gold.

I want to have a room at the top of my house filled with it—
filled with gold sovereigns. I would like to go into that room
night after night, when everyone else is asleep and bury myself in yellow sovereigns up to my neck, and play with them,
toss them about, to hear the jingling music of the thing I love
best!"

Nothing in the literature of the times is as expressive as that conversation of the truth that money was the poetry of the age and that
its creator was the American businessman. Enamored of this figure,
the Parisian magazine *La Revue* took the photographs of eight American industrial organizers and created a composite picture. The men
were J. Pierpont Morgan, Andrew Carnegie, Charles R. Flint, John
W. Gates, August Belmont, Henry C. Frick, William M. Rockefeller,
and Charles M. Schwab. Of them all, the composite most clearly
resembles the face of Henry Clay Frick.

CHAPTER 11

Management Genius at Work

EITHER Henry Clay Frick's fabled business foresight deserted him or his fastidiousness about manners and dress got the better of him on a spring day in 1891. Standing hat in hand in his Pittsburgh office was a burly bumpkin from the backwoods of Minnesota. The man who gave his name as Lon Merritt was spouting what sounded like nonsense about a Bessemer ore as fine as baking powder lying right on the surface in the Mesabi Range. He and his brothers, according to Merritt, had acquired a whole mountain of the stuff that they called Mountain Iron. It could be scooped up with a steam shovel; half a dozen or so men working a shovel could load more iron in an hour than a couple of hundred men could bring out from underground in a day. Merritt figured it would cost him only five cents a ton to mine his ore instead of the going rate of three dollars. Trouble was, Merritt said, they were fifty miles from the nearest railroad. Wouldn't the Carnegie people like to give them money to build a spur line in return for an interest in Mountain Iron?

Unfortunately, nobody recorded Frick's response to this proposition. It must not have been delivered in his usual polite, soft-voiced style. As Merritt told it later, "Frick did not use me like a gentleman and cut me off and bulldozed me." Frick would have lived to regret that momentary loss of temper if it had not been for a flamboyant Pittsburgh entrepreneur named Henry—"Harry"—Oliver. A handsome man with a full mustache and hair stylishly parted in the middle, Oliver had a cheerful, friendly personality like Charlie Schwab's. He had been a boyhood friend of Tom Carnegie and had started out in life as a telegraph messenger boy in the same office as Andy Carnegie. He was in and out of businesses, losing money with the same joyous gusto that he made it. Blessed with something called "the Oliver luck," he was also blessed with affection from the people he worked with. On one occasion when he was in the nut and bolt business, his employees worked two weeks without wages to save him from failure. According to author Herbert Casson, who personally interviewed all the early steelmakers, Oliver had "the luck of a man who falls out of a three-story window and invents a flying machine. His creditors were always the first to lend him more money when he was in difficulties."

In the summer of 1892 Oliver got himself elected as a delegate to the Republican national convention in Minneapolis. While the convention was going through the dull routine of renominating President Harrison, Oliver was socializing in the halls. There was so much excited chatter about the ore discoveries in the Mesabi Range that, instead of going back to Pittsburgh, Oliver headed for Duluth. There he found a town so overflowing with prospectors and speculators that he had to spend his first night on a hotel billiard table. The next morning he hired a horse and rode out to the Merritt camp on Mountain Iron. Although the brothers had managed by hook or crook to build their spur line, they had yet to ship a pound of ore to Pittsburgh. When they showed Oliver mines containing possibly millions of tons of iron that could be scraped up like sand from a beach, he knew that he had run into his greatest stroke of luck. To be sure, existing blast furnaces would have to be adapted to handle the powdery substance, but Oliver knew enough about steelmaking to estimate that the savings in the mining process would more than make up for the cost of adaptation. Although he was going through one of his periods when his bank account was totally devoid of funds, Oliver blithely wrote a check for five thousand dollars to the Merritts as option money on a lease of a large stretch of their property. When he got back to Duluth, he phoned the bank in Pittsburgh and asked them to cover the check and consider it a loan. They were only too happy to oblige.

Although Oliver doesn't sound like the sort of man who would appeal to Frick, who, as Judge Mellon once said, could be too "cautious in his dealings with others disposed to take chances" to make a good banker, it's likely that he considered Oliver's friendship with Tom Carnegie a good recommendation. Besides, Frick had by then begun hearing talk of the Mesabi ore from other steelmakers. Rather casually, Frick asked Oliver when they met on the street in Pittsburgh shortly after his return from Duluth, "Why can't we go in with you in this Mesabi ore business?"

"On what terms?"

"Well, give us five-sixths of your ore stock, and we'll lend you half a million dollars to develop your mines," Frick said.

"Done," said the fundless Oliver.

As in the celebrated purchase of the Duquesne works, Frick got an extremely valuable property for the Carnegie Steel Company for absolutely nothing. It was a coup that should have gladdened Carnegie's Scotch heart. Instead, it angered him. Carnegie's reaction may have been conditioned by the fact that Frick was negotiating the Mesabi deal in the wake of the trouble at Homestead. In any event, Carnegie vented his distrust of a wheeler-dealer like Oliver in a letter from Rannoch Lodge in Scotland dated August 29, 1892. "Oliver's ore bargain is just like him—nothing in it," he wrote. "If there is any department of business which offers no inducement it is ore. It never has been very profitable, and the Massaba [sic] is not the last great deposit that Lake Superior is to reveal."

But Frick, who had already pushed through a reorganization of the Carnegie companies, had a vision of an enterprise in control of every process from raw material to finished product. He wasn't about to lose the opportunity Oliver was offering, and he ignored Carnegie's complaint. Apparently fearful of losing Frick, Carnegie did not countermand the arrangement, but for years he kept grumbling about it. In 1894, writing from England, he predicted that "this ore venture, like all our other ventures in ore, will result in more trouble and less profit than almost any branch of our business." This prediction was so totally wrongheaded that it became a source for subdued laughter in the Carnegie boardroom. Backed by all the other partners, Frick went right ahead and, by 1896, he and Oliver worked out a deal with John D. Rockefeller to lease Rockefeller's Mesabi mines for a a royalty of twenty-five cents a ton, forty cents below the going rate, in return for shipping the ore on Rockefeller railroads and steamships. The millions of dollars this saved the Carnegie enterprise are hard to calculate, and the Rockefeller connection it established would turn out to be very important in Frick's personal life and the development of American industry.

In some ways, Carnegie could be a good loser. By the time Casson talked to him, the immense value of the Mesabi arrangements was glaringly apparent, and Carnegie said, "Harry Oliver was a man who saw far ahead. He could not carry all the game he had captured, and appealed to the Carnegie company to join him. It did, and carried the treasure safely through with its money and credit." Although he might have mentioned Frick, too, Carnegie was right in giving Oliver most of the credit. By acquiring the Merritt properties, Rockefeller became Oliver's landlord, and in 1894, when the recession was still hurting business, Oliver fell some forty thousand dollars behind in payments. When Rockefeller agents demanded immediate settlement, Oliver hurried to New York to employ his persuasive personality on John D. himself. The result, as recounted by Casson:

> Oliver was not allowed to see Rockefeller.
>
> "I trust you will remember that this is not a charitable insitution, Mr. Oliver," said one of the junior partners.
>
> As Oliver walked out of the office, he met a negro porter in the hall. Slipping a twenty-dollar bill into the porter's hand, he said, "See here, George, is Mr. John D. Rockefeller in that inside room?"
>
> "Yes, sir."
>
> "Well," said Oliver, "when these other men go to lunch, you might accidentally leave his door unlocked, that's all."
>
> Oliver waited in the hall until he saw the junior partners vanish down the elevators; then he slipped into the inside room and found his dreaded creditor asleep, with a handkerchief over his face. In about ten minutes Rockefeller awoke, and Oliver told his story. It impressed Rockefeller favorably, and in a few minutes more he wrote a short note, affixed his magic signature, and Oliver was saved.

By 1912 when he appeared before a Senate committee, Carnegie was publicly boasting, again without mention of Frick, about the Mesabi deal. Testifying with his customary inaccuracy that he had leased Rockefeller's ore at fifteen to twenty cents a ton, he told the senators, "Don't you know, it does my heart good to think I got ahead of John D. Rockefeller on a bargain." Carnegie and his wife had dropped in on Rockefeller at his Westchester home unannounced just a week before he appeared before the committee. They found the old gentleman "tall and spare and smiling, beaming." Rockefeller gave the Carnegies two paper jackets, saying, "I can go out in the coldest day and be fully protected from the cold wind."

Carnegie added: "Positively it is a delight to meet the old gentleman. But I did not refer to the ore purchase I made from him."

Consistency was not a Carnegie virtue. Despite his protestations during the embarrassing Homestead strike that he was out of business, Carnegie, as owner, remained on top of everything that went on in Pittsburgh no matter how far afield he might be in body. Carnegie's often unexpected and always unwanted intrusions into company affairs could be an infuriating trial to a man of orderly mind like Frick. Carnegie was a born competitor. As his Senate testimony showed, he read his own nature well when he wrote in that memo at the age of thirty-three, "Whatever I engage in I must push inordinately." He never questioned the morality of ruthless competition. Like many other thinking men of his age, Carnegie welcomed Darwin's relatively new theory of evolution with its doctrine of survival of the fittest. Carnegie was a personal friend and disciple of the British philosopher Herbert Spencer, who preached what was called "social Darwinism." Spencer saw business consolidation as part of the natural order of things, and his writings on business structure must have been soothing for many a captain of industry, as for instance:

> A business partnership, balanced as the authorities of its members may theoretically be, presently becomes a union in which the authority of one partner is tacitly recognized as greater than that of the other or others. Though the shareholders have given equal powers to the directors of their company, inequalities of power soon arise among them; and often the supremacy of some one director grows so marked that his decisions determine the course which the board takes.

Carnegie's competitive spirit undoubtedly had a lot to do with a matter of contention between him and Frick for most of the decade. Although it had been his first important employer and remained one of his most important clients, Carnegie had come to hate the Pennsylvania Railroad, which had a monopoly in the Pittsburgh area. When he discovered that it cost two and a half times as much to bring coke from Connellsville to his furnaces in Pittsburgh as it did to haul it all the way to his competitors in Chicago, he went into a rage. His first response was to make a deal with William H. Vanderbilt of the New York Central. Each of them would put up

$5 million to build a new road from Reading to Pittsburgh to be called the South Pennsylvania. The Pennsylvania promptly began construction of a railroad from New York to Albany just across the Hudson River from Vanderbilt's New York Central. At this juncture, the great railroad pacifier J. P. Morgan stepped in to hold a summit meeting on his yacht *Corsair,* at which the Pennsylvania agreed to turn over the West Shore Line to Vanderbilt if work was stopped on the South Pennsylvania. It was a defeat and humiliation for Carnegie.

All this happened shortly before Frick joined the Carnegie companies, but he was evidently aware that Carnegie was still smoldering with hatred. In his first letter to Carnegie, Frick took pains to inform him that he did not agree with the boss's attack on the Pennsylvania Railroad. Frick did his best to make peace with the Pennsylvania executives, and he was considerably embarrassed when Carnegie made an impassioned speech to the Pennsylvania legislature asking for state regulation of railroad rates. To Frick himself, Carnegie wrote, "If you would call public meetings and denounce the railroads, you would create such an outburst as has never been seen, and it may be necessary for us to begin such an agitation, but I hope not. If these rates have to be forced, it will not be our fault; peacefully if we can, forcibly if we must; but competitive rates we shall have." With the support of the other partners, Frick ignored Carnegie's ranting. As a realist, he was fully aware that the Pennsylvania Railroad had virtually owned the legislature for a generation; as a believer in law and order, he regarded the idea of inciting a public demonstration as madness. Frick admired the efficiency of the Pennsylvania—always ready with the necessary equipment, always on time. He thought that Carnegie would have been wiser to spend the $5 million on freight costs and look elsewhere for saving money. In fact, he was doing just that for the company by prevailing in another disagreement with Carnegie and cutting the heaviest cost—labor.

There was another factor that Carnegie either didn't know or didn't consider. Fortunately, Carnegie did not show the same interest in detail in the operations of the H. C. Frick Coke Co., despite his majority ownership. All he seemed to want was a guaranteed supply of coke at a price that would improve his competitive position with other steelmakers. Thus, it was quite likely that Carnegie wasn't even aware of the secret rebate that the Pennsylvania Railroad was giving to Frick's coke company, and it was unlikely that Frick would call his senior partner's attention to it. In the strange and sometimes strained relationship between the coke company and the steel company, Frick's heart was always with coke and Carnegie's with steel, purely emotional attachments that would have serious repercussions.

In managing both steel and coke companies, Frick always had his eye on the bottom line. He regarded natural resources much as he regarded labor—free gifts of God in unlimited supply to be manipulated in the interests of private profit. Once plant manager Charlie Schwab proposed installing meters on the natural gas used to fire the furnaces, and chairman Frick rejected the idea. It would be a useless expense, Frick argued, since the company owned the gas and the supply was "limitless." No man to take no for an answer when there was any way around it, Schwab discovered that the cost would be within his own powers of authorization, installed the meters, and proved their value in making the workers conscious of waste. At about the same time, Frick made a much more important negative decision in the coke business, a decision that stuck because there was no Charlie Schwab to stand up to him. The beehive ovens cooking coke in the Connellsville area were spewing more than eye-stinging, lung-blackening grime into the atmosphere; they were wasting useful by-products like gas, sulfur, and coal tar that could be captured in more expensive ovens for which the technology was being developed in Europe. Kenneth Warren, an Oxford University lecturer in history who writes admiringly of Frick's business acumen, spelled out his reaction to the new technology in an article for the magazine *Pittsburgh History:*

> Frick's company received numerous reports on by-product ovens and suggestions to shift to them. Frick was adamant that the company shouldn't. An interesting example of the firmness of his opinion concerns improvement, rather than abandonment, of the old process. In July 1890 his General Manager, Thomas Lynch, queried his boss about building an "Adams patent" coke oven at Frick's Leisenring 3 facility. "I made an examination of the Adams ovens at Dunbar (in the Connellsville district) and I believe that more can be produced per day with these ovens than from the Bee Hive, but it seems to me it would be worth our while to try a few of them...."
> Within two days, Frick had written a note on Lynch's letter. It read, "Answered verbally said not to build." One result of

continuing this primitive process, however justifiable commercially, was that first rate mineral resource was savagely wasted. Profit margins remained high.

An interesting postscript would eventually be written to this Frick decision. William Larimer Mellon, nephew and biographer of his uncles, Frick's "Mellon boys," Andrew and Dick, attributed one of the Mellons's most lucrative enterprises—the funding of the Koppers Company to develop coke by-products—to Frick. Uncle Andrew's interest in buying control of a business started by a German named Heinrich Koppers first revealed itself when he returned from a summer vacation spent at Pride's Crossing, Massachusetts, near Eagle Rock, the Frick summer place, according to the younger Mellon. But this was in 1914, long after the profits of the company bearing his name were of no concern to Frick. Nevertheless, Mellon wrote that even then "it would have been well-nigh impossible to find anywhere one better informed about the coke industry than Mr. Frick. . . . If this waste had gone on under Mr. Frick's eyes, it had certainly not gone on unobserved." Judging by a witness who knew him well, it has to be concluded that Henry Clay Frick knew exactly what he was doing in turning down Lynch's suggestion. He was making money the old-fashioned way—by stealing it from the future.

From any overview of Frick's life, it is apparent that the Mellon connection was far more important than the Carnegie connection. Whereas Frick and Carnegie were a business team in uneasy harness, Frick and Mellon were like-minded friends. Their shared silence and shyness was a wall against the outside world but not between themselves. Telling of those convivial Duquesne Club luncheons where there was always a whiskey bottle in the middle of the table for those in need of relaxation, William Larimer Mellon recalled that "the one A.W. looked for almost wistfully any time he wasn't there was Henry Clay Frick. The two would talk about coke or banking or Rembrandts, Whistlers, El Grecos, and Raphaels, or mutual friends abroad and at home." They would also have discussed their many joint ventures.

In addition to the land deals that were sweetened by the political influence of Magee and Flinn, one of which would be a fuse to the eventual explosion at the Carnegie Steel Company, and Frick's Overholt distillery, the fortunes of the two friends were entwined in the Mellon banks. In the eighties, well before Carnegie recruited him into the steel business, Frick became a significant stockholder in Fidelity Title & Trust Co., an offshoot of T. Mellon & Sons that was created to handle the estates and trust funds of the wealthy Pittsburghers who had come to trust Judge Mellon. Fidelity prospered, and by 1889 its directors and management found themselves forced by law or ethics to turn over a lot of business to rival trust companies. For instance, a trust company was prohibited by law from acting both for an estate and for minor beneficiaries of the estate. In addition, a trust company acting as registrar of the stock of a corporation had to find another trust company to act as its transfer agent. The idea of establishing its own "rival" to retain some of this business was the brainchild of Fidelity's president, John B. Jackson. Named Union Transfer & Trust Company, it was capitalized at $100,000; its stockholders were Fidelity stockholders, and its unpaid president was a reluctant Andrew W. Mellon, who agreed to go along only when Jackson promised him he would have no duties to perform. With $274.75 worth of furniture, $4,500 in deposits, and two upstairs rooms in the Fidelity Building, one of history's most successful banking enterprises came into being.

For the first years of its existence, the new trust company was close to being a well-kept secret. Misled by the word "transfer," people who stumbled over its name in the telephone directory or chanced to see its offices were more likely to think it was a moving company than a bank. The spin-off from Fidelity business proved to be less than anticipated. The name was changed to Union Trust Co., but by 1893, when recession set in, Union had earned only two thousand dollars, and the stockholders were getting restless. Most of them being fellow club members, they teased, or grumbled to Mellon about their profitless investment when he showed up for lunch. Angered and embarrassed, Mellon went to Jackson and said, "There are just two things you can do. One is to liquidate. The other is to allow the Union Trust Company to locate on the street floor; let it go into business on its own account." In choosing the latter, Jackson told Mellon, "Go ahead, but don't be too aggressive."

Like Frick's, Mellon's gentlemanly, retiring manner was very deceptive. Mellon had inherited his father's iron-jawed attitude about losing money on anything, and he had acquired much of the competitive spirit he observed in his mentor, Frick, and the other industrialists and entrepreneurs around him like Carnegie, Oliver, George Westinghouse, and H. J. Heinz. Although he could never resort to swearing and bluster as Frick and his brother, R.B., could do when the occasion demanded, A. W. Mellon was incapable of being anything but aggressive in business. His ruthlessness and tactics were a match for those of Rockefeller, Morgan, Harriman, Stillman, and anybody else in the Eastern establishment, and his judgment may well have been better. At any event, Mellon's first act was to replace himself as president of Union Trust with James McKean at a salary to which his fellow stockholders objected. With Frick solidly behind him, Mellon's answer to that was to buy the disgruntled stockholders out with the result that he held 2,400 and Frick 1,500 of the original 5,000 shares. In the next year, with customers flooding into its ground-floor offices, Union Trust Company made a profit of $31,000, and there was no more kidding at the Duquesne Club from the Fidelity crowd, who began to think that they had missed a big boat.

As the nineties wore on, Frick's relations with Mellon were both pleasurable and profitable. The same could not be said of his relations with Carnegie. It was probably inevitable that two men possessed of so much self-confidence and different temperaments would clash. When he was still in the mood to praise his manager, Carnegie once likened Frick to George Washington. Like Washington, Frick was for the most part calm and dispassionate in his dealings but occasionally given to outbursts of violent temper, according to Carnegie. With this insight and with his confidence in Frick's abilities, it is surprising that Carnegie was so careless of the younger man's feelings. But Carnegie was evidently afflicted with the blindness common to absolute rulers. From the time he left the employment of the Pennsylvania Railroad, Carnegie was a principal owner in all his enterprises. Dependent on him for their very livelihood, let alone promotions and bonuses, his partners generally went along with his whims and wishes. Although he was open to argument, Carnegie wasn't used to outright opposition. In addition, he had an optimistic outlook and a sunny, mercurial temperament. Sharp disagreements could come and go with him like summer thunderstorms. He had the ability to change his mind in an instant, to forgive and forget. A man of steely purpose like Frick was evidently a puzzlement to him.

As a benevolent dictator, the one virtue Carnegie prized most in his partners and employees was loyalty—not so much to himself as to the enterprise. When he discovered that one of them had outside interests or investments, especially in the stock market, he would complain and quite often get rid of him. In this respect, Frick was the exception that proved the rule. He was the only partner at a high level brought in from outside instead of being homegrown through Carnegie's careful cultivation. Quite apart from the Carnegie connection, Frick was an admired figure in business circles as King Coke, a respected member of the highest social circles as the husband of a Childs and friend of a Mellon, and, as Carnegie himself acknowledged, a "genius" at management. Carnegie wasn't alone in this opinion. Virtually all of the other partners—and especially the most senior of them, Henry Phipps—were inclined to favor Frick's opinion over Carnegie's when they differed. Carnegie had a tiger by the tail, and he must have been unpleasantly reminded of the fact when he entered Frick's office and saw the painting of a predatory tiger hanging there.

Carnegie's method of running his business in absentia was to have the minutes of every managers' meeting sent to him. He would read them carefully, critique them in his own hand, and send them back. Called "Thoughts on Minutes," these productions were bittersweet mixtures of cruel criticism and effusive praise. James Howard Bridge quotes samples:

> Mr. Hunsiker's interesting but very detailed reports occupy far too much space. There is a good deal of repetition in them. It is not possible that Mr. Hunsiker can have anything interesting to say every week.
>
> Mr. Schwab's reply to Moreland's figures is not thorough. He jumps at four percent decrease, which is a mere guess. He should go thoroughly into this question and solve it by proof.
>
> I notice that the Board has been engaged in the delightful task of making dividends ahead of time. I only wish, when the time comes, that we may have enough money to pay on these. It does not look so to me.
>
> Hearty congratulations on August net. Great!
>
> Clemson's report on our gas properties admirable. Deserves encomium of the Chairman.

One of the ways by which Chairman Frick endeared himself to his fellow working partners in Pittsburgh was his tongue-in-cheek treatment of some of these Carnegie thoughts. On one occasion they were subjected to a long memo finding fault with nearly everybody about everything. Although they agreed during a thorough discussion that some of Carnegie's criticisms were well taken, they also agreed that he was out of line in many instances. Summing it up, Frick employed his gift of caustic wit when he said, "I think we have blundered about in proportion to our interests in the concern."

More than his great coups such as acquisition of the Duquesne works and Mesabi ore deposits, it was Frick's ability to keep the ever growing Carnegie enterprise functioning smoothly and economically on a day-to-day basis that impressed his colleagues. There was such complete cooperation among the executives of its various parts that the company ran like a well-oiled machine. Typical of Frick management was the appointment of an overall troubleshooter named P. R. Dillon after the Homestead strike was won. A veteran of the company's Union Iron Mills and Beaver Falls works, Dillon had a mandate to study every department and make recommendations for increasing efficiency, whether mechanical or human. His fine-tuning caused a reduction of more than fifteen hundred workmen without curtailing production by a pound.

In the end, the bottom lines of both profit and production are more persuasive than opinion in judging a manager. Carnegie could hardly fault Frick on these figures. Even with the crippling Homestead strike and the great recession, profits in round numbers amounted to $4 million in 1892, $3 million in 1893, and $4 million again in 1894. Production in gross tonnage for the same years was 877,602, 863,027, and 1,115,466 respectively. In 1894, the Carnegie Steel Company was quite evidently just taking off from the launchpad Frick had constructed when it began to wobble in flight.

However useful Frick's victory at Homestead was proving to be in allowing for efficiencies and economies, the bitterness it aroused in the workers was continually surfacing in annoying ways. Not a week passed, according to Frick, but that some subversive plot or conspiracy was brought to his attention. Convinced that they were communist inspired, he called them "vermillion hued." There was no suitable response other than to ignore them and fire the troublemakers if identified. This was Frick's reaction when a local attorney came to him and said he represented four Homestead workers who had witnessed acts of fraud in the making of armor plate for the Navy. Before he went to Washington with the information, the lawyer wanted to give Frick an opportunity to buy it himself. An outraged Frick showed the man the door, but he did warn Superintendent Schwab to increase the spy system he had set up in the plant and to make sure that the plates were being made to specifications. Frick also alerted the Navy inspectors to the situation even though he was sure that he was just dealing with another case of sore heads.

Frick was wrong. The attorney did go to Washington, where he made a deal with Secretary of the Navy Hilary A. Herbert for his clients to get 25 percent of any fines levied on the Carnegie Steel Company if their information proved correct. The secretary appointed a board of inquiry, headed by the chief of the Bureau of Naval Ordnance. After a hasty, secret investigation relying mostly on the informants, the board declared the company guilty of producing substandard plates, and the secretary levied a fine of 15 percent of all the armor delivered. Frick's first knowledge of the verdict and fine came when he was summoned by telegraph to Washington to receive it. Surprised and indignant at being convicted without trial, Frick said he would appeal to President Cleveland and went back to Pittsburgh to launch his own investigation.

An embarrassed and enraged Carnegie jumped in ahead of Frick and wrote a very personal appeal for justice to President Cleveland. The matter, as it turned out, was very complicated. All but three plates had been up to the Navy's minimum standard, and these had been rejected. What the Navy was complaining about was that although a few plates were 20 percent better than the specified standard, most were only 5 percent better. As Cleveland put it in writing out a Solomon-like decision upholding the Navy but reducing the fine to 10 percent, "I am satisfied that a large portion of the armor supplied was not of the quality which would have been produced if all possible care and skill had been exercised in its construction." At that point, Frick thought it best to drop the matter and pay the $140,484.94 fine promptly; he was more interested in getting continuing Navy orders than in justice.

But the matter wouldn't end there. Still burning over what he considered the part Frick and Carnegie had played in his election defeat by their refusal to negotiate at Homestead, Whitelaw Reid had his *New York Tribune* call for a congressional investigation of the armor plate affair. In preparation for hearings by a House committee, there was a good deal of buck-passing within the Carnegie

Steel Company. Frick rightly claimed ignorance and innocence. As superintendent at Homestead, Schwab was singled out as the person to bear responsibility although he claimed that he had delegated the project to William E. Corey, head of the armor division. In the end, Schwab took the heat at the hearings on the grounds that he had at least overlooked, if he hadn't caused, such irregularities as secretly reinforcing plates selected for ballistic testing. Since Schwab and Corey couldn't honestly deny the charges, they tried to explain them away on technical grounds, as practices that anybody who knew anything about steel making would understand. The real problem, Schwab charged, was the ignorance of Navy inspectors. Schwab's explanations didn't wash with Congress or the public, and Carnegie Steel Company remained stigmatized. But both Carnegie and Frick, who hated government interference of any kind above all else, understood Schwab perfectly. Their boy could do no wrong.

Late in that same year of 1894 while the company was still reeling a little from public disgrace, Carnegie let his insensitivity get the better of him. He proposed inviting into the Carnegie partnership the operator of a coke company with which Frick had maintained a bitter rivalry. This was more than Frick would take. He resigned as Chairman of Carnegie Steel Company. This was more than Carnegie would take. He accepted the resignation. In a few days, Frick cooled off and tried to withdraw his resignation. By then, however, the Board of Managers had elected a new chief executive with the title of president—John G. A. Leishman, the Frick assistant who had saved his life during Berkman's attack. Rather than contest this action, Frick suggested that he be given some nominal post in acknowledgment of his holdings. Carnegie agreed, and Frick was named Chairman of the Board without specific power or duties other than to preside over meetings.

One man thrown into a panic by Frick's resignation was Henry Phipps. "Mr. Frick is first, and there's no second, nor fit successor. With him gone a perfect Pandora's box of cares and troubles would be on our shoulders," Phipps wrote to Carnegie. It was this letter plus a possible belated realization of his own blunder that caused Carnegie to reinstate Frick. Once that was done there was little need for Phipps to worry. Frick was too strong a personality with too many friends inside the company, including Leishman, to be a figurehead. Frick went right on running the company through sheer influence.

Apparently a weak but charming personality, Leishman lasted only two years during which he was continually harassed by Carnegie. Hearing that Leishman was borrowing from a subordinate in the company to take a flier in pig iron, Carnegie wrote a withering letter ending with the warning that "you have much to do before you can regain the confidence of your partners as a safe man to be the Executive head of the Company." Unfortunately for Leishman, the partner with no confidence in him was Carnegie, and Bridge felt that the real reason was the fact that Leishman had been brought along by Frick. In any event, Leishman was prevailed upon to resign in 1897, and he was shortly thereafter named ambassador to Switzerland by President McKinley.

Frick's not-so-hidden hand can easily be detected in the Leishman diplomatic appointment. The President owed Frick just about any favor he might ask. In 1893 when businessman Mark Hanna was grooming McKinley to be the Republican candidate in 1896, it was discovered that the then governor of Ohio was deeply in debt. Both an honest and a kind man, McKinley had endorsed notes for a friend whose business failed and wound up owing $130,000 that he couldn't cover from his modest personal resources. Frick was one of the anonymous "friends" rounded up by Hanna to bail McKinley out. Frick was also a contributor to the enormous campaign fund Hanna raised from big businessmen frightened out of their wallets by Democrat Bryan's free silver talk in 1896.

Even with Leishman out, Frick was not restored to nominal power at Carnegie Steel Company. Carnegie picked thirty-five-year-old Charlie Schwab to be president and chief executive officer. The sweet singer who used to drive Carnegie to his country estate in a livery wagon had come a long way. Schwab's intimate knowledge of steel making, his production records at both E.T. and Homestead, his good-natured handling of men, seemed to justify the appointment. There would be no friction with Frick since Schwab agreed with the chairman's policies. As ferocious a cost cutter as either Carnegie or Frick, Schwab was also as tough on labor as Frick, but he sugarcoated the bitter pill he made the workers swallow with a backslapping, joking, personal approach. A few months after he took office in 1897, a year when a return to prosperity was enriching Carnegie Steel beyond belief, Schwab cut wages across the board despite Carnegie's objections. He congratulated Corey, who replaced him at Homestead, for spying out and firing union organizers and decreed that "we will have no labor organization in our works." The sharp contrast between the grim and silent Frick and Schwab, who was called "a man with a golden tongue," was only on the surface. When it came to making money, they were both men of steel.

When McKinley was elected in 1896, Mark Hanna crowed in a congratulatory telegram to his candidate: "God's in his heaven—all's right with the world!" He wouldn't get any argument from the executive offices of the Carnegie Steel Company. The reason is evident in the figures for profit and production. Profit: $5 million in 1895, $6 million in 1896, $7 million in 1897, $11.5 million in 1898, $21 million in 1899. Production soared in those same years from 1,464,000 gross tons of steel to 2,663,412. Not only had a general prosperity returned to the country, but the uses of steel kept multiplying. The era of the skyscraper had begun, and the Carnegie people cleverly celebrated and symbolized this development by leaving the delicate steel skeleton of their new fifteen-story office building in downtown Pittsburgh stand silhouetted against the sky for a year before filling it in.

Carnegie business was also enhanced by the outbreak of war against Spain in 1898. Frick's decision not to pick a fight with the Navy turned out to be wiser than he could have known. But once again, Carnegie was proving an embarrassment. A lifelong pacifist, he couldn't refrain from speaking out against the war and the annexation of the Philippines while his factories were going all out to fill military orders and stuff dollars into the company's treasury. As at Homestead, there was no such hypocrisy to be found in Chairman Frick's statements or, presumably, his thoughts. Solely in the interests of achieving maximum earnings, he had argued Carnegie into producing armor even in peacetime, and the coming of war had provided patriotic justification for his point of view. Could the nation have sunk the Spanish fleet and overturned an empire in a few months without the kind of arsenal to which the Carnegie works had contributed? The question answered itself.

With the decade and the century coming to such a promising end, it is not surprising to find an aura of harmony and optimism in the verbatim transcript of a Carnegie board meeting on January 16, 1899. Prior to Frick's arrival on the scene, meetings of the Board of Managers, as it was called, had been sporadic and unrecorded. Frick instituted a system of luncheon meetings every Tuesday. "Around the friendly board it was impossible for two important officers to refuse to speak to each other for five years, as happened more than once in the past," Bridge reported. Although what transpired at these meetings was held in strictest confidence by the participants, the proceedings were recorded for the benefit of those who didn't attend such as Carnegie and senior partner Phipps, and they later came to light when totally unanticipated events in that year of 1899 exposed all the eggs in Carnegie's tightly held basket.

First order of business at one meeting was discussion of estimated costs of $500,000 for changes in a newly purchased plate mill and $800,000 for ten new open-hearth furnaces at Homestead. When a motion was made for authorization of $1.3 million to pay for these projects, the following exchange occurred between Chairman Frick and President Schwab:

> *Frick:* That cost appears high.
> *Schwab:* Mr. Corey admits that it is high, but does not want to get caught again with an insufficient appropriation. He will not waste money, and, if all is not needed, so much the better.
> *Frick:* We must have the Furnaces anyway, and may as well appropriate the outside cost. These are large amounts but the whole matter has been thoroughly discussed outside of the Board Meetings, and all appear satisfied.

The motion passed, as did another authorization of $218,000 for improvements at the Carrie Furnaces. This drew a similar comment from Frick: "It is a large amount, but to our willingness to spend large amounts in improvements, we owe our success." That his demotion had not caused Frick to have any greater fear or respect for Carnegie is apparent in his response to a letter from Carnegie to Schwab that Schwab read to the board:

> Several times I have been upon the point of writing you about settling with James C. Carter, the lawyer here.
> We consulted him in regard to our claim against the Government for remission of the fine imposed [for supplying defective armor plate]. I suppose it is the general feeling that we had better not disturb that question, better just let it pass. If you find this to be so in the Board, then I should like a note to be written to Mr. Carter stating that we do not wish the case pursued any further and to send us his bill.

Frick: Suppose Mr. Phipps should write to Mr. Carter in effect as follows: "We have not yet decided whether or not we wish to abandon our claim, but, should we decide to press we would wish to retain him. Meantime, however, as the case has been hanging fire for some time, we would be glad to have a bill for his services to date, which we will pay."

That complies with Mr. Carnegie's wish, and, at the same time, does not close the matter absolutely.

Frick's suggestion was moved and passed by the board. At the close of the meeting, Chairman Frick read a lengthy statement dealing with the question of whether the Carnegie and Frick companies would, could, or should be sold. For a long time, Carnegie had been on record, whether truthfully or not, as desiring to get out of business and into full-time philanthropy. Throughout the nineties, beginning with President Harrison's dedication of the first Carnegie Library in Allegheny in 1890 and culminating in the Carnegie Institute—a combination of library, museum, and music hall—in Pittsburgh, the bustling little Scotchman had been scattering libraries all over America and the British Isles. Two of them were in Braddock and Homestead, presumably to provide a leg up to higher things for the nonunion workers, who were too tired to read after twelve hours on the job every day. Nearing sixty, Henry Phipps, the most senior of Carnegie's partners in age and ownership, was weary of worry about the vicissitudes of business and wanted to put his money into as safe, sound, and long-term investments as he could find. Presumably, Frick, too, was ready to extricate himself from the squeeze between an ambitious young president and a hostile old owner. Whether or not outsiders had any inkling of the enormous profitability or internal dissension at Carnegie Steel, offers and rumors of offers to purchase the flagship of world steel production were always on the table, and they had to be considered seriously. Failing a sale of the property, consolidation of the steel company and the coke company with an increase in capitalization from an unrealistic $25 million to what everybody agreed was a market value of at least $250 million would make a great deal of sense in Frick's view and therefore deserved study.

The board agreed and showed its faith in Frick by making him one of the four members of a special committee to examine and report back on these weighty questions of the company's future.

Aided and abetted by Henry Phipps, Frick took on the assignment with enthusiasm. Arriving at a profitable reorganization of such a thriving enterprise ought to have been easy, but, as it turned out, the story of Frick's efforts throughout the next fourteen hectic months would be one more proof of the old adage that life is what happens when we've made other plans.

CHAPTER 12

"You Are a Goddamned Thief"

FOR most Americans, and for most of the rest of the world as well, the year 1899 was a special time. It was the last year of a dying century, a time to take stock of the past and think of the future. Although there would be mathematically minded types who would argue that the twentieth century would not begin until 1901, the average citizen would welcome it after the last stroke of midnight on December 31, 1899. Whether it was coincidental or related to the temper of the times, the world's largest and richest organization for the production of steel products went through agonizing changes appropriate to the death of the old and the birth of the new. But, despite its position of power and leadership in a product increasingly vital to the development of industrial civilization in the Western world, the drama of the transformation of Carnegie Steel Company would take place on a stage behind closed curtains until the harsh winds of a new year and new century blew them open.

Even in Pittsburgh, the happenings in the new Carnegie building were not known or recorded in the history of that year. Its citizens were more interested in its first golf course, a six-hole affair that was significantly laid out in the Homewood section where millionaires' row was located; in the city's first automobile races conducted in Schenley Park; in the Pittsburgh Orchestra's concerts under the baton of its new director, Victor Herbert, whose operettas were the rave of Broadway; in a reading by America's uncrowned poet laureate, James Whitcomb Riley. In fact, another poet—from San Francisco—became the national celebrity of the year. Edwin Markham's "The Man with the Hoe" was printed and reprinted in newspapers from coast to coast, used as a text for editorials and sermons and made the subject of literary and artistic criticism. As in the case of Bellamy's utopia, there was irony in the immense popularity of this poem when the Gilded Age was turning into what some would call the Golden Age. Consider Markham's own description of the inspiration he derived from viewing the painting of the same name—a weary peasant bowed over his hoe in a forbidding wasteland—by the French artist Millet at a San Francisco exhibition:

> I sat for an hour before the painting and all the time the terror and power of the picture was growing upon me. I saw that this creation of the painter was no mere peasant, no chance man of the fields, but he was rather a type, a symbol of the toiler, brutalized through long ages of industrial oppression. I saw in this peasant the slow but awful degradation of man through endless, hopeless, and joyless labor.

Obviously Markham and Bellamy appealed to the sentimental strain in the American character—the urge to root for the underdog while really admiring the winner. This same contradiction could be seen in the public reaction to America's new role as empire builder. While a silent majority favored pursuing the nation's "manifest destiny," a vocal minority, including such strong voices as that of Mark Twain, decried the army's deadly pursuit of the Filipino revolutionary leader, Emilio Aguinaldo, who had been a U.S. ally in ousting Spain. An Anti-Imperialist League was founded in a futile effort to empower these voices. The sentimentalists and reformers, the followers of William Jennings Bryan in the Democratic camp and Robert M. La Follette in the Republican, were up against a force for which the right words had yet to be invented—America was "on a roll."

By 1899, the recession of the early years of the decade was only an unhappy memory. With a business-minded President in the White House, a Republican Congress, and a panel of strict constructionists on the Supreme Court, the captains of industry worked their wills without hindrance. Following the lead of the Rockefellers, trusts were formed in sugar, steel, meat, and railroads. Proponents of industrial consolidation like John D. Rockefeller and J. P. Morgan argued that it created efficiency and made possible stabilization and reduction of prices to consumers and job security to workers; opponents claimed that consolidation only created monopoly, allowing a few individuals to take advantage of a public in dire need of their product to ignore the natural conditions in the market and set prices and wages to enhance and protect private profit. Persuaded by opponents, legislatures in Ohio and New York outlawed the kind of trust invented by Standard Oil, but, rightly sensing opportunity, the New Jersey legislature legalized a new form of trust called a holding company. Much simplified, the state law permitted a company to purchase enough stock in any other company or companies of its choosing to gain a controlling interest. This, of course, resulted in directors of the holding company sitting on the boards of its subordinates and dictating a unified policy. One of the first "trusts" to incorporate in New Jersey was the American Sugar Refining Company, which gained thereby a virtual monopoly over the commodity. With Democrats still in power in Washington, a test case to determine whether American Sugar Refining Company was in violation of the Sherman Anti-Trust Act was carried to a Supreme Court that ruled in the company's favor in 1895. There followed a rush to New Jersey that included the massive Standard Oil Company. What with the court decision and the return of the Republicans, the leaders of industry had nothing to fear from the law.

It was against this background that Henry Clay Frick and Henry Phipps, Jr., had to consider an offer that came to the Carnegie Steel Company early in 1899. Having brought order to the railroad business, J. P. Morgan had turned his attention to steel. At the urging and with the advice of Elbert H. Gary, a Chicago lawyer and judge, Morgan began putting together competing steel companies, mostly in the Midwest, to form the Federal Steel Company, the National Tube Company, and the American Bridge Company. At a small gathering in Carnegie's New York home in January, attended by Frick and Phipps, it was decided to put a price of $250 million on Carnegie Steel Company and $70 million on the H. C. Frick Coke Company. Sounded out on this basis, the Morgan people let it be known that they had "too small a tail to wag such a big dog." But these figures didn't bother two of the highest of the high rollers in the fast-moving industrial/financial game—William H. Moore of Chicago and Wall Streeter John W. ("Bet a Million") Gates. It was they who approached Frick and Phipps.

When Frick carried the offer from Moore and Gates to the company's Board of Managers and Carnegie himself, he said that the prospective buyers insisted on secrecy until they could arrange the funding. It is more likely that Frick and Phipps, who knew his boyhood chum and lifelong partner so well, were the ones who advised secrecy. They knew that Carnegie would go up in smoke at the mere thought of having his beloved company fall into the hands of stock speculators. To the point of boredom, they had heard the little reformed stock salesman harangue them and his other partners on the evils of the market. Worse, Carnegie had a special contempt for Moore and his brother, James, who had nearly ruined the Chicago Stock Exchange and gone bankrupt themselves in the organization of the Diamond Match Company. They had covered themselves with a kind of glory by staying in the game and successfully launching the National Biscuit Company and had then confronted Carnegie head-on by devising steel trusts in the form of American Tin Plate, American Steel Hoop, and National Steel. In short, the Moores were hated and despised competitors. Gates, who had made his fame and fortune by creating a steel wire trust and gone on to become a big player in Wall Street, was beneath Carnegie's contempt. His nickname was based on a passion for gambling so great that, looking out of a window during a rainstorm, he would wager thousands on which drop would reach the sill first.

By April Carnegie was still in the dark as to the identity of the buyer, but assumed that it was either Morgan or Frick's good friends the Mellon boys, with whom he did his own banking; and he wanted to take off for Scotland, as usual. Whether he was acting out of suspicion or simply his own canny nature, he offered to give Frick and Phipps power of attorney to complete the sale in his name but only if their client would come up with $2 million for a ninety-day option. The most that the Moore Syndicate was able or willing to raise for this purpose was $1 million, but they encouraged Frick and Phipps to do some creative thinking by offering them a commission of $5 million to split if they could swing the deal. All it took was a little arithmetic to arrive at the conclusion that $1.17 million would cover Carnegie's share in the option money. In presenting the scheme to the company's Board of Managers and the other partners, Chairman Frick said that he and Phipps would personally provide the $170,000 if the rest of them would forgo receiving their shares of option money. Since the sale would increase the value of their holdings tenfold, they all agreed. Frick did not mention the $5 million commission that he and Phipps would split. Before Carnegie sailed, there was an additional $1.17 million in his accounts, and Frick and Phipps were free to dispose of the two companies.

In presenting the proposition to Carnegie, the buyers made one large mistake. They offered him $57 million in cash. This was a very large sum to raise on a gamble that the promoters could find the rest in the market even in good times. While Moore and Gates were making the rounds of the banks, they were visited with a stroke of very bad luck. The head of one of the large brokerage houses died suddenly, throwing the market into a tizzy. By June it became apparent that they could not come up with the $57 million cash payment by August 4, as required in the option agreement.

Although Carnegie would later claim ignorance of details of the negotiations, cables and correspondence show that Frick kept him abreast of everything, including the involvement of the Moores and Gates. On May 20, for instance, Frick sent the following cable to the new castle Carnegie had bought in Scotland, called Skibo:

> Moore's plan cabled was not made public but requiring our aid consented to Pennsylvania charter. Present plan capital Two hundred and fifty millions of one kind of stock to be sold at par subject to bonds. Proceeds of fifteen million to go into treasury and fifteen millions to bear expenses. One third of the balance to Moore, one third to us and one third to be held for deserving young men, thus carrying out your long cherished idea. Expect to offer public soon. After allowing fair premium on bonds you will see we are offering the stock at less than paid to you. Bonds are a serious objection, perhaps fatal. The sum needed is immense, hence uncertainty. Frick. Phipps.

For his share in the purchase money, Carnegie had demanded $100 million in bonds in addition to the $57 million in cash. The bonds would not only guarantee an income but would, in effect, give him ownership of all of the physical assets of the organization in the event that the business failed. Frick and Phipps had to come clean in their cable, because the efforts to raise this kind of money caused so much talk that secrecy was no longer possible. By mid-May rumors of the deal began flooding the press on both sides of the Atlantic. Carnegie was particularly embarrassed by the reaction in

Britain. A popular journalist put out a pamphlet entitled "Mr. Carnegie's Conundrum: L 40,000,000. What Shall I Do With It?" and a soap company sponsored a contest with prizes for the best answer to this question. By June the buyers knew that they couldn't possibly raise the necessary funds before the option expired, and Frick and Phipps set sail to ask Carnegie for an extension of time.

When they arrived at Skibo, Carnegie was, as always, a charming host, displaying with boyish pride the additions and renovations to the old castle that had cost him a million dollars. But when they got around to the purpose of their visit, he turned into the tough Scotchman they knew too well. "You can tell the Moores I won't extend the option—not one hour," he told them. Frick and Phipps pretended to be relieved of their burden by Carnegie's decision, and they spent the rest of their time at Skibo amicably discussing a new plan to reorganize, recapitalize, and sell the company to the partners. Back in New York and eager to get going on the new plans, Frick and Phipps were in for a stunning and infuriating surprise. They were informed by Carnegie's secretary that he would be retaining their $170,000 along with the Moore syndicate's million in option money despite a note he had written to the Carnegie Steel Company board that "any part paid my partners I shall refund." Carnegie's cordiality at Skibo had been a cover-up for his deep-seated anger at their failure to identify the buyer right away and their plot to accept hefty commissions without informing the other partners. Now he was punishing them. In addition to confiscating the money, Carnegie began telling guests who admired the refurbishing of Skibo that it was "just a little present from Mr. Frick."

Used to having the ball land on red when their chips were on black, the Moores and Gates shrugged off the loss of a million dollars and gave up on their effort to buy out the great Carnegie. Frick and Phipps couldn't take the matter so lightly. Despite, or perhaps because of, his considerable unrealized holdings in Carnegie Steel, Phipps complained that raising $85,000 had caused him great difficulties. It may not have been easy for Frick, either. He had tried and failed to persuade the Moores to let Andy Mellon have a piece of the action, and he tried and failed again to persuade his partners to let Mellon buy into the Carnegie Steel Company. So business was being conducted as usual in the Carnegie Building in Pittsburgh when the laird of Skibo returned to America in the fall. Almost as usual, that is. As Carnegie had pointed out to Frick and Phipps to cheer them up after losing a sale, the company's figures promised a profit of forty to fifty million in 1900, twice the projected profit for 1899 and nearly twice the entire evaluation of Carnegie Steel Company. Was there ever in history so profitable an enterprise? If they tried to sell to an outsider again, the price would have to be a lot higher.

In order to present a facade of harmony while negotiations for a sale were in progress, Carnegie's president Charlie Schwab had simply ignored an ongoing disagreement between the steel company and the coke company. During one of their New York meetings in the fall of 1898, Frick and Carnegie had reached a verbal agreement for the H. C. Frick Coke Co. to sell coke at $1.35 a ton to the Carnegie Steel Company for three years. Although this was some 15 cents lower than the market price, cautious Henry Phipps didn't like the deal. "What if the price goes below $1.35?" he asked Carnegie. It was a good question, and Carnegie instructed Schwab to take it up with Frick. Regretting the agreement in hindsight since the price was as likely to go up as down, Frick dodged the issue. "Take it up with Tom Lynch [the H. C. Frick Coke Company president]," he told Schwab. "Neither Carnegie nor I are authorized to make contracts." Not anxious to enter into a contract with Lynch until he had discussed it with Carnegie, Schwab let the matter drag. When coke prices began rising in 1899, the Frick Coke Company billed the Carnegie company $1.45, $1.65, and $1.75 a ton—reasonable amounts in view of the fact that they were selling on the open market as high as $3.25. With Carnegie in Scotland and the sale in trouble, Schwab told the company's treasurer to pay the coke bills but to designate everything over $1.35 a ton as "payment on advance accounts only." If the sale fell through, there would be time enough to settle the matter when Carnegie returned in the fall.

Already disturbed by what he considered the failure and dishonesty of his two main partners, Carnegie was enraged to learn that the H. C. Frick Coke Company was not abiding by his agreement with Frick, and he ordered them to do so immediately. At an October 1899 meeting of the coke company's board of directors, presided over by Frick, there was sharp disagreement between Frick, Lynch, and representatives of the minority stockholders, who had no shares in the Carnegie Steel Company, and Carnegie's handpicked directors. One of the latter, Carnegie's cousin George Lauder, almost pleaded with his fellow directors to let Frick and Carnegie settle the matter between them, but Frick again argued that under the by-laws of both companies he and Carnegie were not empowered to make contracts. Eventually and by a narrow margin, the board passed a resolution introduced by Lynch that read as follows:

> That the President be authorized and instructed to notify the Carnegie Steel Company that the existence of any Contract is denied, and that no claim to settle in accordance with the terms of the alleged contract for past or present or future deliveries of coke to the said Carnegie Steel Company will be recognized or entertained by this Company.

Lynch followed through on this resolution, but at the next meeting of the Board of Managers of the Carnegie Steel Company, on November 6, 1899, Chairman Frick presiding and Carnegie attending, coke prices were not even mentioned. The only action of substance taken at the meeting was a vote to buy from Frick a Peters Creek tract of land along the Monongahela River some six miles from Homestead. Frick had had the land assessed at $4,000 an acre but offered it to the steel company for $3,500—a total of $1.5 million, which represented a cool million-dollar profit to him and his silent partner in the land deal, Andrew Mellon. Although he didn't open his mouth at the meeting since he was not a member of the board, Carnegie did a lot of talking in the halls afterwards, and what he said drifted back to Frick. He called the chairman a coward for not bringing up the coke pricing question, and he suggested that it was unethical for Frick to profit personally—how much, of course, nobody knew then—by selling the Peters Creek land to his partners. Frick was so incensed that he refused to respond to a note Carnegie sent from New York. Not making an outright apology, Carnegie proposed a quick settlement of the coke problem, which he described as "only business with nothing personal in it," and he closed by saying that "we've never had friction before—it annoys me more than dollars—even than Philippines."

But the accelerating disagreement between the two men was clearly personal. Carnegie biographer Joseph Frazier Wall concluded that pride rather than money was the root of the coke pricing stand-off since it threatened the personal holdings of both men in both companies. Rightly calling "self pride—the pride a man has in his own name, be it borne by a son he has sired or by an organization he has created"—a powerful motivation, Wall wrote:

> Carnegie Steel and the Frick Coke Company might be economically complementary and have essentially the same group of men as owners and managers, but each remained a separate creation; each flew its own proud ensign bearing its creator's name. It is strange that Carnegie could never understand the thrill of pride that some of his jingoistic compatriots felt in knowing that the American flag was flying over the Philippine Islands, for it was precisely the same thrill of pride he felt in knowing that the rails connecting East with West, and the structural beams in the Brooklyn Bridge, all bore the imprint of that magical name Carnegie. Both Carnegie and Frick were quite prepared to do battle to protect their respective ensigns, no matter what the cost might be.

Pride there was, but there would be money, too—globs and globs of it—in the clash of two strong wills. Like Carnegie, many of the men around Frick misread his true nature. "He was to me a curious and puzzling man," Charlie Schwab said. "He seemed more like a machine, without emotions or impulses. Absolutely cold-blooded. He had good foresight and was an excellent bargainer. He knew nothing about the technical side of steel, but he knew that with his coke supply tied up to Carnegie he was indispensable—or thought he was." Sharing this view of their usually cool, courteous, and laconic chairman, President Schwab and the other partners on the Carnegie Board of Managers were surprised and shocked when Frick read a lengthy and very personal statement at their regular meeting on November 20:

> I learn that Mr. Carnegie, while here, stated that I showed cowardice in not bringing up the question of the price of coke as between the Steel and Coke Companies. It was not my business to bring that question up. He is in possession of the minutes of the Board of Directors of the Frick Coke Company, giving their views of the attempt, on his part, to force them to take practically cost for their coke. I will admit that, for the sake of harmony, I did personally agree to accept a low price for coke; but on my return from that interview in

New York, President Schwab came to me and said that Mr. Lauder said the arrangement should provide that in case we sold coke below the price that Mr. Carnegie and I had discussed, the Steel Company was to have the benefit of the lower price. I then said to Mr. Schwab to let the matter rest until Mr. Carnegie came out (he told us he intended to come), and we would take up the question of the coke contract. He changed his plans, and did not come out. I saw him in New York before he sailed, and told him that Mr. Lauder had raised that question, and suggested that he write Mr. Schwab, and let Messrs. Schwab and Lynch take up the question of the coke contract. Mr. Schwab, I believe, never heard from him on the subject, and Mr. Lynch very properly, has been billing the coke, as there was no arrangement closed, at a price that is certainly quite fair and reasonable as between the two companies, and at least 20 cents per ton below the average price received from their other customers. Why should he whose interest is larger in Steel than in Coke insist on fixing the price which the Steel Company should pay for their coke? The Frick Company has always been used as a convenience. The value of our coke properties, for over a year, has been, at every opportunity, depreciated by Mr. Carnegie and Mr. Lauder, and I submit that it is not unreasonable that I have considerable feeling on this subject. He also threatened, I am told, while here, that if the low price did not prevail, or something was not done, that he would buy 20,000 acres of Washington Run coal and build coke ovens. That is to say, he threatened, if the minority stock holders would not give their share of the coke to the Steel Company, at about cost, he would attempt to ruin them.

He also stated, I am told, while here, that he had purchased that land from me above Peters Creek; that he had agreed to pay market price, although he had his doubts as to whether I had any right, while Chairman of the Board of Managers of the Carnegie Steel Company to make such a purchase. He knows how I became interested in that land, because I told him, in your presence, the other day. Why was he not manly enough to say to my face what he said behind my back? He knew he had no right to say what he did. Now, before the Steel Company becomes the owner of that land, he must apologize for that statement. I first became interested in that land, as I told you, through trading a lot in Shady Side that I had owned for years.

Harmony is so essential for the success of any organization that I have stood a great many insults from Mr. Carnegie in the past, but I will submit to no further insults in the future. There are many other matters I might refer to, but I have no desire to quarrel with him or raise trouble in the organization; but in justice to myself, I could not at this time, say less than I have done.

Here again was the Clay Frick who came out swinging in the schoolyard for his honor. There was no apology from New York, and the land deal did not go through. Silence from the voluble Carnegie was more ominous than sound. When finally Carnegie let cousin Lauder know that he meant to seek "divorce under 'Incompatibility of Temper,'" from Frick, a very worried Charlie Schwab, who admired both of his older mentors, persuaded Phipps to go with him to New York on Saturday, December 2, and try to talk Carnegie into making peace. Schwab had thoughtfully prepared the way for his mission with a letter to Carnegie pledging his undying loyalty but also warning Carnegie that he would have to make his intentions very clear to the junior partners. Still in his thirties and relatively new in his job, Schwab felt obliged to be very diplomatic. Carnegie had the ultimate power to fire, yet Frick had been the man on the spot who brought him along. Since Carnegie and Frick had made up their differences before, Schwab couldn't afford to offend either man. Unhappily, Carnegie wasn't in a mood to listen to Schwab or Phipps. He had decided that a division of power was bad for the company, and he wanted Frick's resignation. The office of chairman would be abolished and all power put into Schwab's hands. Schwab was given a prize he greatly coveted and a job he hated; as head of the company, he would have to get rid of Frick.

Back in Pittsburgh on Monday morning, Schwab wrote to Frick:

I write you confidentially. I just returned from New York this morning. Mr. Carnegie is en route to Pittsburgh today— and will be at the offices in the morning. Nothing could be done with him looking towards a reconciliation. He seems most determined. I did my best. So did Mr. Phipps. I feel certain he will give positive instructions to the Board and Stockholders as to his wishes in this matter. I have gone into the matter carefully and am advised by disinterested and good authority that, by reason of his interest [i.e., his majority ownership], he can regulate this matter to suit himself—with much trouble no doubt, but he can ultimately do so.

I believe all the Junior members of the boards and all the Junior Partners will do as he directs. Any concerted action would be ultimately useless and result in their downfall. Am satisfied that no action on my part would have any effect in the end. We must declare ourselves. Under these circumstances there is nothing left for us to do than to obey, although the situation the Board is thus placed in is most embarrassing.

Mr. Carnegie will no doubt see you in the morning and I appeal to you to sacrifice considerable if necessary to avert this crisis. I could say much more on this subject but you understand and it is unnecessary. Personally my position is most embarrassing as you well know. My long association with you and your kindly and generous treatment of me makes it very hard to act as I shall be obliged to do. But I cannot possibly see any good to you or anyone else by doing otherwise. It would probably ruin me and not help you. Of this as above stated I am well advised by one most friendly to you. I beg of you for myself and for all the Junior Partners, to avoid putting me in this awkward position, if possible and consistent.

I write you instead of telling you because I cannot under the circumstances well discuss this subject with you at this time, and I wanted you to know before tomorrow. Please consider confidential for the present, and believe me

As Ever

C.M.S.

Instead of attending the Tuesday board meeting on December 5, Frick sent this communication:

Gentlemen:

I beg to present my resignation as a member of your Board.

Yours very truly,

H. C. Frick

The sighs of relief from Schwab and the Junior Partners must have been audible. They had no way of knowing that this was only a beginning rather than an end of the fight between Frick and Carnegie. Among other things, the issue of coke prices had yet to be settled. Frick was still chairman of the company bearing his name and presumably still had the support of the board members that repudiated the contract with Carnegie. Schwab solved this problem by transferring shares of H. C. Frick Coke Company held by Carnegie Steel Company to selected individuals and then "packing" the annual meeting in January 1900 with Carnegie men. At this meeting, a new and larger board was elected. Although Lynch and Frick were reelected, two Frick men representing minority stockholders were dropped and five Carnegie men elected. Convening immediately, the new board named Lynch president, abolished the office of chairman, and instructed the president to enter into a contract to deliver coke to Carnegie Steel Company at $1.35 a ton.

Frick arose and stalked out of the meeting, saying over his shoulder, "You will find that there are two sides to this matter."

It was Frick's intention to seek a court injunction to prevent the H. C. Frick Coke Company from delivering any coke to Carnegie Steel Company under that contract. Before he could take action, Carnegie dropped into his office on the morning of January 8 and once more tried to smooth things over. Frick was having no more sweet talk from the man who had just driven him out of a second chairmanship and was proceeding to plunder the company he had created.

"And what if I succeed in enjoining the Frick Coke Company from making deliveries? What then?" he asked quietly.

"I'm afraid I would have no alternative but to put the Iron Clad Agreement into force and take over your shares of Carnegie Steel Company at book value."

Schwab, sitting in the next office, heard clearly the rest of a meeting that he described as "not harmonious." Frick almost literally exploded. He jumped from his chair and started around the desk toward Carnegie with raised fists.

"For years I have been convinced that there is not an honest bone in your body," Frick said in a voice breaking with emotion. "Now I know that you are a goddamned thief. We will have a judge and jury of Allegheny County decide what you are to pay me."

Carnegie literally ran out of Frick's office and down the hall toward the boardroom. Frick followed for a few steps until he got himself under control. It was the last time that the two men who had together created the most efficient moneymaking machine in history would ever speak to each other. The men and women in the Carnegie Building who saw or heard this extraordinary exchange wondered in fear whether their own lives would ever be the same again. It was no way for a new century to start.

CHAPTER 13

Manufacturing Millionaires

ONE of the greatest assets of Henry Phipps, Jr., was his size: he was shorter than Andrew Carnegie. By an odd coincidence, the number of inches of his stature—fifty—was almost exactly equal to the number of millions of dollars he finally acquired. As a small man himself, Carnegie had a noted preference for small men, including Henry Clay Frick, and he also seemed to favor men with personalities complementary to his own. Again like Frick but unlike Carnegie, Phipps was a quiet man, an unblinking realist, a man with a mind for detail. He was a nervous worrywart, the fussbudget of the Carnegie enterprises. Charlie Schwab called him "a little, dandified man, who was not assertive. He had no vigor or initiative." But there was justification for Phipps's meek character in the circumstances of his life. He could never quite believe all that had happened to him, and was always afraid that some unforeseen event or some careless mistake would bring the edifice that he had helped to build crashing down around him.

Although he was born in Philadelphia, Phipps grew up in a small house in Allegheny next door to the Carnegies. Harry, as he was called, was a chum of his age-mate, Tom Carnegie, and Mrs. Carnegie would often augment the family income by four dollars a week by binding shoes for Harry's father, a master shoemaker. Like the rest of the Allegheny gang, Phipps went to work at thirteen. After some lean years of clerking for a jeweler and working for a news vendor, Harry borrowed twenty-five cents from his brother and advertised for a position. A firm of iron dealers responded and, at seventeen, Phipps went to work as a bookkeeper in the business that would consume his life. In this respect, he was ahead of Andy Car-

negie, who was still working for the railroad. In 1861, Phipps borrowed eight hundred dollars to buy into an iron forging and axle business
run by the Kloman brothers. Renamed Kloman & Phipps, the company prospered during the war, but in 1867, during a postwar slump,
it was merged with Carnegie's newly formed Union Iron Mills.

It was then that Phipps, an experienced and expert borrower, and
his black mare Gypsy became a familiar sight on Pittsburgh's Wood
Street as they zigzagged from bank to bank. Phipps did not have
the Frick guts for gambling or the Carnegie flair for impulsive
spending. He wanted to pay his borrowings back. As a result,
Phipps's major contributions to the partnerships over the next thirty-
odd years were to act as a brake on spending and a demon at cost
cutting. In order to play the latter part well, Phipps became far more
than a tight-fisted bookkeeper. He studied the processes and chemistry of making the product, looking always for ways to save money.
A typical case in point had to do with the operation of the Lucy
Furnaces. By mixing about 80 percent expensive Lake Superior ore
with 20 percent cheap puddle-furnace cinder, it was possible to create
a product called mill iron, but the large amount of phosphorous in
the puddle-furnace cinder limited the use of this mixture. Knowing
that the Union Iron Mills made heating-furnace or flue cinder that
was being thrown away as waste, Phipps had it secretly analyzed
and discovered that it contained as much iron but only a fifth as
much phosphorous as puddle cinder. This made possible a mixture
of 60 percent flue cinder and only 40 percent Lake Superior ore, an
enormous saving. Phipps's discovery was a closely guarded trade secret for years while the company sold its puddle cinder at a dollar a
ton through brokers to competitors and bought the competitors' flue
cinder at fifty cents a ton to feed the Lucy Furnaces. Such a thumb
in the eye delighted a fierce competitor like Carnegie, and this, along
with similar economic strategies, accounts for why Phipps could
seemingly do no wrong in the senior partner's eyes.

In late 1886 when Tom Carnegie died and Andy Carnegie almost
died, Harry Phipps began to worry about the real possibility that
paying off departing partners could bankrupt the company, then
organized as Carnegie Brothers & Co., Ltd. It was an association of
working partners, not a corporation. There was no outside ownership. Each partner held a percentage share of the "book value" of
the company as determined by the Board of Managers on the basis
of the physical assets. Profits above the dividend, also determined by

the board, were either retained by the company or spent on expansion and improvement of facilities, which, of course, enhanced the book value. Older partners like Carnegie, Phipps, and Lauder owned their shares outright and collected dividends for personal use, but in 1884 Carnegie began creating debtor partners in order to reward what he called his "young geniuses"—men like Charlie Schwab. Dividends on the percentages assigned to these partners would be used to pay up their shares over a period of years. In order to keep the company entirely in the hands of the men who worked it, no partner, including Carnegie, could retain his shares in the event of discharge, retirement, or death; the company would buy them back. Once a man became a partner, he couldn't be fired unless the owners of three quarters of the outstanding shares agreed. Since Carnegie owned 58 percent, he was the only man who couldn't be fired, and it obviously wouldn't take many other partners in agreement for Carnegie to dismiss any one of the rest. Of all of Carnegie's partners, Phipps—with 11 percent—had the most to worry about in terms of the value of shares, and his worry led to his becoming chief architect of the Iron Clad Agreement of 1887.

There was something almost diabolical in the Carnegie way of doing business. As a voracious reader, he may well have had in mind Alexander Pope's insight when he wrote, "Hope springs eternal in the human breast; Man never is, but always to be, blest." Except for Captain Jones, who refused to be made a partner, salaries were never high in the Carnegie companies. (In lieu of a partner's share, Carnegie rewarded Jones with the salary of the President of the United States—$25,000 a year.) The spur for Carnegie men was the knowledge that their shares would grow in number and value as long as they could hold on to their jobs and to the extent that the company prospered. It was also clear to all of them, from Phipps on down, that they served at the whim of Andrew Carnegie. Without losing the life potential of his work, a man couldn't afford to quit or be fired, and what with rapid growth and ballooning profits, the potential was beguiling. In addition, attention on the job to enhancing profit rather than other factors such as safety, environmental harm, or employee morale was individually and demonstrably rewarding to superintendents, most of whom were partners. Because of his choice to go on salary, Captain Jones was the only Carnegie subordinate with enough independence to push for profit-threatening arrangements such as the eight-hour day.

Under these circumstances, it was important for partners to have at least some sense of security in the form of an apparently legal agreement as to the dispensation of ownership. Hence, the Iron Clad. Signed by all the partners at the time—or so it was thought—the Iron Clad affirmed the system roughly outlined earlier, and it stipulated that shares would be paid off to partners or their heirs over varying periods of time depending upon the amounts in question in order to avoid the bankrupting drain on the treasury that worried Phipps. This agreement was in force when Henry Clay Frick came aboard as chairman and into an 11 percent ownership (it would be reduced to 6 percent in 1894 when 5 percent was spun off to Leishman, his replacement as chief executive). Frick valued the Iron Clad and was one of the board who agreed that it would have to be updated and reaffirmed in July 1892, when Carnegie Brothers & Co., Ltd., was folded into the Carnegie Steel Company, Limited. Indeed, this was one important bit of routine business that was accomplished despite the Homestead strike—or almost accomplished. The signatures of Carnegie, Phipps, and Lauder, who were all abroad, were not affixed.

Since it was felt that the 1887 agreement remained in force, there seemed to be no urgency to get these signatures. In fact, the supposed updating in 1892 was soon clearly out of date again. With the assets of the company appreciating, book value had risen to $45 million by 1897, which meant that the shares of Carnegie ($25 million) and even Phipps, Lauder, and Frick would have to be liquidated over a much longer term. With Frick's full backing, Carnegie produced a new draft of the Iron Clad in September of that year, in which he agreed to take his share in 5 percent debenture gold bonds over a fifty-year period and fixed other periods of liquidation down to eight years for partners with 4 percent or less. To everybody's surprise, Phipps, the original Iron Clad author, politely but firmly refused to sign, even though all the others were agreeable. What Phipps objected to was the provision for paying off partners at book value, a value that he had come to regard as totally unrealistic since the company's fantastic earnings were not capitalized. Despite efforts by both Frick and Carnegie to change his mind, Phipps remained firm in his refusal down to that January day in 1900 when Andrew Carnegie told Henry Clay Frick that he would use the Iron Clad to relieve him of his holdings in Carnegie Steel Company, Limited.

Better than anyone else, Frick knew the full meaning of that threat. He himself had used the Iron Clad to separate fifteen partners during his term of office. At the book value on that date, Frick's share would amount to $4.9 million; with capitalization of "earning power" and "good will," as Phipps had been proposing, it would be worth another $10 million. In view of the amount involved, Frick must have felt that "thief" was a mild epithet to use on Carnegie. But, as usual, Frick had some regret as soon as Carnegie disappeared down the hall. He was in need of consolation and confirmation of his action, and he went to see John Walker, leader of the minority stockholders in H. C. Frick Coke Co. When he told Walker that he had lost his temper, Walker said half jokingly, "I knew you had one to lose." But Walker lost his own temper after Frick told him the whole story. Seething over being thrown off the coke company board and the damaging contract with Carnegie Steel, Walker was already contemplating a stockholders' suit. There and then, the two men decided that they would hit Carnegie with a double-barreled legal volley. Frick would sue for rightful compensation from the steel company, and Walker would sue the coke company.

While Frick's spirits were being lifted by this kind of support, Carnegie was getting a similar lift from a hastily summoned Board of Managers meeting. With accurate foresight, Carnegie had prepared for this meeting during a secret rump meeting of the board a few days earlier when the 1897 Iron Clad, unsigned by Phipps, was rescinded and the original agreements held to be in force. At the January 8 meeting, the board members present agreed to invoke the Iron Clad against Frick. As Carnegie recalled in a memorandum:

> It was late in the afternoon when I left the office. Our legal department brought the necessary agreement under the "Iron Clad" agreement. I signed it and Mr. Schwab signed it; perhaps one or two others did before I left the room, but I am not clear about that. But I never asked a man to sign it; I never saw any man on the subject; I learned that the necessary three-fourths had signed it promptly and our legal department took charge of the matter.

Wanting always to be loved and respected, if not revered, Andy Carnegie would have been upset had he seen a few men on the subject. Although thirty-two of thirty-six associates in the company signed the board's resolution to require Henry Clay Frick to "sell, assign and transfer to Carnegie Steel Company, Limited, all of his interest in Carnegie Steel Company, by 31 January 1900," four did not. One was Frick, who was not asked to sign. Another was H. M. Curry, a partner so ill that the resolution had to be taken to his bedside. "I intend to go to my grave with the marks of an honest man, just as I lived," he told the bearer of this document. A third— a shocking surprise to Carnegie and Schwab—was Francis T. F. Lovejoy, the secretary of Carnegie Steel Company, Limited. Not only had Lovejoy been Frick's closest associate and supporter during the Homestead strike, but he had examined the Iron Clad agreements closely at Frick's request when they were trying to convince Phipps to sign the 1897 version and had discovered an interesting, if not fatal, flaw. The lawyers told Lovejoy that the Iron Clad would have to have the signatures of every partner to establish full mutuality of the pledge to surrender an interest on demand. Missing on the 1887 document was the signature of John W. Vandervort, then a partner. Although still a believer in the Iron Clad, Frick had passed Lovejoy's discovery along to Carnegie in a letter on June 10, 1898, when he wrote that "the present Iron-clad Agreement [that of 1892, unsigned by Mr. Phipps and dependent for validity upon assumed continuance of the Agreement of 1887] is not binding on anybody and never has been; while we have purchased interests of deceased partners under it, if objection had been raised by their estates, it could not have been enforced." Although he was kept in the dark about Lovejoy's finding at the time, it was precisely the kind of thing that Phipps, the fourth defector, suspected. He not only refused to sign the board's resolution but reluctantly in view of his continuing friendship with Carnegie joined Frick in filing suit.

When he found that he couldn't sign the resolution of January 8 because he considered it unfair and probably illegal, Lovejoy felt obliged to resign his position on the board and his office, which would have required him to act on behalf of the board. Schwab took over. On January 12, he officially notified Frick and Phipps of the board's action, prompting this exchange:

> To The Carnegie Steel Company, Limited.
> On Friday evening, January 12th, 1900, for the first time I learned that the Board of Managers of your Company secretly and without notice to me, at a meeting on Monday, January 8, 1900, passed a resolution offered by Andrew Carnegie, re-

scinding a former resolution of October 19th, 1897, touching
the agreement of September 1st, 1897, and at the same time
your Secretary was directed to procure the signatures of the
present members of the association who had not signed the
same to what is now for the first time in your minutes called
"the Supplemental Iron Clad agreement dated July 1st, 1892."

This is to notify you that all the said action on January 8th,
1900, was taken without my knowledge or consent and I do
hereby protest against and object to the same. In some respects
the recitals or statements therein contained are untrue in fact.
The action did not and could not as the resolution asserts, re-
instate the so-called agreement of 1887. At the instigation of
Andrew Carnegie you now speciously seek without my
knowledge or consent and after a serious personal disagreement between Mr. Carnegie and myself, and by proceedings
purposely kept secret from me to make a contract for me
under which Mr. Carnegie thinks he can unfairly take from
me my interest in The Carnegie Steel Company, Limited.
Such proceedings are illegal and fraudulent as against me, and
I now give you formal notice that I will hold all persons
pretending to act thereunder liable for the same.

H. C. Frick

Pittsburgh, January 13th, 1900.

To The Carnegie Steel Company, Limited:
I have read a copy of the minutes of the Board of Managers
of the Carnegie Steel Company, Limited, dated January 8th,
1900, handed to me on Friday afternoon, January 12th, 1900,
and I desire particularly to call your attention to certain actions of the Board regarding the so-called agreements as to
partners' interests, dated 1887, 1892 and 1897.

I dissent from some of the statements of alleged facts
therein contained, and I, certainly, do not agree, but object to
and deny, that the said action of the Board of Managers on
January 8th, 1900, and, indeed, any action of the Board of
Managers, could or did re-instate the so-called agreement of
1887.

As I have heretofore stated, I am opposed and object to
any attempt not only to force from any partner his interest in

our Company, but, also, to the right of our Company to use its capital in the purchase of any such interest.

> Henry Phipps, Jr.
> Pittsburgh, January 15, 1900.

> The Carnegie Steel Company, Limited
> General Offices, Carnegie Building
> Pittsburgh, Pa. February 1st, 1900.

Mr. H. C. Frick
Dear Sir:—I beg to advise you that pursuant to the terms of the so called "Iron Clad Agreement" and at the request of the Board of Managers, I have to-day acting as your attorney in fact executed and delivered to the Carnegie Steel Company, Limited, a transfer of your interest in the capital of said Company.

> Yours truly,
> C. M. Schwab.

Before Schwab wrote this terse note, Frick and Phipps had jointly requested a reevaluation of the company "as a whole and going concern." Claiming that this value would exceed $250 million, they proposed having the matter settled by a three-man board of outside businessmen. This request and proposal, which constituted the substance of the case that would be brought against the company, were totally ignored. The battle was joined, and there followed an almost comic scramble for lawyers. Frick's former and future friend and political front, Philander C. Knox, took the position that he couldn't be involved with either side since his firm, Knox and Reed, were the company's attorneys. Frick turned first to D. T. Watson, a local attorney who had drawn up the first Iron Clad at Phipps's request, and Watson advised him to hire the most famous trial lawyer in the country, John A. Johnson, of Philadelphia. When Frick promised to write Johnson immediately, Watson said, "Don't write—phone." While Frick was on the phone closing the deal, Carnegie was on a train from New York to Philadelphia with the same purpose in mind. It was one of the few times that Andy Carnegie was ever beaten to the draw. He ended up engaging a team headed by George T. Bispham that included one in-house Carnegie lawyer, Gibson D. Packer.

Leaving the whole affair in his lawyers' hands, Carnegie entrained in mid-February for his usual visit to his sister-in-law, Mrs. Thomas M. Carnegie, on Cumberland Island, off the coast of Florida. Since Packer had assured him that the Iron Clad would live up to its name in court, Carnegie was able to give his undivided attention to golf and yachting. Frick, meanwhile, worked with his lawyers on the brief he would file that month with the Court of Common Pleas of Allegheny County in an Equity Suit against The Carnegie Steel Company, Limited, and its shareholders. It would be fair here to use the old cliché that all hell broke loose when the Frick complaint was made public through the courts.

It was unquestionably *the* trial of the young century, and the papers played it as such, calling it "the clash of the steel kings." Up to that moment, nobody—even competitors in the trade—had any idea of the enormous profitability of Carnegie Steel. Industrialists generally were so embarrassed by the revelation of how much wealth was being stuffed away in private pockets that fellow Pittsburgher George Westinghouse offered to mediate to prevent further details being aired in a courtroom. Once again, the leaders of the Republican Party felt threatened by happenings in the Carnegie enterprises. It was an election year and their candidate for reelection, President McKinley, was identified in the public mind as Mr. Tariff. The Bryan forces and their allies in the press were using Frick's charges to ridicule the fact that steel had tariff protection as a so-called infant industry. The fact that Carnegie himself in some of those writings that Frick found so annoying had said that American steel no longer needed tariff protection was unknown or ignored. A worried Mark Hanna sent emissaries to plead for a settlement. One of these might have been Philander Knox, who, while staying technically aloof from the case, frequently was seen conferring with Frick and company representatives.

What was it that Frick said in his complaint to cause such a stir? Much of it consisted of a recital from Frick's point of view of the foregoing events. Frick cited statistics of profitability—expected to be $40 million in that year of 1900 against a book value of only $25 million—in support of his contention that his own interest in a properly capitalized company would be at least $15 million. He reported that Carnegie had asked for $157 million as his share during the negotiations of 1899 that failed and that Carnegie had then predicted that the business could be sold on the London market for $500 million. But as titillating to the public as these figures was the strong language Frick used to describe the personal enmity between him and Carnegie and Carnegie's autocratic control of the company through the Iron Clad that Frick was challenging.

Frick said that "Carnegie has recently conceived a personal animosity toward your orator." He claimed that "this attempt of Carnegie to expel him from the firm and seize his interest therein at but a mere fraction of its value is not made by him in good faith" but "to punish your orator" and "to make gain for himself by seizing your orator's interest at very far below its real and fair value." As for the action of other partners, Frick said that many "were unable or unwilling to incur [Carnegie's] animosity lest he might attempt to forfeit their interests in the association. Some of them were practically unable to resist his will because of their large indebtedness thereto." The only reason Frick spelled out for Carnegie's action against him was the failure of the sale to the Moore syndicate, but he promised to go into others during the taking of testimony.

One of those was contained in another suit filed simultaneously in the Court of Common Pleas by John Walker on behalf of the stockholders of H. C. Frick Coke Company. Although he was an old friend and associate of Carnegie, Walker's language was as strong as Frick's. He claimed that Carnegie was personally responsible for "the execution of their evil design to cheat and defraud, not honestly or in good faith for the Coke Company but dishonestly and in bad faith for the benefit of said Carnegie."

These assaults on his integrity got under Carnegie's thick skin. He finally had to give up fun in the sun to answer them. While he was pondering this, he met Judge Elbert H. Gary, the president of Federal Steel, in a railway car. Unable to keep much of anything to himself but the profits of his company, Carnegie told the judge, "Frick has filed an abusive bill against me and here is the reply which I want you to read." As he later told his biographer, Judge Gary read the document "and found that Mr. Carnegie had excoriated Mr. Frick in violent language. I advised him not to file that reply; it was too abusive. Mr. Carnegie was plainly disappointed, for he believed he had done a fine thing, but he agreed to show the paper to his counsel, and it was never filed in that form." The happenstance of Gary's intervention and its outcome would be of far more importance than either man could have imagined at the time. When Carnegie's attorneys did proceed to file a response in early March, all parties to the suit were beginning to realize that they were into a no-win situation.

Phipps and Walker, on Frick's side in terms of legalities and fairness, were on Carnegie's in terms of friendship. They persuaded another old partner loyal to Carnegie, W. H. Singer, to warn Carnegie that the Iron Clad probably wouldn't stand up in court and that a trial would only be "a rich thing for the lawyers and a great gratification to our competitors and the public." Suggesting that he might after all be fit for the high government posts he would eventually occupy, Knox was working behind the scenes on both Frick and Schwab and giving Schwab the courage to write to Carnegie:

> Knox told me this morning that he had decided to leave for California tonight as he was satisfied that Frick could not be brought to any reasonable position. Knox very strongly advised settlement with F on any reasonable basis. Says that if at any time we want to dispose of our reorganized stock proceeding in court to show low valuation will injure us. Knox evidently gets this from Frick. My own impression is that Frick is much more anxious for a settlement than we are. But I can't help think that reorganization at an early date is the proper step.

Reorganization was, of course, the true basis of the Frick/Phipps suit. No doubt aware of this pressure on Carnegie from his own allies, Phipps decided to play the Harry and Andy trump card in this high-stakes game. Through all of their long association they had had many differences like the present one as to business policy but none as to their liking and respect for each other. During their preparation for the case, Phipps had suggested that Frick look up the record on the termination of Superintendent Abbott's partnership after he went against Carnegie's wishes in the settlement of the first Homestead strike. Frick found a forgotten letter to himself in Carnegie's own handwriting:

> Mr. Abbott came from Washington to see me as a friend.
> He thought that if he retired his half was worth far more than the books and I could not say otherwise.
> I said of course it was worth 20% more than the books and

if he decided to retire and sell, I should see he got that
for it.

Confronting Carnegie with the evidence of his own interpretation
of the Iron Clad in the Abbott case, Phipps was able to talk his old
friend around to the point of saying, "Make your own plan, Harry,
I only want what is fair."

Phipps hurried back to Pittsburgh to give the good news to Frick,
who, according to biographer Harvey, said, "It is useless now to talk
about anybody buying or selling. The fair thing to do is to make the
consolidation of the two companies upon the terms agreed to by
everybody a year ago before the Moore offer was received. That will
solve the whole problem justly and honestly. I am willing."

This, of course, was what Phipps wanted all along. He lost no
time in arranging a meeting at Carnegie's New York home on March
17 with Carnegie and Schwab. Phipps and Lovejoy represented
Frick. When Carnegie agreed to the plan in principle, another, larger
meeting to include the Board of Managers and attorneys was arranged for the following Monday. Ever since the filing of the Frick
suit, the press had been keeping a kind of death watch on Carnegie
Steel. To outwit them until the agreement could be formalized, Carnegie booked rooms in an Atlantic City hotel and instructed the men
from Pittsburgh to travel to the resort over the weekend with their
wives, as if going on holiday. This ruse worked, but it would have
failed utterly if any newspaperman had got wind of the fact that
another Carnegie guest at Atlantic City was a round, rosy-faced little
lawyer from New Jersey named James B. Dill. Held in nearly as
much awe in Wall Street as J. P. Morgan, Dill invented and shep-
herded through the legislature the laws that made New Jersey the
haven of the new trusts or holding companies. Dill was in Atlantic
City to draft the charter of The Carnegie Company, combining The
Carnegie Steel Company, Limited and the H. C. Frick Coke Company, capitalized at $320 million—$250 million for steel and $70
million for coke.

In this process, Carnegie's beloved association of partners was dissolved as each of them became stockholders in the new corporation.
It appeared to be an outright victory for Phipps and Frick, and the
suits were called off, including Walker's since the coke company
prices were readjusted in "the spirit of Atlantic City." Carnegie did
demand some concessions, one of which nearly sank the negotiations.

He wanted Frick so completely removed from the company that he insisted upon having his stocks delivered to him through a trustee. After some hot argument, Lovejoy, who was in constant phone contact with Frick in Pittsburgh, conceded the point. In another respect about which he would boast in the future, Carnegie got his way. None of the stock, pegged at a thousand dollars a share, went on the market; it all stayed in the hands of men in the company. Moreover, not a cent was paid in commissions—the lifeblood of Morgan's operation—for establishing the new corporation.

The immediate increase in fortunes of all concerned was staggering. Carnegie's share soared to $174,529,000; Phipp's to $34,800,000; Frick's to $31,284,000, with $16,604,000 representing his interest in the coke company. Smaller fry did very well, too. George Lauder was on the books for $11,075,000; honest Henry Curry for $5,715,000; courageous Francis Lovejoy for $1,786,000; John Walker for $1,459,000; Charlie Schwab's little brother, Joe, for $893,000, putting him very close to the magic million mark. Schwab, of course, was a big winner. Although still clinging to his power as owner, Carnegie made Schwab czar of the new corporation and increased his shares to equal Frick's 6 percent. On the day the conference ended, a happy Schwab telegraphed orders for a banquet to the Bellevue Hotel in Philadelphia, where he and his newly rich colleagues celebrated.

Because Carnegie fought reorganization almost to the courthouse door, one of his biographers, Joseph Frazier Wall, argued that he was acting out of principle rather than avarice, as Frick charged. "For the first time, Carnegie's authority had been openly challenged, and his response had been ruthless in its totality," Wall wrote. "For Frick and Phipps, on the other hand, it must be said that it was not 'the principle but the money of the thing' that motivated them. As for Schwab and the lesser partners, their behavior could be interpreted as being opportunistic." In letting Carnegie off the hook of greed, Wall overlooks his willingness to go back on his word and confiscate the option money Phipps and Frick gave him, his willingness to ignore the Iron Clad in a relatively minor settlement with Abbott. The whole affair, in fact, had the character of a falling out among thieves, a falling out that ironically increased the loot for all of them. Everybody was happy except perhaps a public cheated out of the drama of a trial.

A sad footnote to this creation of instant millionaires is provided by the fate of Francis Lovejoy, the only one who acted against his own self-interest. Like Frick, Lovejoy could no longer be an active participant in the company and eventually took his interest out. For reasons unrecorded, he ran through the money, and eight years later his wife humbled herself to write to Carnegie and ask for a loan so that they wouldn't lose their home. Of course, it was granted since a real Carnegie virtue was that he seldom held a grudge. He and Phipps, for instance, were back on a close friendship basis before the ink was dry on the Atlantic City agreement. But Lovejoy was beyond salvation. A man helping Carnegie to collect material for his autobiography—in which the name of Frick appeared only once—noted: "All agree needless to talk to Lovejoy. He seems to have gone all to pieces, physically and mentally."

CHAPTER 14

Mr. Morgan's Billion-Dollar Bargain

IF Henry Clay Frick and Andrew Carnegie ever were to come back from wherever they've gone, chances are that they would deplore the uses to which the last great invention of their times—the flying machine—have been put. Theirs was the heyday of the luxury ocean liner, and they were guaranteed a few weeks rest at sea whenever they made a trip abroad. For top executives in the Carnegie enterprises, going to see Andy in Scotland or wherever he was for six months during every year came close to being an annual ritual— what would be classified as a perk today. It was an opportunity that Frick, who was becoming increasingly fascinated with searching out European works of art that he liked and could afford, certainly enjoyed, and it was a respite from work that he undoubtedly needed. Although he always managed to maintain a show of energy and a stiff-backed posture of command in public, Frick would sometimes literally collapse as soon as he crossed the sheltering threshhold of Clayton after an exhausting business day. One of the Mellons reported seeing him crawl to the nearest couch, where he would lie until his strength returned, on more than one occasion. Stress could bring on recurring attacks of his boyhood illness. Aboard ship, Frick could relax and always find congenial company for his favorite pastime—playing cards. If he wanted to talk business, there would be a Morgan or a Rockefeller or a Stillman or a Phipps or a Mellon on the passenger list. Frequent and lengthy sojourns abroad were the common lot of both the new and the old rich in America. The steamer trunk never stayed long in their attics.

The friendship that Frick and Andrew Mellon cemented during their first European trip together twenty years before was still holding strong on land and sea at the turn of the century. In 1898 during a crossing on the White Star ship *Germanic* with Mellon, Frick got to know a British couple, the Alexander McMullens, of Hertfordshire, and their twenty-year-old daughter, Nora Mary. McMullen was a brewer, and no doubt the grandson of a distiller would find some common ground with him. As for Nora Mary, she was not only beautiful and spirited but something of a princess in that the McMullens lived in Hertford Castle, on which they had a ninety-nine-year lease. Frick introduced the McMullens to his friend, Andrew Mellon. Unknowingly, he was returning the favor that Mellon had given him when he arranged an introduction to Adelaide Childs. Back then, Mellon had also been in love with a Pittsburgh girl, but she had died of tuberculosis and his romantic life had been totally nonexistent ever since. Whether Frick could have anticipated anything coming of a meeting between a lively young woman and a shy, forty-three-year-old bachelor or not, he did know that his friend was lonely from the way he haunted the child-filled houses of the Fricks and his brothers and nephews. An only daughter with seven older brothers, Nora was not easily impressed by men, however rich and handsome. Mellon spent much time in England courting her during the two years that his friend, Frick, was wrestling with Carnegie, and they were finally married in 1900.

Fortunately for Frick, Mellon did not allow his expensive courtship with its idle crisscrossing of the Atlantic to interfere with business. Pittsburgh was the steel capital of the world, and Mellon was *the* banker to Pittsburgh. So Mellon felt frustrated, if not outright angry, that Frick had not been able to shoehorn him into the wheeling and dealing going on at the Carnegie companies. When William Donner, an experienced metal maker, came to him for a loan to build a rod and wire mill on the banks of the Monongahela in 1899, Mellon was quite interested. Before granting the loan, however, he consulted Andrew Carnegie to make sure that Donner's plant could get the steel ingots it would need. Delighted to have somebody go into competition with the Morgan mills in the Midwest, Carnegie agreed to a five-year contract to supply Donner with ingots. Within months of that agreement, Carnegie manipulated Frick's ouster as chairman of his companies; within days of Frick's dismissal, Andrew Mellon called a very rare press conference to announce the formation of Union Steel Company, in which Henry Clay Frick would have a quarter interest, the others being A. W. Mellon, R. B. Mellon, and William H. Donner.

Since there were so many other bones of contention between Frick and Carnegie by that time, it is doubtful that Frick's participation in Union Steel had much to do with the final dissolution of their partnership. It did, however, rankle with Carnegie when he realized the contract he had negotiated with Mellon was going to enrich Frick. Initially capitalized at $10 million and funded with expertise from Frick and the Mellons, Union Steel made quick progress. A whole town named Donora—Donner's name combined with Mellon's wife's—was built to accommodate the works and the workers. Before long, Union acquired the Sharon, Pennsylvania, steel plants of William Flinn, the Pittsburgh Republican boss and longtime associate of the Mellons and Frick in various projects. Anyone *au courant* with the steel business knew that, regardless of what happened in the Carnegie companies, Henry Clay Frick was a force and factor to be reckoned with.

With the suit settled and Frick out of the way, Carnegie, working through Schwab, felt free to indulge his fierce competitive instincts. He decided to attack both his new enemies—the consolidations Morgan was creating in the steel business—and his old ones—the Pennsylvania and B. & O. railroads, which monopolized traffic in the Pittsburgh area. Carnegie had property and facilities at Conneaut, the Lake Erie terminus of his Bessemer railroad, for the transhipment of Lake Superior ore to Pittsburgh. The trains were running virtually empty from Pittsburgh back to the lake, and it seemed obvious that they could carry Carnegie coal and coke back with them to supply a steel operation at a very low cost. One of the Morgan enterprises that threatened Carnegie's supremacy was the National Tube Company. With the Conneaut site in mind, Carnegie asked Schwab, "How much cheaper can you make tubes than the National Company?" When Schwab came up with a figure of ten dollars a ton, Carnegie said, "Go ahead and build a tube plant at Conneaut." This was an order leaked to the press, as were the plans Carnegie began making with George Gould to build yet another railway line to the east and west. As Carnegie probably intended, the news of these projects was very upsetting to J. P. Morgan.

Somebody advanced the surprising and rather interesting theory that the only difference between the socialists and Morgan and Rockefeller had to do with who would run the show. For both

Morgan and Rockefeller, the establishment of order and centralized control over large segments of productive society such as transportation, steel, and oil was a motivation nearly as compelling as making money. Where they differed with the socialists was in thinking that the profit for achieving these desirable ends should go to the private citizens smart enough to do it. To them a loner like Carnegie was a spoiler. Not only did he appear to really believe in democracy, free enterprise, survival of the fittest and all the rest, but he had turned his beliefs into so much money that he could afford to carry out just about any plan that came into his head. They didn't know what to do with him. He *would* build a plant at Conneaut and another railroad unless some way of stopping him surfaced.

This was the situation in December of 1900 when two New York financiers, J. Edward Simmons and Charles Stewart Smith, felt obliged to reciprocate the hospitality of Charles M. Schwab, president of Carnegie Steel, who had shown them around his installations in Pittsburgh. They staged a dinner at the University Club in Schwab's honor on December 12 and invited the leading lights of New York's financial community. Although Andrew Carnegie, who had another engagement, was not among them, some said that his hidden hand was behind the affair. Seated on the guest's right hand was none other than J. P. Morgan, a sure sign that something more important than mere socializing was involved. Morgan's stature as a manipulator of men and money was of nearly superhuman proportions, and he was not a man to waste his valuable time knowingly.

Physically, Morgan was an impressive and striking figure. At sixty-three, he still held his six-foot, two-hundred-pound body stiffly erect. Although the handsome features of his youth had long been scarred by a skin disease that left him with an ugly, bulbous, red nose, Morgan's piercing hazel eyes and regal bearing immediately captured the attention of anyone he confronted. He radiated a supreme self-confidence, and virtually all of the affairs in which he was engaged were of national or international significance. Like so many of his peers, including Henry Clay Frick, Morgan was a man of few words. When he did speak, men around him listened—and acted.

In many respects, Schwab, still shy of forty, was a match for Morgan. He, too, had what we now call charisma. He hadn't been born into what passed for an American aristocracy, as had Morgan, but his rapid and continuing success in every endeavor had given him a nearly equal measure of self-confidence. Also a commanding figure physically, Schwab parted company with Morgan in that he loved to talk. As guest of honor at the Simmons-Smith dinner, Schwab would have the privilege—and in his case, real pleasure—of addressing the company. Gifted with his famous golden tongue, Schwab liked to speak without notes or manuscript—a pity in this instance since he delivered a truly historic talk. Wherever and whenever Schwab spoke, he always opened with a statement that all he could talk about was steel. On this December evening, he ad-libbed what amounted to a prose poem about the glorious future of a properly organized steel industry, an industry that would control every process from the mining of ore and coal to the manufacture of the entire range of steel products down to needles and nails. He must have sounded almost like the socialist utopian Bellamy when he argued that the savings generated by this rationalization of the industry would provide cheaper products for the American consumer and permit American industry to undersell British and German competitors in foreign markets. Schwab did not dwell on the fact that the Carnegie Company was at that very moment doing all it could to undermine and break up the consolidation in steel that the impressive old gentleman on his right had already achieved.

Nobody in America better understood the subtleties of business transactions than J. P. Morgan. He knew exactly why he was there and what Charlie Schwab was saying: that old buccaneer Carnegie was ready to put down his blunderbuss. Morgan was fascinated by the profit picture that the knowledgeable Schwab painted for the kind of structure he was trying to erect in steel—and probably by the man himself. A Morgan peculiarity that may have been related to his own disfigurement was a penchant for surrounding himself with handsome and charming young men. This night Morgan did not escape the gathering as soon as politely possible but pulled Schwab off into a corner where he belied his reputation for silence by pestering the young man with pointed questions. The only form of intellectual interest or superiority ever noted about J. P. Morgan throughout his academic career and thereafter was—again reminiscent of stories about Frick—an exceptional ability to handle mathematical facts and computations in his head. Morgan wasn't above fooling others who were less precise in their calculations, but he seldom fooled himself. He wanted to know the facts beneath Schwab's rhetoric.

Obviously, Schwab was able to satisfy Morgan, because he had barely arrived back in Pittsburgh before he got a call from a most unlikely source—the infamous "Bet a Million" Gates. According to Gates, Mr. Morgan was interested in having a further discussion with Mr. Schwab. If Carnegie really was lurking behind the scenes of this drama, the main actors weren't aware of it. Schwab hadn't discussed his appearance or his speech with Carnegie at all, and he was reluctant to meet Morgan without his superior's knowledge. "What if you just ran into him?" Gates suggested. On that basis, it was agreed that Schwab would appear at a Philadelphia hotel where Morgan would be staying. It was a cold day in early January when Schwab showed up for the rendezvous only to get another call from Gates. Morgan was laid up with a cold. (This was not unusual. Despite his robust appearance, Morgan was subject to frequent colds and other ailments.) Gates suggested that Schwab hop a train and meet with Morgan in his home at 219 Madison Avenue. Having come that far, Schwab felt that he had no alternative. Cold or no, Morgan was attentive and alert that night when, along with one of his handsome young partners, Robert Bacon, and Gates, they talked the whole night through about the properties that would be needed to arrive at the kind of organization Schwab had envisioned. The essential core would be the Carnegie Company, and Schwab found himself out on the street at dawn with a commission from Morgan to find out whether and for how much Andrew Carnegie would be willing to sell.

Within a few days of the meeting rumors abounded on Wall Street and made their way into the press. On January 14, Carnegie wrote Schwab that he had read what sounded like a "cock & bull story" in the *New York Tribune* about him and Morgan. He wanted a letter assuring him that Charlie wouldn't be diverted from their plans to build at Conneaut and work with Gould on a new railroad. Schwab's instant response was to the effect that "am anxious to get at Conneaut. Are finishing plans rapidly & will be ready for a stand in spring. Hope to see you next week." Schwab did show up in New York the next week on a day that he knew Carnegie would be up at his cottage on the St. Andrews Golf Club in Westchester. Schwab wanted a chance to talk to Louise Carnegie alone before he met the master.

Schwab told Mrs. Carnegie the whole story, and she became his instant ally. Her Andy was sixty-five and for years she had been hoping to extricate him from business so that he could spend more time with her and their daughter. From her point of view Mr. Morgan's interest could not have surfaced at a better moment. They were in the act of building a new house on Ninety-first Street to replace their Fifty-first Street home, and it would be most appropriate to move on to a new phase in their lives together as well. Despite the calendar and the temperature, Andy was up at the cottage so that he could play golf on any good day. "As you must know, Mr. Schwab, he likes the cold and the game is a perfect passion with him," Louise said. "I'm glad because it makes him feel so good. He's only been at it for two years but he already calls it 'Dr. Golf.' I'd suggest you go up there and play a round with him before you get down to business. He'll be in the right mood then—especially if he wins." There was a conspiratorial twinkle in her eye when she delivered the last phrase, and Schwab followed her advice to the letter.

Over lunch after a Carnegie victory, Schwab again told the whole story as he had told it to Louise. For once Carnegie was silent. This was a proposition he had to take very seriously. He had no particular liking for a Wall Street figure like Morgan, but he had done much business with Morgan's father in London and considered the son more reputable and reliable than, say, the Moores and Gates. He said he would spend a night thinking it over and give Schwab an answer in the morning. It was a sleepless night for both men, and when Schwab returned, Carnegie handed him a piece of paper with the following message scribbled boldly in pencil:

Capitalization of Carnegie Company:
$160,000,000 bonds to be exchanged at
par for bonds in new company $160,000,000

$160,000,000 stock to be exchanged at
rate of $1000 share of stock in Carnegie
Company exchanged for $1,500 share of
stock in new company $240,000,000

Profit for past year and estimated profit
for coming year $80,000,000

Total price for Carnegie Company and
all its holdings $480,000,000

In addition to what he had written down, Carnegie told Schwab
that he would require as a form of payment for himself, his cousin
Lauder, and his sister-in-law Lucy first mortgage, 5 percent gold
bonds. He wanted no stocks and no participation in the new company that might be required of a major shareholder; he also wanted
protection in the event of failure. He asked Schwab to take the paper
and his verbal message right down to Morgan's office at 23 Wall
Street. Schwab undertook the mission immediately. With only a
glance at Carnegie's notes, Morgan said, "I accept this price."

That was it—it was a done deal! It was days later before Morgan thought that he and Carnegie ought at least to shake hands
on it. Arranging for this simple ceremony involved a problem in
protocol for the King of Steel and the King of Finance. When
Morgan phoned to invite Carnegie down to Wall Street, Carnegie
suggested that the distance between Fifty-first and Wall streets was
the same in either direction. Concerned that the question of who
should visit whom could cause a rift between two men of pride,
some underling who stood to profit from the deal reminded Morgan that he was two years younger than Carnegie and could,
therefore, gracefully accede to riding uptown. The identity of this
industrial diplomat hasn't been made part of the history. Years
later Schwab claimed to have come up with the age differential,
but all the other details in Schwab's account are so at variance
with those of others as to descredit it. However it actually came
about, Morgan did summon a carriage and ride up to Fifty-first
Street, where he and Carnegie spent not more than fifteen minutes
in private conversation. On the way out where he could be overheard, Morgan shook Carnegie's hand and said, "Mr. Carnegie, I
want to congratulate you on being the richest man in the world!"

It may have been hyperbole, but not by much. One of the Rothschilds later wrote that Carnegie had amassed in about thirty years
more money than his family had acquired in centuries. Sent by letter
from Carnegie to the Board of Managers, the news was greeted in
Pittsburgh with elation. God and the markets willing, each stockholder was getting five hundred dollars more per share. But more
important psychologically than the monetary gain was that all of
them were free from bondage to Carnegie. They could start living

it up on their new wealth. At the February 4, 1901, meeting of the board of managers of the Carnegie Company a joint response to Carnegie's letter was drafted. In it, they agreed to Carnegie's desire to be paid in bonds and to accept stock in the new company in exchange for their own holdings. They didn't gloat over suddenly becoming half again as rich as they had been. Instead, they piously informed Carnegie that "whatever pecuniary benefits we may derive from a new organization such as outlined, our first and most natural feeling is the keen regret to all of us in the severance of our business relations to you, to whom we owe so much. Your sound judgment and profound business sagacity have been the foundation stones on which has been built the fabric of our success."

Acquiring the Carnegie Company and subsidiaries such as the H. C. Frick Coke Company was slightly less than half the package that Morgan, Schwab, Gates, and Bacon planned to wrap up during that meeting in the Morgan home. Of course, Morgan's Federal Steel would be part of the new company, and Morgan wanted its chairman, Judge Gary, to take the same position in what he would call the United States Steel Corporation. Gary would be the organization's front man; Charlie Schwab, as president, would be the steelmaker. Once he had settled with Carnegie, Morgan turned the working out of details over to Gary and Bacon. The last weeks of February and the early weeks of March were busy and anxious times at 23 Wall Street. At one point, for instance, there were hints that Carnegie was getting cold feet. Learning that neither Morgan nor Carnegie had thought about putting their agreement on paper, a nervous Judge Gary managed to get lawyers for both sides together to hammer out an agreement.

More troubling was a standoff between Morgan and Gates. Gates wanted more for his American Steel and Wire Company than Morgan was willing to pay. After prolonged and frustrating negotiations, Morgan stomped out of the room and told Gary to take over. Despite a conciliatory attitude, Gary was getting nowhere while an impatient Morgan kept sending him messages that he wanted to get it over with and go home. Finally, Gary went out to Morgan and suggested that he return and give Gates an ultimatum. As recounted by Gary:

> Morgan reappeared big and fierce, his eyes like coals of fire.

"Gentlemen," he said, pounding the desk, "I am going to leave this building in ten minutes. If by that time you have not accepted our offer, the matter will be closed. We will build our own wire plant." And he turned and left the room.

John W. Gates scratched the top of his head and said, "I don't know whether the old man means that or not."

"You can depend upon it, he does," I said.

"Then," said Gates, "I guess we will have to give up."

I sent for Mr. Morgan. "The gentlemen have accepted your proposition," I told him when he came in.

"Is that right?" Mr. Morgan snapped.

"Yes," they all said.

Never have I seen Mr. Morgan more elated. "Now," he said, "let's go home." We went up on the Elevated to Fiftieth Street, where his old electric car met him. He was like a boy coming home from a football game.

There was yet another hitch when Judge Gary added the Rockefeller Mesabi ore lands to the list of properties that they ought to acquire. This time Morgan's personal power turned out to be useless, even counterproductive. Although he disliked Rockefeller, Morgan went hat in hand to call on the older man at his home at 4 West Fifty-fourth Street. Rockefeller told him politely that he was no longer active in the business and that any arrangement would have to be made with his twenty-seven-year-old son, John D., Jr. Probably because of the age protocol observed by business royalty, young Rockefeller went to see Morgan in his Wall Street office. With him was Standard Oil's top hit man, H. H.—known on Wall Street as "Hell Hound" for his fierce practices in private speculation—Rogers. Busy talking to an aide when they arrived, Morgan let his visitors stand unnoticed until he finished. When Rogers introduced Rockefeller, Morgan growled, "What's your price?"

Unruffled by the Morgan manner, John D., Jr., said, "Mr. Morgan, I think there must be some mistake. I did not come here to sell. I understood you wished to buy."

After a start like that and with a bold bargainer like Rogers in attendance, there was no chance for an agreement. The very top offer that Judge Gary had advised Morgan to make was simply shrugged off. To have a squirt like that walk out on him must have rankled Morgan, but he wasn't a man to let pride get in the way of profit. He decided that the best next move would be to find an acceptable ambassador, a plenipotentiary, to work out a treaty between two powerful forces. The man whose name came to mind for this office was Henry Clay Frick. Whatever had passed between Carnegie and Frick, Frick's reputation as the master manager who was responsible for much of the Carnegie Company's astounding profitability remained intact. Besides, Frick would be a major stockholder in United States Steel, and gaining some access to his expertise had been one of the factors in Morgan's thinking about the whole deal. Quite apart from these considerations, it was known throughout the business world that old John Rockefeller admired Frick for his stand at Homestead.

As he had so frequently in the past, Frick approached this assignment boldly and in person. He took a carriage out to the Rockefeller estate at Pocantico Hills, told the coachman to wait at the gate, walked in and found Rockefeller out inspecting the grounds. Between two men of such directness, the fact that Rockefeller was supposed to be retired didn't come up. Instead, the old man asked, "I would like to know of you, Mr. Frick, if you do not consider the price that I have heard named for my ore properties as below their value."

"I do consider that price below their value," Frick agreed.

"Then, I will trust you to represent me," Rockefeller said. "I do not wish to stand in the way of any improvements or progress, but I will turn my properties over to you. Represent me and you can dispose of them as you wish."

With only slight resistance to make sure that Rockefeller meant what he said, Frick accepted the commission. The whole conversation took about fifteen minutes. Frick returned to his carriage, went back to the city and down to Wall Street, where he told Morgan that he could have the Rockefeller properties, ore, ships, railways—the works—for about $5 million more than Gary had proposed. When confronted with this deal, Gary objected, and Morgan asked him: "Well, put it this way: Would you let those properties go?"

"No," Gary said.

"Well, write out an acceptance," Morgan ordered.

It was the last important acquisition. With it, capitalization had run slightly over a billion dollars—the first billion-dollar corporation in history. It was a worldwide wonder. Writers struggled to describe the magnitude of a billion dollars. Awed by it all, Bridge, the Carnegie insider, wrote:

> If the authorized capital of the United States Steel Corporation ($1,404,000,000) could be turned into solid gold it would weigh 2,330 tons, or over 5,200,000 pounds!
>
> This gold would have a cubic content of 3,880 feet!
>
> With it you could build a pillar six feet square and towering 108 feet in the air; or a Cleopatra's needle of virgin gold six feet square at its base and tapering to a point at a height of over 430 feet!
>
> A train of fifty-eight railroad cars would be required for transporting the precious metal, with two big engines, one before and one behind, to move the train!
>
> For storage room the gold would require a vault eight feet high, twenty feet wide and 24½ feet long—and there wouldn't be an inch of spare room!
>
> Placed at one end of a scale the gold would need 30,000 men of average weight to balance it!
>
> If the corporation's capital were coined into Five Dollar gold pieces they would pave a road 17 feet wide for more than 15½ miles!
>
> Stacked one on the other these coins would reach a height of over twenty miles!

The companies comprising the new U.S. Steel Corp. were only worth that kind of money in the imagination of a man like Morgan, who was always bullish on the potential of the American economy. The corporation's tangible assets were only worth $682 million to support $303 million in mortgage bonds, $510 million in preferred stock, and $508 million in common stock. This amounted to "water" in copious quantities. The savings for the consumer and/or better wages and conditions for workmen that were supposed to have come from the increased efficiency of a large organization would have to go into servicing debt. Although, according to Schwab, the Carnegie works could turn out steel rails at a cost of $12 a ton and sell them for $23.75, the price rose to $28 a ton after the formation of U.S. Steel. None of this would have mattered much to Morgan, whose off-the-top reward for arranging the deal included a syndicate fee of $12.5 million and subscription profits of $50 million. What with fees paid out to other bankers and promoters involved, the total cost of creating the Trust was $150 million.

Andrew Carnegie, who could easily hear the water sloshing around in this new industrial beast, enjoyed crowing over his feat of creating the Carnegie Company the year before without paying a cent in promoters' fees and his wisdom in insisting on taking his payment in bonds. When the water spilled out, he would be left with the meat. "Pierpont is not an iron-master," he told a visitor to Skibo shortly after the sale was consummated. "He knows nothing about the business of making and selling steel. I managed my trade with him so that I was paid for my properties in bonds, not stocks! He will make a fizzle of the business and default in payment of the interest. I will then foreclose and get my properties back, and Pierpont and his friends will lose all their paper profits. Pierpont feels that he can do anything because he has always got the best of the Jews in Wall Street. It takes a Yankee to beat a Jew, and it takes a Scot to beat a Yankee!"

Doubtless Morgan would have chuckled when that remark got back to him. As a broad-scale financier, he never pretended expertise in any given business. But he did pride himself on an ability to recruit the right people. This was evident in the names of U.S. Steel's first board of directors. The Rockefellers, who became the owners of the largest block of stock through the $80 million Mesabi purchase, were therefore given strong representation in the persons of John D. Rockefeller, John D. Rockefeller, Jr., and Henry H. Rogers. Directors knowledgeable about the metal business included Charles M. Schwab, William H. Moore, Elbert H. Gary, Abram S. Hewitt, and Henry Clay Frick. As a stockholder, Frick came close to the Rockefellers with his $61 million, and for that reason alone would seem to deserve a place on the board. But Charlie Schwab, already chosen as president, objected when Morgan brought up Frick's name. "If he's on the board, count me out," he said. Not about to lose touch with Frick, who had brought the Rockefellers aboard, Morgan came up with a Frick-like bit of diplomacy. "It's necessary to have his name for the public eye. Will it be all right if Frick doesn't attend the meetings?" he asked Schwab. The fact that Frick was a quarter owner of the rival Union Steel made a convenient "conflict of interest" excuse for him to stay away from U.S. Steel board meetings.

There was another good reason for Frick to keep a low profile in the new business. He and his cautious partner in bringing all this about, Henry Phipps, were worried about that water in the securities. They began quietly unloading their shares on a public that expressed its trust in the financial wizardry of names like Morgan, Rockefeller, and Frick himself by gobbling up U.S. Steel stock as fast as it came on the market. Speculation was wild. Half a million shares changed hands in the first two days, a million in the first week. Prices soared—common stock from 38 to 55; preferred from 82¾ to 101⅞.

A desire to own part of the first billion-dollar corporation was the most significant public reaction. But there were expressions of alarm at the power it placed in a few private hands. Typical was the *London Chronicle's* claim that "it is little less than a menace to the commerce of the civilized world; it sets the seal to the triumph of the millionaire." Writing in the magazine *Cosmopolitan,* John Brisben Walker said that "those who control the concentrated portion of the money supply" had become the world's real rulers instead of the "so-called statesmen." This same thought received wider circulation when Dunne's "Mr. Dooley" gave it voice:

> Pierpont Morgan calls in wan iv his office boys, th'prisidint iv a national bank, an' says he, "James," he says, "take some change out iv th'damper an' r-run out an' buy Europe fr me," he says. "I intind to re-organize it an' put it on a paying basis," he says. "Call up the Czar an' th' Pope an' th' Sultan an' th' Impror Willum, an' tell thim we won't need their savices afther nex' week," he says. "Give thim a year's salary in advance. An', James," he says, "ye betther put that r-red headed boookkeeper near th' dure in charge of th'continent. He dosen't seem to be doin' much," he says.

Morgan became, if not a hero, even more of a celebrity than he had ever been before. Newsmen hounded him, and crowds stared as he passed through the streets. He had to use the second-class gangway to dodge the press when he boarded the *Teutonic* on April 4, 1901, just a month after the formation of U.S. Steel was announced. Although he wasn't setting sail to buy Europe, as Mr. Dooley suggested, one of his first acts when he was settled into his London home at Prince's Gate was to buy a bit of European culture—Gainsborough's portrait of the Duchess of Devonshire. Whether it was on that crossing to England or another of the many they took at approximately the same time every year, Morgan and Carnegie met on deck and engaged in the kind of truth-telling session that is only possible in the relaxation and detachment provided by a slow voyage on the high seas.

"I made one mistake, Pierpont, when I sold out to you," Carnegie said. "I should have asked you $100,000,000 more than I did."

"If you had, I should have paid it to you—if only to be rid of you," Morgan said.

Although some authors have labeled it legend, this conversation between two tough men has been reported by too many sources and is too characteristic to be doubted. Adept as they were at the money game, both men knew that Morgan had made a bargain. The question was whether it would stick—a question that, in large part and in the long run, would be answered by Henry Clay Frick.

CHAPTER 15

"No Rest f'r th' Rich an' Weary"

MOST of the thirty-odd Carnegie men who became instant multi-millionaires in that spring of 1901 when their shares were exchanged for U.S. Steel stock, which kept climbing on the market, knew nothing of being rich. Almost without exception they had started out in the lower reaches of the company as laborers or clerks, and Carnegie's system of compensation had kept them hard at work and living in modest circumstances. The ingestion of a large amount of wealth acted on their heads like champagne in the stomach of a teetotaler. Casson, an eyewitness to the scene, reported that their spending sprees turned Pittsburgh into a "Klondike for artists, book agents, curio dealers, and merchants who had expensive gewgaws for sale. A young [Carnegie] partner would say: 'See that painting? Cost me $22,000; but I could get $28,000 for it. Have a cigar. Fine brand. Seventy-five cents apiece wholesale.'" One instant millionaire celebrated by rising between acts of a theatrical performance and draping an expensive pearl necklace on his wife; another by importing Cuban cigars with his name and a coat of arms on each wrapper. In addition to these frivolities, they created a lively market for Tudor style mansions and "grand tours" of Europe. In her novels of the stylish old rich of Newport and New York, Edith Wharton used the "Pittsburgh millionaire" as a stock figure in possession of more money than good taste.

These people suddenly overwhelmed by wealth didn't invent their lives. They probably got their ideas of how the rich behave from the popular press. The outrageous extravagance of the very rich was a staple of the print media at the turn of the century, much as it would be again in the 1980s on television with shows like "Lifestyles of the

Rich and Famous." At one stag dinner costing an estimated $50,000 on the upper floor of a fashionable New York restaurant, guests were served on horseback. Each mount came equipped with a miniature table and rubber pads on its hoofs to protect the floor. Another dinner with animal overtones was given by the host in honor of his black-and-tan mongrel dog. While men and women in tails and shimmering ball gowns stood around to applaud, the host decorated the dog with a $15,000 diamond collar. In the matter of diamonds, a man who sparkled with as many on his person as he dared in the way of stick pins, rings, and the like had his dentist bore holes in his teeth and install twin rows of diamonds. In the early days of motoring, a Southern millionaire unknowingly invented today's popular RV. After looking over his $12,000 imported car and finding it wanting, he called in decorators and engineers and ended up with a $30,000 vehicle that contained a living compartment, a sleeping room, a kitchen, and a small bathtub.

It would be foolish to believe that any of these spenders read Veblen, the caustic and critical observer of the rich, but it is certain that they were his inspiration. In *The Theory of the Leisure Class,* Veblen cites animals—dogs and fast horses in particular—as prime examples of what he called "conspicuous consumption." Owning and bestowing unusual expense and attention on animals that are economically useless, as in the case of the bejeweled black-and-tan, is a sure and visible sign of wealth; the breeding of dogs and riding horses were two favorite pursuits of J. P. Morgan. Dress, too, is a form of conspicuous consumption, according to Veblen. For those who wish to prove their material worth, clothes should be of a cost and quality in evident excess of their function in covering the body and providing warmth. But they should have another attribute, as Veblen wrote:

> If, in addition to showing that the wearer can afford to consume freely and uneconomically, it can also be shown in the same stroke that he or she is not under the necessity of earning a livelihood, the evidence of social worth is enhanced in a very considerable degree. . . . Much of the charm that invests the patent-leather shoe, the stainless linen, the lustrous cylindrical hat, and the walking-stick, which so greatly enhance the native dignity of a gentleman, comes of their pointedly suggesting that the wearer cannot when so attired bear

a hand in any employment that is directly and immediately of any human use.... It needs no argument to enforce the generalisation that the more elegant styles of feminine bonnets go even farther towards making work impossible than does the man's high hat. The woman's shoe adds the so-called French heel to the evidence of enforced leisure afforded by its polish; because this high heel obviously makes any, even the simplest and most necessary manual work extremely difficult.

Throughout the Gilded and Golden ages in which Henry Clay Frick had his being, the kind of dress that provided strong support for Veblen's theories prevailed. From the age of eight, Frick himself was seen by others as a model of sartorial splendor. It will be remembered that one of the prizes that he and Andrew Mellon brought back from their first trip abroad was the fashionable beaver hat that proved offensive to puritanical Pittsburghers. Nowhere was dress flaunted so conspicuously as in Newport, Rhode Island, the fashion-setting summering spot of the very rich. Every pleasant afternoon Newporters would take a drive along mansion-lined Bellevue Avenue and scenic Ocean Drive in their various equipages (also, along with the horses drawing them, evidence of conspicuous consumption) to show off their finery. Edith Wharton, who spent childhood summers there at a home called Pencraig, left this memorable description of the rite:

> For this drive it was customary to dress as elegantly as for a race-meeting at Auteuil or Ascot. A brocaded or satin-striped dress, powerfully whale-boned, a small flower-trimmed bonnet tied with a large tulle bow under the chin, a dotted tulle veil and a fringed silk or velvet sunshade, sometimes with a jointed handle of elaborately carved ivory, composed what was thought a suitable toilet for this daily circuit between wilderness and waves.
>
> The dress of the young ladies perched on the precarious height of a dog-cart or phaeton was no less elegant than that of the dowagers; and I remember, one hot summer afternoon seeing one of the damsels who were staying at Pencraig appear for the drive arrayed in a heavy white silk dress with a broad black satin stripe, and a huge hat wreathed with crim-

son roses and draped with a green veil against the sun. It is only fair to add that my brother, who helped her to the giddy summit of the T-cart, and climbed to her side while a tiny groom in snowy breeches clung to the bridle of the impatient chestnut—my brother, like all the young gentlemen of his day, was arrayed in frock-coat, a tall hat and pearl-gray trousers.

Ward McAllister, a social gadfly who is credited with creating "the four hundred" to descibe all the people who mattered in New York, told a story illustrative of the attention to dress among men as well as women. Riding the ferry across the Hudson from his summer place in New Jersey, McAllister met a friend who invited him to dinner at the Union Club that night in honor of two visiting British gentry. McAllister declined. "I have no dress suit in the city," he explained. "My dear man, it will be an event in your life to meet these distinguished men. Jump in the first train, return to your country home, and get your dress coat." McAllister did just that at the cost of several boring hours, because it would have been unthinkable to wear street clothes for such an occasion.

Perhaps the food itself, if not the company, in the highest social and business circles of those days demanded the tribute of formal dress. Meals served at the balls where wives and daughters were paraded and the stag dinners where so much business was conducted constituted a form of actual consumption to be conspicuous. In today's cholesterol-conscious climate the wonder is not that so many of yesterday's rich died at a relatively young age but that so many of them lived as long as they did. Consider, for example, the menu of dinner at the University Club in New York at about the same time and in the same place as the one at which Schwab charmed Morgan:

Amontillado Sherry	*Moet & Chandon, 1893*
Cotuit oysters	Terrapin, Maryland Club
Bisque of crabs à la Norfolk	Grapefruit au Kirsch
Consommé de volaille Sévigné	*Clos-Vougeot, 1893*
Hors-d'oeuvres varies	Canvasback ducks
Rhine Wine, 1893	Fried hominy
Soft clams à l'ancienne	Celery à l'université

Chateau-Latour, 1878	Parfait noisettes
Saddle and rack of spring lamb	Cheese
Mint sauce	Fruit
Peas à la Francaise	Coffee
Bermuda potatoes rissolées	*Cognac, 1805*

In the late nineties and early twentieth century by far the most conspicuous form of consumption was the vast city palaces and country villas that the rich constructed and stuffed with paintings, pieces of sculpture, oriental rugs, and all sorts of collectibles acquired in their extensive travels. Particularly fabulous were the estates like Rockefeller's Pocantico in New York, William Randolph Hearst's San Simeon in California, and George Vanderbilt's Biltmore in North Carolina, which prompted some wit to say, "They show you what God could do if he had money." The miraculously enriched Carnegie partners were not immune to infection by the building bug. Frick was one who caught the fever, and he would eventually prove to be as masterful in this pursuit as he had been in running the steel company. But it was Charlie Schwab who first stole the show. Almost as soon as the deal was closed making him president of U.S. Steel, Schwab began building a magnificent residence to cover a whole city block at Seventy-second Street and Riverside Drive in New York. Copied from Chenonceaux, a chateau on the Loire in France, it was four stories high with a 116-foot lookout tower, contained ninety bedrooms, a 60-foot swimming pool and 50-foot gymnasium, a wine cellar, and its own power plant. Andrew Carnegie was moved to say that it made his own new house on Ninety-first Street look like a cottage, and *Harper's Weekly* to opine that it "may strike the average observer as a burdensome possession, oppressive to maintain, and likely to be embarrassing to heirs, but if Mr. Schwab can stand it, we can."

It's to be wondered whether the *Harper's* editor knew a wealthy man of a generation earlier named Frederick Barreda, as did Charles R. Flint, a financier and author of a memoir full of insights about the Gilded Age. Barreda, according to Flint, owned a residence on Madison Avenue in New York, a summer place in Newport, an estate in Maryland, and a place in Paris, and he lived "more extravagantly than any man in this country." On one occasion, Flint was Barreda's guest, and he later wrote:

In my youthful inexperience I said; "Mr. Barreda, you have magnificent facilities for enjoyment."

"Magnificent discomfort!!" he replied. "I have worked up the most elaborate system for irritation and trouble that could be devised. In business you excite the earnest industry and loyalty of young men by picturing attractive prospects. I can inspire but little interest and loyalty in a large retinue of servants—my property is neglected, many of my belongings have been stolen, more are misused, and most of the entertaining is done by servants in my absence and at my expense."

Admired as they might be by people getting along on subsistence incomes, the lifestyles of the very rich were often found wanting by contemporaries close to them who did not have the "predatory animus." A sampling of their voices:

Author Henry Adams:

Newspapers might prate about wealth till commonplace print was exhausted, but as a matter of habit, few Americans envied the very rich for anything the most of them got out of money. New York might occasionally fear them, but more often laughed or sneered at them, and never showed them respect. Scarcely one of the very rich men held any position in society by virtue of his wealth, or could have been elected to office, or even into a good club. Setting aside a few, like Pierpont Morgan whose social position had little to do with greater or less wealth, riches were in New York no object of envy on account of the joys they brought in their train.

Boston-born novelist Henry James, who lived as an expatriate in England, after revisiting America:

The preliminary American postulate or basis for any successful accommodation of life . . . is that of active pecuniary gain and of active pecuniary gain only—that of one's making the conditions so triumphantly pay that the prices, the manners, the other inconveniences, take their place as a friction that it is comparatively easy to salve, wounds directly treatable with the wash of gold. What prevails, what sets the tune, is the American scale of gain, more magnificent than any other, and the fact that the whole assumption, the whole theory of life, is that of the individual's participation in it, that of his being more or less punctually and more or less effectually "squared." To make so much money that you don't "mind," don't mind anything—that is absolutely, I think, the American forumla. Thus your making no money—or so little that it passes there for none—and being thereby distinctly reduced to minding, amounts to your being reduced to the knowledge that America is no place for you.

Clarence W. Barron, leading business journalist of the day:

Spent the afternoon with Mr. and Mrs. John Shepard, Jr. Dr. Billings of Chicago called while I was there. He told Shepard some years ago that he had never seen a very rich man who died happy. He named five big men, including George M. Pullman, whom he had attended on their death beds, and they had all been unhappy, notwithstanding their millions. There was always family trouble, or woman trouble, or some other trouble.

Charles Francis Adams, businessman and railroad executive:

As I approach the end, I am more than a little puzzled to account for the instances I have seen of business success— money getting. It comes from a rather low instinct. Certainly, so far as my observation goes, it is rarely met with in combination with the finer or more interesting traits of character. I have known, and known tolerably well, a good many "successful" men—"big" financially—men famous during the last half century; and a less interesting crowd I do not care to encounter. Not one that I have ever known would I care to meet again, either in this world or the next; nor is one of them associated in my mind with the idea of humor, thought or refinement.

It's possible—but not very likely—that these comments were inspired by envy. They come from men of good background, high intelligence, modest fame, and adequate means. Charles Francis Adams did acknowledge that moneymaking required a special talent and temperament—that "pecuniary animus" again?—and a high level of concentration, which might well preclude involvement in noncommercial aspects of life. However accurate their observations might be, the attention paid by these prominent people to the pleasures and problems of getting rich is indicative of its dominance as a theme in American life. Where these observers opened themselves to error may have been in judging the rich by their own motivations and values. Except perhaps in some writings by Carnegie, the rich did not talk about happiness, knowledge, justice, kindness, refinement, democracy, and the like as the end and reward of their efforts. What they wanted and worked for was money and the one intangible thing that money could, and did, buy—power.

An interesting aspect of the very rich of that time was that they were so much like one another. A characteristic that the richest of them—John D. Rockefeller, John Pierpont Morgan, Andrew Mellon, James Stillman, Henry Clay Frick—shared was silence. Whenever possible, they said nothing and whenever necessary they said very little. Although what they did say was often obvious and trite, the words gained unusual weight by the fact that they said them at all. Amusing anecdotes about silence have been passed down about all of them, but Stillman, president of National City Bank, produced the best. Telling a colleague about his vacation in Egypt, a New York broker said, "At the foot of the Sphinx I met James Stillman." The other broker said, "I'll bet the Sphinx spoke first." Known as the Rockefeller banker, Stillman might have had little in common with Morgan, whose distaste for Rockefellers and their minions was common knowledge, but on one trans-Atlantic voyage the two of them disappeared into Morgan's cabin for hours at a time. This provoked wild rumors of some unlikely financial deal until Stillman told a friend, "Oh, we play patience—and we don't exchange ten words." Stillman himself admitted that one of his bonds with William Rockefeller, John D.'s brother, was that they could sit together for fifteen minutes before either of them broke the silence. Thus it is that Stillman's pronouncement on his own motivation and that of his fellow moneymakers carries conviction: " 'Twasn't the money we were after; 'twas the power. We were all playing for power. It was a great game."

There were likenesses other than silence among the new rich. In pursuit of money for power, they were all ruthless, which is one reason why they admired Henry Clay Frick to a man. Frick's stand at Homestead had impressed Morgan, Stillman, William Rockefeller, and H. H. Rogers as well as old John D., and he was welcomed with open arms into the inner circle of American financial power. Perhaps nobody was more representative of this circle than Rogers.

A large, powerfully built, handsome man of sixty at the turn of the century, Rogers almost literally had a finger in every tasty financial pie. As a representative of Standard Oil and/or his own personal investments, he sat on innumerable boards of directors, including the newly formed United States Steel Corporation, was possessed of a sizable fortune, and commanded almost unlimited borrowing power. In the conduct of business, Rogers was said to have an eye and presence as fierce and formidable as Morgan's. He acquired them through long practice since, like all of his peers but Morgan, he eschewed higher education to go to work in his early teens. The son of a Massachusetts sea captain, Rogers pulled off a business deal in his home town of Fairhaven at the age of fourteen that was typical of his whole career. Then a newsboy, he read in the papers he picked up one morning that a ship carrying five hundred barrels of sperm oil consigned to a local dealer had sunk. Instead of peddling the papers, Rogers rushed to the dealer and offered to sell him the lot in order to suppress the news long enough for the dealer to corner the local whale oil supply. Although both of them knew that the papers had cost Rogers only fifty cents, the dealer readily agreed to the boy's asking price of two hundred dollars. It's prophetic that the profitable deal involved oil. Rogers later joined a fellow Bay Stater, Charles Pratt, in establishing a refinery in Brooklyn that they sold to Rockefeller, becoming themselves part of the Standard Oil establishment in the process.

With his sharp eye for a good deal and belief that anything goes in the way of business, Rogers, a profane and humorous man in contrast to his pious boss, became a Rockefeller hatchet man. Again like virtually all of his peers, including Frick, Rogers developed a dual personality. Out of the office and in social situations, he was a good family man, loyal friend, and kindly charmer. His severest critic was a renegade capitalist from Boston named Thomas W. Lawson. A diamond-in-the-rough type as unprincipled as the rest of them, Lawson rose from rags to riches by playing the market. Although excluded from the charmed circle of Rogers and his cronies, Lawson was chosen by them to market the securities of a $200 million supertrust called Amalgamated Copper Company designed to "organize" copper as the Standard had organized oil. It was a fiasco, and in a series of magazine articles and a book that went unchallenged Lawson charged Rogers and banker Stillman specifically, and "the System" they represented, with illegal procedures and mismanagement that resulted in the loss of $100 million, thirty suicides, and twenty jail sentences. Some $36 million of what he called little people's savings went into the bank accounts of the promoters, according to Lawson. As a result of this experience, Lawson wrote of Rogers:

> Away from the intoxicating spell of dollar-making this remarkable man is one of the most charming and lovable beings I have ever encountered, a man whom any man or woman would be proud to have for a brother; a man whom any mother or father would give thanks for as a son; a man whom any woman would be happy to know as her husband, and a man whom any boy or girl would rejoice to call father. Once he passes under the baleful influence of "the Machine," however, he becomes a relentless, ravenous creature, pitiless as a shark, knowing no law of God or man in the executions of his purpose. Between him and coveted dollars may come no kindly, humane influences—all are thrust aside, their claims disregarded, in ministering to this strange, cannibalistic money-hunger, which, in truth, grows by what it feeds on.

That soft side of Rogers caused considerable intellectual and emotional difficulty for Mark Twain. By instinct and experience a sympathizer with the underdog and a caustic critic of the morality of acquisitiveness, Twain became a bootlicking apologist for the most egregious excesses of capitalism in his writings about Rogers. In what may have been either a genuine act of friendship or a shrewd public relations maneuver on behalf of a beloved celebrity, Rogers took over when Mark Twain's publishing company went into bankruptcy in the early 1890s. The author felt that he was morally, but not legally, responsible for his debts. Rogers agreed. He admitted that standard business practice then—as now—would be to let the creditors carve up whatever was left in the physical property of the company and walk away. An embarrassed Mrs. Clemens, Mark Twain's wife, wanted to add their home she owned in Hartford, Connecticut, to these assets, and Mark Twain was willing to include his copyrights. Rogers disagreed. Because Twain was an artist and not a business-

man, Rogers argued, his most valuable asset was his personal reputation, and he could salvage that only by going on a worldwide
lecture tour to pay off his debts in full. Meanwhile, it would be silly
to give up the home that was needed as a base for moneymaking
operations and the copyrights that were a guarantee of future income.
Rogers summoned a meeting of Mark Twain's creditors, fixed them
with that fierce eye (and enormous financial power) of his and persuaded them to go along with his plan—full restitution from future
earnings if they would let the Clemens house alone and consider
assignment of copyrights to Mrs. Clemens as proper repayment for
her position as number-one creditor on account of a loan of $63,000
to her husband's publishing company. Everything worked out as
Rogers predicted and, thereafter, Roger's office in the Standard Oil
Building became Mark Twain's *pied-à-terre* when he was in New
York.

It's not hard to understand why Henry H. Rogers was one of the
few heroes in Mark Twain's blunt and despairingly cynical autobiography. Rogers charged the author no fees for his services and was
always a delightful companion to Samuel Clemens, the man. But it
raises difficult questions about the intellectual integrity of Mark
Twain, the author, to read a passage like the following:

> I was never able to teach him [Rogers] anything about fi-
> nance, though I tried hard and did the best I could. I was
> not able to move him. Once I had hopes for a little while.
> The Standard Oil declared one of its customary fury-breeding
> 40 or 50 percent dividends on its $100,000,000 capital, and the
> storm broke out as usual. To the unposted public a 40 or 50
> percent dividend could mean only one thing—the giant Trust
> was squeezing an utterly and wickedly unfair profit out of
> the helpless people; whereas in truth the giant Trust was not
> doing anything of the kind, but was getting only 5 or 6 per-
> cent on the money invested in its business, which was eight
> or ten times a hundred millions. In my quality of uneducated
> financial expert I urged that the nominal capital be raised to
> $1,000,000,000; then next year's dividend would drop to 4 or
> 5 percent, the year's profit would be the same as usual, but
> the usual storm would not happen. If I remember rightly, I
> think he offered the objection that the ten-fold increase in
> taxes would be too heavy, and I rejoined that by the ill-veiled

exultation in his eye I knew he regarded my suggestion as of vast value and was trying to invent some plausible way of getting out of paying a commission on it.

Rogers was right to worry more about what taxes on a realistic capitalization would do to profits than public opinion. For most Americans, the ability to make money by any means was considered a sign of virtue. Even single taxer Henry George, who was looked upon as a socialist, was resigned to this fact. Concentration of great amounts of wealth in a few hands was given intellectual sanction by combining the economic theories of Malthus with the scientific theories of Darwin, according to George. But, theory aside, George claimed that "the sting of want and the fear of want make men admire above all things the possession of riches, and to become wealthy is to become respected, and admired, and influential. Get money—honestly, if you can, but at any rate get money! This is the lesson that society is daily and hourly dinning in the ears of its members." As for the rich themselves, most of them probably said a silent amen when John D. Rockefeller was quoted as saying, "God gave me my money."

Another shared characteristic of the very rich was their public piety. Virtually all of them were WASPs—white Anglo-Saxon Protestants—in good standing. One exception was the financier Jacob Schiff, but he was so pious that he ruined a deal for his best client, railroad tycoon E. H. Harriman, by being in synagogue on a Saturday when he should have been out playing the market. Another exception often cited was Andrew Carnegie, who subscribed to no church, and yet the Sunday routine at his Skibo castle always included evening hymn singing to the accompaniment of the organ. Childhood friends of Henry Clay Frick recalled that he didn't often attend Sunday school; his religious experience was something of a mixed bag between his grandparents' Mennonite church and an uncle's Baptist church. But with unintended foresight, Frick joined the Calvary Episcopal Church in Pittsburgh and entered into the faith of the old aristocracy of the East. Morgan was the leading layman of America's Episcopal Church. Rockefeller was a psalm-singing, tithing Baptist, and Frick's good friends, the Mellons, stuck to Pittsburgh Presbyterianism. Indeed, when their money built what could pass for a Presbyterian cathedral in Pittsburgh's East Liberty section, it was promptly dubbed "Mellon's fire escape."

How the very rich could square their piety with their business practices and, in cases such as Morgan's well-known philandering, with their private lives has been a subject of much speculation down to this day. However they made their peace with it personally, they obviously appreciated and supported religion as a stabilizing force in society and a resource for their wives and children. As a Presbyterian elder in Pittsburgh once said of an absentee rich man in his congregation, "He took out religion in his wife's name." Still it remains a mystery that men of such intelligence could blandly ignore all the biblical injunctions against amassing wealth so neatly summed up in Jesus' metaphor of the camel and the needle's eye. Playing with this paradox in his old age as he wrote his autobiography, Judge Mellon came up with an argument in defense of his peers and heirs that would still stand up in the case of *Wealth* v. *Christianity.* He eased into the subject by describing his reaction to a death threat from a lawyer he defeated in a trial:

> I prepared myself to meet it, and certainly would have killed him had he attacked me and it became necessary. I am aware of no duty, either legal, moral or religious, which requires one man to submit to personal violence at the hands of another. The fault lies in giving provocation; but no matter what the provocation, a man is not bound to submit unresistingly. Every man's person is sacred to him; and the right of self defense is consequently sacred also. Although the assault may not be likely to kill, yet the assailed party is not bound to take that risk: he is not bound to suffer the infliction of personal indignity and injury of any kind. Every one's manhood resents that; and every man has the right to resort to the most efficient means within his power to defeat the purpose of the assailant. If the physical power of the assailant is the greater, the assailed is under no moral or legal obligation to interpose his lesser physical power against him, but may resort to the most convenient weapon of defense within his reach. The law of self defense in all countries rests on this priniciple. Our moral duty to ourselves and society justifies it. The spirit of violence is not to be fostered and encouraged by abject submission to it. Nor does religion require such submission: passages of the Scripture to the contrary are either interpolations or erroneously interpreted. The nature which

God has implanted in us contradicts them; and the uniform practice of the Christian world for over eighteen hundred years contradicts them. I have given this supposed Christian doctrine very considerable attention, and made what research was possible regarding it in history contemporary with the origin of Christianity; and I find it, as also the doctrine of community of goods, was derived from a sect of Jewish ascetics then rather extensive, called "Essenes," and by some "Essenians," to which the family of Jesus belonged. And I have discovered also that historians of those times, and until a much later date, were in the habit of putting sentiments and words and speeches in the mouths of their chief characters which they supposed they would or ought to have used under the circumstances. How this may have been in regard to the doctrines referred to is uncertain. The church has from time to time eliminated many things in the Old Testament and some in the New as apocrypha; and it may be that some things still remain to be expurgated. Sentiments repugnant to the best regulated minds, contrary to common sense and the nature which God has implanted in his creatures, as well as contrary to the interests of society, may fairly be regarded as apocrypha, and part of the old leaven of the Essenians which has crept into some of the manuscript copies of the Scriptures of the early church.

The proposition that we should encourage wickedness and violence by extending safety and immunity to its perpetrators: as by exposing one side of the face to blows because we have been beaten on the other; or encouraging idleness and indolence by dividing all we have among the poor and consequently adding ourselves to their number; or giving away our clothing even to the coat off our back to any tramp who may ask for it, is too great an absurdity in the line of religious teaching to be imputed to Christ. Besides it is in conflict with the reasonableness of his instructions elsewhere; as for instance the declaration that he who provides not for those of his own household is worse than an infidel. If a man should follow the practice of giving all he hath to the poor, and even the coat off his back to the first who asks for it, it is not possible he could make provision for those of his own household. No, these extremes of non-resistance and charity cannot be sound doctrines; but if apocrypha, that circumstance does not impugn the authority of the Scriptures in other respects. Good temper and gentle and peaceable habits are Christian, and liberal charity according to our means to the deserving poor as taught in our Christian churches is a Christian virtue. But that is very different from the degrading communistic principle of having all goods in common and of non-resistance to every insult and indignity that is offered us. Neither Christian charity nor Christian forbearance can be carried to extremes any more than human laws, in regard to which one of the oldest and best founded maxims is, that "needle points of law are not law."

This legalistic rationalization by Judge Mellon deserves being cited fully and considered carefully in the context of this book. The judge was Henry Clay Frick's mentor in the business world and father of Frick's best friend. Whether he preached his kind of thinking to the young men or not, he certainly practiced it, and they could have learned by observation to shuffle off into apocrypha any inconvenient moral injunctions in their religion. In this regard, Scott Fitzgerald's famous assertion that the rich are different from the rest of us is probably not true; few adherents to any religion take its precepts with them into the marketplace. The difference lies in the power and influence exerted by the rich on the political processes and social structure around them. In making it appear that God was on their side, that the making of money any which way was sanctified by religious observance, they exonerated greed. By themselves leading ostensibly righteous lives, they created the impression that their participation in illegalities, fraud, deception, and all the other rough stuff of moneymaking would be incredible. As he so often did, Mr. Dooley covered the whole subject of the business ethics of his day in a sentence when he said of Rockefeller: "He never did wrong save in th'way of business."

Although they may have rationalized their sins and done their best to deceive the public, most of the rich—Frick among them—did not deceive themselves. Financier Flint recalled a delightful incidence of their mutual frankness when he took a group of notables for a cruise on Long Island Sound in his steam yacht *Arrow*. Reading the log, one of the guests, Chauncey M. Depew, attorney for the Vanderbilts and U.S. senator from New York, came upon an entry by publicist Frank A. Munsey: "To a New England Boy. The New England boy is born with two great overshadowing purposes in life—purposes that are his whole life from the cradle to the grave: getting on in the world and getting into Heaven." For his own entry, Depew wrote under Munsey's: "But the methods of one close the door to the other." In the annals of true but bitter humor this ranks with Frick's "see him in hell" message to Carnegie. Through the hindsight of nearly a century, humor comes into focus as the best and sharpest depiction of the daily drama of the times and its actors.

So it's Mr. Dooley who rightfully laid claim to the last word on the life into which the Pittsburgh millionaires were thrust by the creation of the U.S. Steel Corp. Dooley was discussing the fate of their mutual acquaintance Alonzo Higgins with his friend Hinnissy:

> Now that Higgins has got th' money, he's took th' brewery man's job with worse horses an' him barred fr'm dhrivin' with more thin wan hand. An' does he get anything fr it? On th' conthry, Hinnissy, it sets him back a large forchune. An' he says he's havin' a good time an' if th' brewery man come along an' felt sorry fr him, Higgins wudden't exactly know why.
>
> Higgins has to sail a yacht raymimberin' how he despised th'Swede sailors that used to loaf in th'saloon near his house durin' th'winter; he has to run an autymobill, which is th'same thing as dhrivin' a throlley car on a windy day without pay; he has to play golf which is th' same thing as bein' a letther-carryer without a dacint uniform; he has to play tennis, which is another wurrud fr batin' a carpet; he has to race horses, which is the same thing as bein' a bookmaker with th'chances again' ye; he has to go abroad, which is the same thing as bein' an immigrant; he has to set up late, which is th'same thing as bein' a dhrug clerk; an' he has to play cards with a man that knows how, which is th' same thing as bein' a sucker.
>
> He takes his good times hard, Hinnissy. A rich man at spoort is a kind iv non-union laborer. He don't get wages fr it an' he don't dhrive as well as a milkman, ride as well as a stable-boy, shoot as well as a polisman, or autymobill as well as th' man that runs th'steam-roller. It's a tough life. They'se no rest fr th' rich an' weary. We'll be readin' in th' pa-apers

wan iv these days: "Alonzo Higgins, th'runner up in las' year's champeenship, showed gr-reat improvement in this year's brick layin' tournymint at Newport, an' won handily with about tin square feet to spare. He was nobly assisted by Regynald Van Stinyvant, who acted as his hod carrier an' displayed all th'agility which won him so much applause arlier in th' year. . . .

"Raycreations iv rich men: Jawn W. Grates an' J. Pierpont Morgan ar-re to have a five days' shinglin' contest at Narragansett Pier. George Gold is thrainin' f'r th' autumn plumbin' jimkanny. Mitchigan avnoo is tore up fr'm Van Buren sthreet to th'belt line in priparation f'r th' contest in sthreet layin' between mimbers iv th'Assocyation iv More-Thin-Rich Spoorts". . . .

An' why not, Hinnissy? If 'tis fun to wurruk why not do some rale wurruk? If 'tis spoort to run an autymobill, why not run a locymotive? If dhrivin' a horse in a cart is a game, why not dhrive a delivery wagon and carry things around? Sure, I s'pose th' raison a rich man can't undherstand why wages shud go higher is because th' rich can't see why annybody shud be paid f'r anything so amusin' as wurruk. . . .

No, sir, what's a rich man's raycreation is a poor man's wurruk. Th'poor ar-re th'on'y people that know how to injye wealth. Me idee iv settin' things sthraight is to have th'rich who wurruk because they like it, do th' wurruk f'r th'poor who wud rather rest. . . .

CHAPTER 16

The Quintessential Capitalist

IN the early months of the first year of a new century, Americans were riding a high wave of euphoria. It was only fitting that the world's first billion-dollar corporation was organized in a nation that had become both a world power and a world leader. Figures from the 1900 census showed that the country was still growing rapidly— a 21 percent increase in population to 76,212,168 in ten years; an additional three states, to make a total of forty-five. By a victory over Spain, these United States had acquired an empire. Lesser victories in 1900 were almost equal sources of pride. American athletes won the second revival of the Olympic Games at Paris and the first international lawn tennis match for the Davis Cup at Longwood, Massachusetts. Business recessions like the one in 1893 were events of the distant past. The man who presided over this surge of prosperity and power, William McKinley, was installed in the White House for another four years on March 4. As Mark Hanna had crowed four years before, "God's in his heaven and all's right with the world!"

Although history has not accorded him a place in the front row of the pantheon of presidents, McKinley may well have been the most beloved chief executive in his own time. "Kind," "gentle," and "warm" were the adjectives used in describing the man. To be sure, McKinley was pictured by political cartoonists as a child of the Trusts with Mark Hanna lurking in the background as his nurse, but he was never accused of personal dishonesty. That business deserved the support—and occasionally the blind eye—of government was simply an article of faith with him. With things going so well, McKinley saw no use to meddle in the private affairs of businessmen by invoking the Sherman Anti-Trust Act or other regulatory powers. In fact, he ran for reelection on a platform that his manager, Hanna, neatly summarized in a sentence: "All we need to do is stand pat." The fact that his margin of victory over William Jennings Bryan increased by 200,000 votes over his 1896 margin is evidence of his popularity.

McKinley was Middle America personified. The seventh of nine children born to an iron-founder in Niles, Ohio, he managed to make his way through Allegheny College at Meadville, Pennsylvania, and teach for a while in a rural school before enlisting as a private for Civil War service at age seventeen. He rose to the rank of major, read law after he was mustered out, and went into practice in Canton, Ohio, in 1867. In and out of Congress from 1876 to 1890, he was elected governor of Ohio in 1891. One of his political assets was a smile that would melt icebergs and another was a spotless personal life. His loyalty and gallantry toward his wife, who became a chronic invalid after the early deaths of their two daughters, was a romantic legend. He wore religion on his sleeve but with a sincerity few could match. To a gathering of fellow Methodists, he explained how he bore the burdens of war and arrived at the decision to sanction American expansion in these words: "I walked the floor of the White House night after night, and I am not ashamed to tell you, gentlemen, that I went down on my knees and prayed Almighty God for light and guidance."

There was nothing McKinley enjoyed more than getting out among the people and shaking their hands. In September 1901, a great Pan-American Exposition was staged in Buffalo, New York, to celebrate the community of interests in the hemisphere, and the President seized upon it as an opportunity to indulge in his pleasure of pressing the flesh. Although his secretary, George B. Cortelyou, tried to persuade the President not to expose himself to the kind of unscreened crowd that would be found at a fair, McKinley asked, "Why shouldn't I? No one would want to hurt me." So on the afternoon of September 6, he stood between two large potted bay trees in the Temple of Music shaking hands at the rate of forty-five a minute. There were two Secret Service agents facing the President, two more at each end of the receiving line, and four city detectives, nine soldiers, and eighteen guards along the makeshift aisle through which the people were shuffling. It was hot, and many of them were using handkerchiefs to wipe sweat from their faces and hands. Nobody thought anything of a thin, young man with a handkerchief in his right hand approaching the President until they saw smoke coming from under the cloth. For a few seconds all action was frozen until McKinley sagged into the arms of the Exposition's president, and a knot of men, including a black waiter standing right behind him, jumped the gunman.

There was more than one echo of the attempt to assassinate Henry Clay Frick nine years before in this event. While people piled on his assailant, McKinley, now slumped in a chair, said, "Go easy with him, boys," just as a wounded Frick, leaning against his desk, had ordered his people to do with Berkman. It was very quickly learned that the man was a twenty-eight-year-old Polish-American anarchist named Leon Czolgosz. For a few days, there was a nationwide woman hunt for Emma Goldman, the girl behind Berkman, when it was learned that Czolgosz was acquainted with Ms. Goldman, who might have inspired him as well. There were never any grounds for charging her with anything but the most casual contact with Czolgosz, but it is evident that he was emulating Berkman in pursuing the anarchist tradition of the *Attentat*. In this, he was far more successful than his model. President McKinley died on September 14, 1901, after a week of suffering, and his death brought to an end the era when unchallenged big business could dominate American government and society.

The mourning public may not have been aware of the real significance of McKinley's death, but the man who loved him most, Mark Hanna, certainly was. A senator by then, Hanna's comment as Vice President Theodore Roosevelt took the oath of office was: "Now look, that damned cowboy is President of the United States!" At forty-three, Roosevelt was the youngest man ever to enter the White House, and he was as much of a cowboy as anyone born to a rich merchant family in New York City and graduated from Harvard was likely to become. For the sake of his health at first and then for the love of it, Roosevelt had spent a great deal of time in the saddle out West and had recruited the cowboy friends he made there for the Rough Riders he led to glory on San Juan Hill in Cuba. Hanna's adjective "damned" was an expression of his fear that Roosevelt would not stand pat. Always a Republican, Roosevelt was a maverick, a "reformer" as a member of the New York legislature, police commissioner of New York City, and governor of the state, a post he won on the basis of his heroic war record in Cuba. Before going off to war, he was McKinley's assistant secretary of the Navy

Top left: Henry Clay Frick's reign as chairman of the Carnegie companies was peaceful and very prosperous until the killings during the Homestead strike in 1892 brought him national attention and the hatred of Alexander Berkman, an anarchist who tried to assassinate Frick on a Saturday afternoon in July 1892. *The Carnegie Library of Pittsburgh*

Top right: Berkman's assault on Frick took place behind the windows marked with crosses in what was known as the Chronicle-Telegraph Building in Pittsburgh. Passers-by on the street could hear the shots and watch the men struggling in Frick's office. *The Carnegie Library of Pittsburgh*

Above: The harsh treatment given Private Iams of the National Guard forces occupying Homestead, for cheering, "I hate Frick" upon the news that Frick had been shot, turned public sentiment against the imperious Carnegie chairman once again. *The Carnegie Library of Pittsburgh*

When a break came between Frick and Carnegie in 1900, Carnegie's boyhood friend and oldest partner, Henry Phipps, Jr., joined Frick in his suit to receive fair market value for his shares in the Carnegie enterprises. *The Carnegie Library of Pittsburgh*

Initially reluctant, young Charles Schwab became Carnegie's lieutenant in ousting Frick. He filled Frick's position and was the catalyst in organizing the U.S. Steel Corporation in 1901, which made millionaires of all the Carnegie partners. *The Carnegie Library of Pittsburgh*

With some of the millions he made from the sale of U.S. Steel, and before he left Pittsburgh, Frick built a skyscraper to dwarf the Carnegie Building. Newspapers viewed the Frick Building as a very expensive thumb-in-the-eye. *The Carnegie Library of Pittsburgh*

One of Frick's most enduring legacies was his influence on the mind and spirit of his lifelong friend Andrew W. Mellon, who outlived Frick by nearly twenty years. Serving under three Presidents as the most powerful Secretary of Treasury in history, Mellon turned the gospel of greed into public policy until it was discredited in the Great Depression. He made a lasting contribution to art history by creating the National Gallery in Washington, D.C. *The Carnegie Library of Pittsburgh*

and an advocate of fighting a conflict that Hanna deplored. The only reason that Hanna, the Republican Party chairman, had agreed to put him on the national ticket was to placate the New York boss, Thomas C. Platt, who wanted Roosevelt out of the state and buried in an office that was then considered a political graveyard.

For Hanna and a great many of the moneyed men from whom he had "fried the fat" to pay for McKinley's election, God had tumbled out of heaven. Some, however, read eagerly and hopefully the signs that Roosevelt might, in their terms, be maturing. In his short time as vice president, for instance, he had held a dinner for J. P. Morgan. Admittedly, Morgan was one of the aristocratic rich with proper manners, as was Roosevelt himself, but he was also the acknowledged power in a Wall Street that Roosevelt mistrusted. Immediately after McKinley's death, Roosevelt announced that he would carry out his predecessor's policies and keep the McKinley cabinet in office. This meant there would be men of old Republican credentials like John Hay at State, Elihu Root in the War Department, and Philander C. Knox, counselor to Frick and Mellon, as Attorney General. Possibly Roosevelt would be all bark and no bite.

At that point in his life, Frick could hardly have cared less. Like all his partners at the Carnegie companies, he was enjoying his freedom as much as his money. No longer tied down to office routine, he could flit from project to project as the spirit and occasion moved him. In his own rather solemn way, he reflected the pleasure he took in this kind of life by giving a rare press interview to deny rumors that he would become president of U.S. Steel. He told *The New York Times*:

> I am much averse to newspaper interviews that my name has been so persistently used in connection with conditions in the United States Steel Corporation that I rather welcome the opportunity of making this statement. I have retired from active business and nothing would induce me to take any position that would claim my time from my own affairs. I am a director in the United States Steel Corporation besides being a large stock holder and am very much interested in its success and while I am willing to give all the time and attention required of me as a director I could not accept any position that required my daily and exclusive attention.

While it was true that Frick had no desire for regular employment, the rest of the statement was misleading to say the least. For
the first two years of its existence, Frick was ambivalent about U.S.
Steel. He allowed his name to be used as a director but stayed away
from meetings to avoid friction with Schwab. Meanwhile, he was
slowly and quietly unloading his steel stock, selling a little more at
each small rise as it slipped into general decline after the novelty and
excitement of the corporation's founding wore off. There were troubles in U. S. Steel's executive suite that couldn't be concealed because
of the press's intense interest in the doings of the new millionaires.
The one they most dearly loved was flamboyant Charlie Schwab,
who, in addition to building his Riverside Drive castle, took off for
a spot of rest and recreation in the fleshpots of Europe in December
1901. He felt he deserved a little fun after the kind of year he'd had,
and he let himself go in the best *belle époque* style.

For a man of Schwab's temperament being Andrew Carnegie's
boy was something of a trial. Not only did Carnegie's work-now-
get-paid-later policy keep him on a comparatively short financial
string, but Carnegie's disapproval of pleasures like womanizing and
gambling forced him to be sparing and very discreet in indulging
his grosser appetites. Schwab felt it was necessary to hide the fact
that he had a daughter after an affair with his wife's nurse. He
supported his daughter well throughout her life, even took her with
him on trips to Europe, but she always lived under another name.
Schwab's wife was an unsophisticated homebody who overate to ease
her sorrow at being unable to have children, and their marriage
became a comfortable companionship. Undoubtedly, Schwab had
heard of the showgirls who kept Morgan content with a marriage
that remained stable but sexless after the children were born. With
some justification, he felt that being Morgan's boy would not call for
such a restricting code of behavior.

Schwab began his European adventure by acquiring a fast and
flashy automobile in Paris, a newsworthy act in itself at a time when
there were only eight thousand passenger cars in all of the United
States. He drove south to Cannes on the Riviera, where he joined a
high-living group that included Baron Henri de Rothschild and Dr.
Griez Wittgenstein, an Austrian steelmaker. When they all crowded
around one of the roulette tables at the casino in Monte Carlo on
the night of January 12, 1902, Schwab had a run of good luck. Hearing about it secondhand, a reporter for the *New York Sun* who hap-

pened to be in Monte Carlo cabled a story that his paper headlined
SCHWAB BREAKS THE BANK. It was said that he made fifty thousand
francs that night and, in a follow-up story, fifty-four thousand the
next. Other papers picked up the *Sun*'s accounts and wrote scolding
editorials condemning such behavior on the part of a man in control
of a billion dollars of supposedly safe securities.

One reader who was even more outraged than the editors by the
stories was Andrew Carnegie. Schwab was like a son to him, and
he vented his shock and anger in a cable urging Schwab to resign
and in a letter to Morgan proposing the same thing. Schwab was
deeply hurt that Carnegie would believe the papers and overreact
before giving him a hearing. Despite their differences, he venerated
Carnegie and felt indebted to him for his whole career. Schwab's
defense was rather lame, however. He claimed that he went to the
casino mostly because he liked the orchestra. He admitted that he
visited the tables but never sat down, only stood up, and he denied
emphatically that he ever came near breaking the bank. If Carnegie's
reaction hurt him, Morgan's possible reaction frightened him. When
he offered to return home at once, Morgan's man, George Perkins,
cabled that Morgan was unmoved by Carnegie's hysteria and added:
"Go ahead and have bully good time." But Schwab's good time was
over. Arriving home a month later, he confessed to Morgan, "I did
gamble at Monte Carlo, but I didn't do it behind closed doors."
Although insisting that he stay on as president, Morgan told him,
"That's what doors are for."

Schwab was too sensitive to believe that the matter would end
there. He had already had differences with Judge Gary, the corporation's puritanical and pious chairman, about policy. Gary used
Schwab's indiscretions, of which he disapproved as much as Carnegie, to force a showdown with Morgan and came away with carte
blanche. "From this time on, when you want me to do anything or
say anything, all you have to do is to tell me," Morgan said. "You
needn't explain. Just say, 'Do so and so,' and I will do it." Already
literally sick—stomach upsets, nervous ticks, insomnia—with worry
over the situation, Schwab took a long leave of absence. Judge Gary
was left in complete command of the world's largest corporation with
William Corey, Schwab's longtime assistant in Pittsburgh, as his
technical man.

The Schwab scandal would clearly have had a bearing on Frick's
decision as to what to do with his money. The bulk of it was going

into railroad stocks, which he would call "the Rembrandts of investments." Having been a man with millions for twenty years or more, Frick did not go on the same kind of spending sprees as his former partners. As far as personal comfort was concerned, it would be hard to improve upon Clayton, which he was slowly turning into a personal art gallery of distinction as his purse and taste improved. About the only problem with living there was the heavy smog that would descend on the property when the wind was wrong. The pollution was tolerable to a person who spent most of his waking hours with a cigar in hand and his working days in and around factories and coke ovens that spewed smoke and flame into the atmosphere, but Frick was beginning to worry about what the noxious gases might do to his paintings. In the matter of building, Frick had other, more profitable, uses in mind than housing for his money.

Almost as soon as the ink was dry on the agreements forming U.S. Steel, Frick began construction of a skyscraper reaching twenty-one stories into the air and three below ground on a lot at Fifth Avenue and Grant Street in Pittsburgh. The lot was next door to the Carnegie Building, and the press immediately saw it as an act of spite. If Schwab's house in New York made Carnegie's look like a cottage, Frick's building in Pittsburgh made Carnegie's look "like a hut," as one observer put it. It was a classic temple to commerce. The entrances, floors, walls, and ceilings of the halls were of Italian marble—220,000 square feet in all. The doors were bronze. Faced with granite over a steel skeleton, the building reflected Greek Doric architecture in overall design and detail. Opposite the main entrance, for instance, was a La Farge window depicting Fortune on her wheel above a marble bench flanked by pale green Greek amphorae. Instead of an altar, this temple housed in the marbled basement the largest armor plate steel vault in the world, hung with two seventeen-ton doors.

Frick had no trouble finding tenants for his building. Half of the first floor was occupied by the Union Savings Bank, of which he was a director. The vault was for the use of the Union Safe Deposit Company of Pittsburgh. Other space was assigned to the Pittsburgh offices of Equitable Life, of which Frick had just been made a director. The twenty-first floor was reserved for the Union Club and part of the basement was occupied by the Union Restaurant, a rather gloomy establishment with medieval German decor. Whether the motive for putting up the building was a mean one—to stick the biggest possible thumb in Carnegie's eye—or not, the result was a solid gold investment.

The Frick Building was precisely the kind of building expatriate novelist Henry James found so distasteful when he walked through New York on his revisit to America about that time. The skyscrapers replacing buildings he remembered "were going to bring in money— and was not money the only thing a self-respecting structure could be thought of as bringing in?" James went on to muse:

> I may appear to make too much of these invidious pres-
> ences, but it must be remembered that they represent, for our
> time, the only claim to any consideration other than merely
> statistical established by the resounding growth of New York.
> The attempt to take the aesthetic view is invariably blighted
> sooner or later by the most salient characteristic, *the* feature
> that speaks loudest for the economic idea. Window upon win-
> dow, at any cost, is a condition never to be reconciled with
> any grace of building, and the logic of the matter here hap-
> pens to put on a particularly fatal front. If quiet interspaces,
> always half the architectural battle, exist no more in such a
> structural scheme than quiet tones, blest breathing-spaces, oc-
> cur, for the most part, in New York conversation, so the rea-
> son is, demonstrably, that the building can't afford them. (It
> is by very much the same law, one supposes, that New York
> conversation cannot afford stops.) The building can only af-
> ford lights, each light having a superlative value as an aid to
> the transaction of business and the conclusion of sharp bar-
> gains. Doesn't it take in fact acres of window-glass to help
> even an expert New Yorker to get the better of another expert
> one, or to see that the other expert one doesn't get the better
> of *him*? It is easy to conceive that, after all, with this origin
> stamped upon their foreheads, the last word of the mercenary
> monsters should not be their address to our sense of formal
> beauty.

If James was right that New Yorkers needed all the light they could get to survive the sharp bargains they drove with each other, they needed even more when they dealt with Pittsburghers. Frick was collaborating with the Mellons in all those Union ventures he was housing in his new building. None was more active than the rapidly expanding Union Steel Company, in which Frick held a quarter interest shared with the Mellon boys and Donner, the president. When they annexed Republican boss Flinn's steel works in Sharon, Pennsylvania, Judge Gary and others at U.S. Steel began to see them as a threat. At Donner's invitation, they boarded a train and came out to have a look at the competition themselves. There were a number of consequences from that visit, but from the viewpoint of this book the most important one was an invitation to Henry Clay Frick to have a sail up Long Island Sound on the *Corsair* with Commodore J. P. Morgan.

Unhappily, the historic conversation between the two taciturn tycoons that took place on the deck of the *Corsair* went unrecorded, which, of course, was the reason for conducting it at sea. Happily, however, its substance can be reconstructed from its results. What with the mess in the executive suite and Schwab away on what might become terminal leave and the stock drifting downward, Morgan's fledgling corporation might not fly at all. Now that he wouldn't have to deal with Schwab, couldn't Frick become a really active director and give U.S. Steel that genius for management that Carnegie used to talk about? Frick felt that it might be perceived as inappropriate, or even illegal, if he became too involved with U.S. Steel while he was part owner of, and an active participant in, competing Union Steel. What if U.S. Steel bought Union Steel, Morgan wanted to know. Well, it would depend on the price and whether his partners agreed to it, but it would make a difference, Frick admitted. Morgan assured Frick that, based on what Judge Gary and the others had seen of the Union Steel properties, a mutually satisfactory arrangement could be made for the corporation to acquire Union Steel if Frick would be willing to come back aboard and help with the steering. What then? What course would he recommend? Frick proposed draconian measures: stopping dividends on the common stock (of which he then owned none), cutting dividends on the preferred stock (of which he had retained a nominal 10,000 shares), and reorganizing the operating command. George F. Redmond of the *Financial Weekly* claimed inside knowledge of this parley when he reported the results:

> Mr. Frick pleaded earnestly and Mr. Morgan listened intently. Finally, rising from the breakfast table and going on deck with Mr. Frick, he said to him, with tears in his eyes, that if the dividends were not paid on the preferred stock, he

could not face going down town on the following day. Mr. Frick was deeply touched. He then realized how keenly Mr. Morgan felt upon the subject and assured him that not another word should be said. At once he threw himself energetically into the task of aiding in steering the great organization through its trouble.

More than a few tears, a lot of dollars attested to how keenly Morgan felt. In a deal arrived at between Andrew Mellon, representing Union Steel, and Attorney James Reed, partner of Philander Knox and longtime acquaintance and legal counsel to Mellon and Frick, representing U.S. Steel, the corporation agreed to pay $30,860,501 for a company capitalized at $10 million two years earlier. The corporation also agreed to assume Union Steel's debts. Having no debts, Union Steel directors authorized a $45 million bond issue at a hastily summoned board meeting. By December 1902, Andrew and Dick Mellon were out of the steel business with more money in their pockets from that one deal than the old judge had made in a lifetime of foreclosing on mortgages. Donner went on to head another company, and Frick was free to devote his attention to the mess at U.S. Steel.

Possibly because he had more balls in the air than he could catch with only two hands, Frick, the Mellons' acknowledged mentor in finance, dropped two of the most enriching opportunities that his friends tossed his way in those first years of the century. In 1901, the Mellons bankrolled Spindletop, the first oil gusher in Texas, and Frick declined to go along on developing it because he didn't like the wildcatter, Colonel Guffey, who was promoting the project. It turned into Gulf Oil Corporation. Although they sold out on steel manufacturing, the Mellons got into steel fabricating when they backed Charles D. Marshall and Howard W. McClintic, two engineering graduates of Lehigh University, with a $100,000 loan to form their own company to make structural steel. Asked to join them, Frick, said, "Don't touch it. There is no chance whatever for success. We have never made money out of our bridge company." In thirty years of operation, the McClintic-Marshall Construction Company, which was involved in building the Panama Canal, Grand Cental Terminal, and the Waldorf-Astoria Hotel in New York, as well as the George Washington and Golden Gate bridges, paid out $8 million in dividends and finally sold for $70 million.

At what they must have considered a considerable risk, the Mellon boys went against the advice of one of America's leading steel experts, who was also their closest friend and colleague, because of a curious character test that the young engineers passed. A. W. and Dick Mellon first offered to put up $50,000 if Marshall and McClintic would match it. When they said they couldn't possibly do that, the conversation went as recorded by William Larimer Mellon:

> "How much can you put up?" asked A.W.
>
> "Ten thousand dollars. Five thousand from each of us."
>
> "But you own your homes? Couldn't you mortgage your homes to increase that?"
>
> Marshall and McClintic glanced at each other as men who find themselves suddenly at the edge of a precipice.
>
> Then A.W. asked another question. "What about having your father's help?" he said to Mr. Marshall.
>
> Mr. Marshall objected to disturbing his father's security.
>
> "Would your father not have faith in you?" asked A.W.
>
> Marshall replied almost indignantly that his father did have faith in him and that he would put the matter up to him. Then A.W. pressed the two again about mortgaging their homes.
>
> "Your reluctance," he said, "makes it appear as if you do not have faith in yourselves in this enterprise."
>
> Again Marshall and McClintic looked at each other. Then they agreed to mortgage their homes. Curiously enough, it was A.W. who then breathed a sigh of relief. He told them he appreciated and sympathized with their feelings, not only as to mortgaging their homes but as to approaching Mr. Marshall's father.
>
> "Neither of these steps will be necessary," said A.W. "My brother and I will lend you the additional money. You should be able to repay us out of profits of the business."

The Frick/Mellon friendship and partnership easily weathered these small storms of disagreement as well as a more serious incident involving the Union Trust Co. When the president who succeeded Andrew Mellon, James McKean, died, Mellon was abroad. Responding to the sad news, Mellon suggested replacing him with Henry C.

McEldowney, the thirty-four-year-old assistant cashier of the Bank of Commerce. Frick, who owned so many shares of Union Trust that it was informally called the Mellon-Frick bank, cabled back: "We think he's too young." Meant to be humorous, Mellon's cabled reply was that Frick thought well of himself at the same age. When this was read out at a meeting, Frick didn't think it was funny. He called his friend Andy the kind of name that gentlemen didn't find acceptable in those days, and Dick Mellon, as open and hot as his older brother was reserved and cold, jumped at him. Others restrained him and no blows were struck. Needless to say, with A.W. owning a thousand more shares than Frick, McEldowney became president and would stay in place a lifetime as one of Pittsburgh's leading bankers.

In 1902, Frick and the Mellons decided that a restructuring of their banking interests was in order. The first step was to turn T. Mellon & Sons, a private bank owned by A.W. and R.B., into the Mellon National Bank to expand its scope. The second step was to increase the Union Trust Co.'s shares from 5,000 to 10,000 and use 3,000 of those shares to buy the Mellon National Bank from A.W. and R.B. The final step was to allot 7,000 of the 10,000 Union Trust Co. shares to A. W. Mellon and H. C. Frick in equal amounts of 2,750, and 1,500 to R. B. Mellon. Thus, three men sat on the top of a very high financial pyramid—a third of all the money on deposit in all Pittsburgh banks was in their hands. It was very propitious timing for Frick, who was able to acquire his power with the cash he was getting from the sale of his steel stocks.

Following the *Corsair* summit meeting, Frick went into action at U.S. Steel as an influential member of the board's Finance Committee. He could hardly have picked a worse time. In the recession of 1903, the stock kept dropping until it reached a low of 8¾ for common and 50 for preferred. The confusion in the executive suite was continuing since Schwab refused to go gentle into the night. What he was doing on his "sick leave" was playing around with the securities of then little Bethlehem Steel Company and the U.S. Shipbuilding Company. When the Shipbuilding Company failed and was placed in receivership by a judge who charged Schwab with "ruinous extortion," the scandal got a play in the press almost equal to Schwab's Monte Carlo adventure. There were headlines like SCHWAB A WRECKER, SCHWAB GUILTY OF BIG FRAUD, and

DEATHLY GRIP OF SCHWAB. Realizing at this point that he couldn't hold on to his job at U.S. Steel, Schwab tried to hold on to his dignity in a letter to George Perkins:

> I think the press treated me shamefully and I ask of you and Mr. Morgan to put me right in the minds of the public. Retiring from active business this becomes important to me. I shall gladly do what I can in return—but I want you to have Mr. Morgan do this for me. A word from Frick would be much appreciated—but I have no right to ask him. I feel I have a right to ask Mr. Morgan to say the criticism is unfounded and that I acted entirely upon my own suggestion.

In short, Schwab didn't want his record to reveal that he had been fired although the directors of U.S. Steel had made clear their intention of doing just that by officially naming Corey "assistant president" and assigning Schwab's duties to him. Although neither Morgan nor Frick, both of whom believed firmly in closed doors, liked to do business in the press, they made an exception when Perkins passed along Schwab's plea. A little lying was a fair price to pay for getting rid of the uncontrollable Schwab. Frick told reporters that Schwab had been seeking his help in leaving the presidency for months. Morgan attributed the resignation to ill health and expressed regret in losing a man of "unequalled powers in the manufacture of steel." This last part of the statement turned out to be true as the people at U.S. Steel watched Schwab develop Bethlehem, which he rescued from the debacle of U.S. Shipbuilding, into a formidable rival. Something else may have been lost, too. Without apology, Schwab went on enjoying his money—building a huge complex at his old home of Loretto, Pennsylvania, to equal Riverside, taking his pleasures where he found them—and eschewing cultural pretenses and good works. A man who could be honest about himself, Schwab liked to tell of an occasion when a banker friend refused his request for a loan. "Why, I got a bigger loan from So-and-So the other day, and he didn't even know me," Schwab said. "That's why you got it," the banker replied.

It may be that Frick developed some sympathy for Schwab after he started attending U.S. Steel board meetings. Aside from their differing lifestyles, Schwab and Gary were far apart on general policy. In accord with common business practice of the day, Schwab saw nothing wrong with running the company to serve the best interests of directors and officers, all of whom were substantial stock-holders. This meant full and free use of inside information to buy and sell company stock in their own interest, regardless of the effect on other stockholders, as Frick had done. It also meant pricing and labor policies determined by what they would do for stock values and profits in the short term rather than what the consequences might be for the long term with respect to such things as stability and public approval. An abstemious and pious Methodist of deep conviction, Gary did not believe in the common business practices of the day, and it brought him into conflict not only with Schwab but with such high-powered directors as H. H. Rogers and Henry Clay Frick, for whom these practices had become a kind of gospel and the main source of their personal wealth.

With that carte blanche from Morgan, Gary had the temerity to preach morality to his board. To men who agreed with Vanderbilt's "public be damned" attitude, he argued that good public relations should be a major policy consideration. To an audience that included a man like Frick, whose high standing with his peers was owing in large part to his brutal repression of labor, Gary insisted that peace with labor at the cost of some profit would pay off in stability. Be-sides, it was the Christian way to go. This sort of thing was hard to take, and one man stopped attending board meetings because, as he said, "I believe in Sunday school, but not in turning a business into Sunday school." When Gary announced that he was making his first annual report public, Rogers cornered him after the meeting and tried to argue him out of it. "What if you have a bad report some year?" he asked. When Gary said he would issue that, too, Rogers went off shaking his head. But the real shocker came when Gary refused to deliver his reports to the directors before they were made public. Indeed, he decreed that the report would always be released after the stock market closed at three P.M. so that outside stockhold-ers and the public would have a chance to react the next morning as soon as the directors.

Frick and Rogers were together in opposing many of Gary's pol-icies; indeed, Gary said that Frick was harder to bring around to share his views than Rogers. In the conduct of the board meetings themselves, there was a rather amusing instance of the continuing ethical conflict that stands as a window into the character of the participants. Payment for attending a meeting was a twenty-dollar gold piece. When any members were absent, their fellow board members, all of them millionaires, claimed a pro rata share of the forfeited gold. This practice amazed and disgusted Gary, but he let it go on in the interest of peace, even taking his own share in order not to appear too stuffy. But Rogers and Frick went too far. Gamblers by nature, they came up with the idea of matching for the forfeited fees, and their suggestion was adopted with enthusiasm by the other board members. Gary couldn't participate in this and after a time, as he recollected for his biographer, "I told them that I was brought up not to believe in gambling and I thought the board of directors of the United States Steel Corporation should set a good example. I think H. H. Rogers was the only one who really listened to me and finally agreed to what I said. Frick finally came around to that point of view, but I don't think the rest ever did."

Somehow U.S. Steel did stumble its way through its early troubles, partly by taking Frick's advice to cut dividends, and Frick himself began buying again until he was down on the books for 100,000 shares of preferred and 50,000 shares of common stock. It was an investment to show his faith in the corporation he was helping to run, but he would keep most of his money elsewhere. A few years later when cornered by the press Frick issued a statement that indicated an agreement with Gary's long-term thinking and explained his own early desertion:

> It should be said that we have had five good years. There has been no panic—no hard year like 1896. If there had been such a year, it is a doubtful question whether or not the young corporation would have come through safely. It began business with less ready cash than it should have had. But trade was wonderfully brisk, and the company is now in good shape—much better than in 1903.
>
> I believe that a great mistake was made in beginning to pay dividends on the common stock from the first. Better have waited a while. But the common stock is today a good investment—not for small investors, but for large ones. It is only for those who can afford to wait—for those who can buy a large block of it and hold on until the big dividends come. It is a speculative stock, not a steady one for those who have small incomes.
>
> If the company were to be mismanaged, we have every

reason to believe that the government would interfere. As long as it is well managed, as now, there will be no slump. There will be fewer ups and downs in the future than there have been in the past. Today, if we have a bad year, we have a whole world market for a dumping ground. A slight depression does not hurt the trade. On the contrary, in my experience, I have found it acts as a stimulant to bring costs down.

Cautious as he seemed to be about steel, Frick bought his "Rembrandts" with an open hand. Before long he had become the biggest single investor in railroads in the nation. He was credited with spreading some forty-two million dollars over seven major roads. In order to protect his investments, Frick accepted active directorships in these lines: Chicago and Northwestern; Union Pacific; Atchison, Topeka and Santa Fe; Reading; Pennsylvania; Baltimore and Ohio; and Norfolk and Western. Daughter Helen remembered her supposedly "retired" father as a very busy man who was always out at some directors' meeting or another. He had become the quintessential capitalist, a man whose occupation and preoccupation was managing the money he owned wherever it could be best employed in the pursuit of gain.

A major difference between Frick, the steel man, and Frick, the capitalist, was that he could manage his own time in addition to his money. Too busy with Homestead to get involved in politics in 1892, Frick's interests were too thickly spread throughout the economy by 1904 for him not to give a good share of his time as well as money to politics. It's said that he flirted with the notion of seeking the U.S. Senate seat vacated by the death of the state's Republican boss, Matthew Quay. Perhaps recalling the advice of Judge Mellon, he settled instead for the role of kingmaker. At a meeting in the offices of President A. J. Cassatt of the Pennsylvania Railroad in Philadelphia attended by Frick, the new state boss Senator Boies Penrose, and the Philadelphia boss "Iz" Durham, it was agreed that Philander Knox would be an ideal replacement for Quay. That decided, the four men went to Cassatt's house for a dinner at which Governor Samuel W. Pennypacker, who was charged with appointing the new senator, was a guest. While the others chatted over brandy after the repast, Penrose took the governor for a walk in the garden and said, "It's Knox." A puzzled business community must have wondered whether they were rewarding Frick's old friend for his services as attorney general or kicking him upstairs where he could do no more harm.

After a very brief period of seeming cooperation, that "damned cowboy" in the White House had started riding roughshod over big business. His unlikely steed was his holdover Attorney General from the McKinley administration whose Pittsburgh firm, Reed and Knox, had represented not only Frick but Carnegie and Mellon and most of the rest of the city's big moneymakers. When Roosevelt discovered that Knox agreed with his interpretation of the Sherman Anti-Trust Act, he ordered his Attorney General to charge the most powerful financial figures in sight—J. P. Morgan, the lion of Wall Street, and James J. Hill and E. H. Harriman, twin tigers of the railroads. In 1901 there occurred a very complicated stock battle for the Chicago, Burlington & Quincy between Hill, who controlled the Great Northern and Northern Pacific and was backed by Morgan, and Harriman, who controlled Union Pacific and was backed by Kuhn, Loeb & Co. The whole stock market was thrown into a frightening tailspin until the wealthy warriors joined forces to create a holding company called the Northern Securities Company, combining Great Northern and Northern Pacific, which had acquired control of the Burlington, and giving Harriman three seats on the Burlington board. Arguing this combination was "in restraint of trade or commerce," as defined in the Sherman act, Knox filed a suit that wound its way through the courts for two years until the Supreme Court in 1904 ordered the company dissolved by a five-to-four decision.

The court's action caused a sensation. It reversed an earlier decision in the American Sugar Refining Company case that had allowed big business simply to ignore the existence of the Sherman act. More stunning to the financial community than the decision itself was the fact that the case had been brought by their own people—a Republican President of inherited wealth and social position and a Republican Attorney General with formidable credentials as a corporate lawyer. The whole court action must have represented a kind of personal betrayal for Frick. When Roosevelt visited Pittsburgh in the same year that the suit was filed, Frick assembled some twenty of the city's leading businessmen for lunch with the President at Clayton. It was a typical Golden Age repast—melon, consommé, radishes, salmon mayonnaise, sweetbreads with peas, filet of beef, new potatoes and asparagus, roast duck, tomato aspic, cheese and crackers, vanilla ice cream, cake, coffee, and fruit, all washed down with proper wines. While the men worked their way through this, Sousa's band serenaded them from the lawn outside. Frick then ushered Roosevelt into a guest bedroom upstairs where he slept off lunch in preparation for another banquet and speech at the Schenley Hotel that night. Yes, in spite of his peculiarities, Roosevelt was one of them.

Coming as it did in an election year, the court decision raised serious questions as to how to treat Roosevelt's bid for reelection. Colorful, courageous, and vastly entertaining, Roosevelt was clearly popular with the people. Renominating him would virtually assure another Republican victory, which had to be weighed in the minds of the business community against the probability that Roosevelt would continue his efforts to make government at least an equal power to business in a democratic society. Knox evidently persuaded Frick and Mellon that the action against Northern Securities was warranted and acted, in fact, as a kind of safety valve to let off the steam of public discontent with big business. In turn, Frick, the plenipotentiary, spread the Knox gospel among his wide circle of associates on boards of directors.

Roosevelt was not unappreciative. He appointed Frick to the Isthmian Canal Commission. To take the curse off the antitrust suit, Roosevelt also consulted frequently with Morgan, John Archbold of Standard Oil, and James Stillman on other matters having to do with the economy. In the end, Roosevelt retained the most effective kind of support from the wealthy: $150,000 from Morgan, $100,000 from Rogers and Archbold, $100,000 from George Gould, $50,000 each from Harriman and Frick. Andrew Mellon acknowledged giving to the Republican Party as if giving to a church.

Frick's support wasn't only financial. On one of those rare opportunities when the press could get at him, he was interviewed in August 1904, returning from Europe on *Kaiser Wilhelm II,* and issued this statement:

> I have always been for Roosevelt and do not see any reason for changing now. He is the safest man. He has the best interests of the government at heart, is sound in his business policies, and is not afraid to follow his convictions. An awful mistake would be made if any other candidate succeeded.

Frick was certainly backing the right horse. Roosevelt was elected over Alton B. Parker, a relatively unknown New York judge, by a plurality of 2,500,000 votes. With Knox in the Senate and a $50,000 lien on White House favors, Henry Clay Frick, capitalist, would be gambling with favorably loaded dice.

CHAPTER 17

"We Bought the Bastard . . ."

ON Sunday, April 16, 1905, *The New York Times* carried a feature story about Henry Clay Frick's tenancy of one of the "famous brownstone twins" at Fifty-first Street and Fifth Avenue built by William H. Vanderbilt. Because Frick wasn't given to talking about himself, the story lacked the element that would have made it a real heartwarmer. Moving with his family into the mammoth stone pile at 640 Fifth Avenue meant reaching an objective he had set for himself some twenty-five years before when he and young Mellon rode together down the avenue. Like making his million before thirty, the move had the character of self-fulfilling prophecy. Mr. Frick was always a man who knew where he was going, and this characteristic gives an eerie resonance to the last message he sent to Carnegie.

What intrigued the *Times* writer was that Frick was willing and able to sign a ten-year lease for a rental said to be in six figures. This wouldn't have bothered Frick, who, it will be remembered, had told Andy Mellon that it would probably cost at least a thousand dollars a day to live in such luxury. And, as usual, Frick was getting his money's worth. To capture a reliable long-term tenant, the owner, George Vanderbilt, was footing the bill for extensive remodeling to Frick's specifications. Among other improvements, electric lights and modern baths would be installed, making the house "quite as modern" as Charlie Schwab's Riverside, according to the reporter.

Presumably the renovations would not put a strain on the exchequer of this Vanderbilt heir, who was living in splendor on his North Carolina estate, Biltmore, an estate so vast that more men were employed for its maintenance than for the entire national Department of Agriculture. By coincidence, Henry James's American tour took him to Biltmore in February of that same year of 1905, and his report on the visit to his soul mate, Edith Wharton, again raises the question as to what the possession of great wealth does to the quality of life and the human spirit:

> The whole land here is bound in snow & ice; we are 2,500 feet in the air; the cold, the climate, is well nigh all the "company" in this strange, colossal heart-breaking house; & the desolation & discomfort of the whole thing—whole scene— are, in spite of mitigating millions everywhere expressed, in- discribable [sic]. . . . I am now alone with the good G V & Huntina; & it has all been verily a strange experience. But I can't go into it—it's too much of a "subject": I mean one's sense of the extraordinary impenitent madness (of millions) which led to the erection in this vast niggery wilderness, of so gigantic & elaborate monument to all that *isn't* socially pos- sible there. It's, *in effect,* like a gorgeous practical joke—but at one's own expense, after all, if one has to live in solitude in these league-long marble halls, & sit in alternate Gothic & Palladian cathedrals, as it were—where now only the tem- perature stalks about—with the "regrets" sighing along the wind, of those who have declined.

Loneliness amid finery would not be a problem for the Fricks if the newspaper's report that they would "entertain extensively in win- ter" turned out to be accurate. Trying to make it into the "four hundred" was not, however, their reason for moving to New York. Helen Clay Frick, then seventeen and old enough to know what was going on and why, said that her father wanted to rescue his art works from Pittsburgh's sea of smog and find a place where they could be better hung and displayed. There was also the fact that Frick, as a newly minted capitalist, wanted to be located in the financial center of the country, if not the world, according to Helen. Close as father and daughter were, the secretive Mr. Frick apparently never told her about his youthful dream of occupying the very house to which they were moving.

In any event, Frick was by then rich enough to have his cake and eat it, too—to use a cliché too apt to resist. There seems to have been no thought whatever given to selling, or even renting, Clayton. The whole family had a sentimental attachment to the "starter house" that Clay and Adelaide had expensively restructured into a turreted mansion where two of their children had died and been buried within the range of sight from the house and where Childs and Helen had grown up. Helen, in fact, would never get over her love affair with Clayton. She would insist on having her "coming out party" there and would devote much of her time and inheritance to it. From a practical point of view, Frick had too many roots, friendships, interests, and influences in Pittsburgh and the rest of Pennsylvania to give up a base there. He would keep Clayton fully staffed and operated so that he, or any of them, could return on the few days a year necessary to establish legal residence and vote or for business and social engagements.

Quite apart from the move to New York, the year 1905 was one of transition for the Frick family. Childs graduated from Princeton University in keeping with the pattern for Frick's peers in the financial world. As noted, only Morgan among the leading money men of the time had any college education to speak of, but almost all of their sons went to Ivy League colleges. The choice of Princeton was a natural for Childs Frick since the pervasive Presbyterianism in Pittsburgh resulted in a natural affinity for Presbyterian Princeton. Although going to Princeton did not inspire Childs to follow in his father's footsteps as a man of business, the Princeton connection was destined to endure with significant results for both the college and the family. Later in that same year, Frick's mother, Elizabeth Overholt Frick, died in Wooster, Ohio, severing ties that never seemed to have been tightly binding with the place and people he left behind (except for the money it produced) as soon as he had his first million in hand.

Henry Clay Frick surfboarded into New York on a wave of the most favorable publicity he would ever have. As reported, he had been made a director of the Equitable Life Assurance Society in 1901. He accepted the appointment from James H. Hyde, controlling owner and vice president, with a cablegram in which he called it "quite an honor to be offered the position on the Board of a company held in high esteem in Pittsburgh, as it is everywhere." In a reciprocal gesture, young Hyde's name appeared on the board of directors of Union Trust, the Mellon/Frick bank that was organized about the same time. Neither man bothered to attend the other's meetings. In the circles Frick was entering, directorships were often honorary, a use of names to assure stockholders that their money was in the hands of solid citizens. Although Frick, still living in Pittsburgh, was probably not aware of it at the time, the adjective more appropriate than "solid" that might be applied to James Hazen Hyde was "colorful."

Son of Henry B. Hyde, the supersalesman founder of Equitable, James inherited 51 percent of the $100,000 in controlling shares of Equitable on his father's death in 1899. In order to step into his father's shoes, Hyde moved back to New York from Paris, where he had acquired a taste for French culture and mannerisms. A fancy-dressing dandy, he was also one of the best four-in-hand coachmen in the country and regularly put on a show for his fellow New Yorkers driving his spirited horses decked out with violets behind their ears along the avenues and through the park. Despite this behavior and the fact that he was only in his early twenties, the business community was quite conscious of his power over some $400 million in Equitable Funds and welcomed him by making him a director in forty-six companies. In Equitable itself, James modestly agreed to serve as vice president in deference to James W. Alexander, son of a minister of the Fifth Avenue Presbyterian Church and longtime president of the company. Having been carefully coached by his father, James knew that it wasn't a title or salary that brought rewards from the life insurance business but how you used all the cash that policyholders paid in premiums to play the markets.

Insider deals were the devices most commonly used by the elite of big business to enrich themselves. None of them acquired a personal fortune by earning and saving and very few, if any, by blindly investing in public offerings of securities. Men who were officers and/ or directors (or trustees, as they were called in life insurance) of multiple companies could manipulate the trading among them to their own advantage. According to Veblen, managing companies to enrich insiders through securities speculation rather than producing good products for reasonable returns became the name of the corporate game at the turn of the century, as it would again some eighty years later. At Equitable and several of the other large insurance companies, officers and directors would form syndicates to buy securities at bottom prices on the market and then prevail upon the company to buy them at a profit.

Henry B. Hyde was more subtle in pursuing this course than his son. He called his personal syndicates "Louis Fitzgerald and Associates" or "George H. Squire and Associates," but the son boldly did business as "James H. Hyde and Associates." And what business they did! A typical operation was to subscribe to $1 million Metropolitan Street Railway bonds at 94 on June 11, 1902, and sell them to Equitable Life seven days later at 97½. Without putting up a penny, James H. Hyde Associates earned $30,000. Working with Alexander in a similar deal that same year, Hyde got $1.5 million in Oregon short line bonds at 96 and resold them to Equitable in five days at 97, splitting a $25,044 profit with the president. Even if the securities eventually lodged in the Equitable portfolio were perfectly sound, profit that should have belonged to the policyholders whose money was used to acquire them had already been skimmed off by the insiders. Not infrequently, the securities in which the syndicates speculated were far from sound. And on occasion, directors arranged for insurance company assets to underwrite their private ventures, as did E. H. Harriman when he had Equitable help fund his acquisition of Union Pacific.

In early 1905 all this was common business practice about which the practitioners felt no guilt when James Hazen Hyde decided to spend some of that money he was earning in the old-fashioned way by throwing a masquerade ball. This was to be a Louis Sherry masterpiece for which Sherry would convert his establishment at whatever cost to Hyde into a near replica of Louis XV's Versailles. Entertainment would be provided by Madame Gabrielle Rejane, imported from Paris, and dancing would be accompanied by the Metropolitan Opera orchestra. It would be *the* party of the year, and the "extras" would include young men about town like the President's cousin, Franklin Delano Roosevelt. Everything went according to plan, and on January 31 costumed guests supped at sixty tables nestled in a garden of roses, danced and dined again at three A.M. while reporters hidden behind the rose bowers recorded every expensive detail. When it all came out in the papers, Equitable president Alexander was not amused; policyholders would suspect rightly that money that should have gone into their dividends paid for the extravaganza. Already divided among more imaginative investors like Harriman and Hyde and Alexander's conservative clique, the board erupted in open dispute as a result of the party, and absentee Henry Clay Frick attended his first meeting in February.

In the midst of charges and countercharges about malfeasance and mismanagement, the board decided to appoint an investigating committee. Because he had never profited in any way from Equitable operations other than to rent office space in his new skyscraper to the Pittsburgh office, Frick was elected chairman of this committee. Other members of the committee included E. H. Harriman, Melville E. Ingalls, Brayton Ives, and Cornelius N. Bliss. It was an unwelcome task for Frick, but he pushed it through in record time, and the committee came up with a stunning report in late May. It was a plague-on-both-your-houses account of company officers using Equitable funds to underwrite syndicates for their own profit in violation of the insurance law and of buying control of trust companies in order to engage in speculative undertakings, again in violation of the law. Involved in matters like this, the top officers had let loose and irregular methods permeate the entire management force. The conclusion: both Alexander and Hyde should resign.

The Frick Report, as it would be called, caused what *The New York Times* described as a "cat and dog fight" at the June 3, 1905, meeting of Equitable trustees. For four hours they wrangled, and Alexander and Hyde got together to save their necks. They managed to persuade enough other trustees to go along with them that they were able to reject the report. At one point when Hyde was criticizing the report, Frick jumped to his feet and said, "I will no longer sit on the same board with that young man."

Frick walked out of the room, and Harriman followed him. Both men resigned on the spot, causing Hyde to say, "By the resignation of these gentlemen, this board stands more truly purified than if I had gone out of it. Now I am willing to offer control of my stock on such terms as may be deemed wise."

Both officers did resign as demanded in the Frick Report, but that was only the beginning of the great insurance scandal. The abuses uncovered by Frick's committee virtually demanded state intervention. An investigation headed by Charles Evans Hughes came in with evidence of similar shenanigans in the other large companies, New York Life and Mutual, and remedial legislation was quickly passed. As a result of his work, Hughes became governor, a candidate for the presidency, and eventually Chief Justice of the U.S. Supreme Court. Soured by his experience, Frick resigned from the boards of Franklin National Bank and Commercial Trust Company in Philadelphia so that he would not have to serve with Hyde. It turned out to be a useless gesture. Even before the results of the Hughes investigation were announced, a deposed Hyde took ship for France, where he would stay for thirty-five years.

Reading the Hughes findings in the White House, President Roosevelt undoubtedly found them fuel for the fire he was setting under big business. In this respect, the man who believed in speaking softly and carrying a big stick was speaking loudly and brandishing the stick of government regulation. As he would explain fully in his autobiography, T.R. was no friend of socialism nor foe of capitalism. Like his Democrat cousin, F.D.R., his concern was to preserve the capitalistic system by curbing the excesses of its greediest practitioners. Indeed, he believed firmly, as did socialistic Henry George and capitalistic J. P. Morgan, in the inevitability of large business organizations achieving efficiency and economy in the manufacture and distribution of goods. But he also believed that in a democracy government should have more power than private enterprise in order to ensure that the nation's resources were being used in the best interests of all of the people.

T.R. put his theory of government's place and power to the test very early in his presidency. When a strike in the anthracite mining regions in the fall of 1902 threatened to leave mostly the poor of the great northeastern cities shivering through the winter, Roosevelt exercised the moral force of his office by bringing the two sides together in the White House and reaching an agreement. Since there was no precedent for such an intervention in private business, nor any legal authority for his action, Roosevelt found the negotiations hard going and developed an abiding dislike for the kind of selfish intransigence displayed by the coal operators, who were represented by George Baer, president of the Reading Railroad. In a letter that found its way into the papers, Baer wrote to a friend that "the rights and interests of the laboring man will be protected and cared for—not by the labor agitators, but by the Christian men to whom God in his infinite wisdom has given the control of the property interests of this country." Roosevelt's high-pitched laugh must have sounded through the White House when he saw the retort his good friend, Finley Peter Dunne, had his Mr. Dooley make to Baer's pious utterance:

Mr. Hinnissy asked: "What d'ye think iv the man down in Pinnsylvanya who says th' Lord an' him is partners in a coal mine?"

"Has he divided th' profits?" asked Mr. Dooley.

With his victory in the courts over Northern Securities, his land-slide reelection, and his Nobel Prize for arranging peace between Russia and Japan, T.R. became a force to be feared by even the biggest of businessmen. A problem with Roosevelt was his inconsistency. It was Roosevelt who had the temerity to stand up at a Washington dinner where H. H. Rogers of Standard Oil and J. P. Morgan sat side by side and, with teeth and eyeglasses flashing defiance, rage against "malefactors of great wealth." But it was also Roosevelt who called journalists like Ida Tarbell, with her exposé of Standard Oil, and Lincoln Steffens, with his articles on political corruption in American cities, "muckrakers." Roosevelt exasperated Mark Twain, who, as noted earlier, was a close friend of Rogers. As perhaps still the greatest of all American writers, Twain's recollections of T.R. are worth quoting because they explain in large part why he was the first President since Lincoln who was able to put public good above private gain:

Mr. Roosevelt is one of the most likable men that I am acquainted with. I have known him, and have occasionally met him, dined in his company, lunched in his company, for certainly twenty years. I always enjoy his society, he is so hearty, so straightforward, outspoken and, for the moment, so absolutely sincere. These qualities endear him to me when he is acting in his capacity of private citizen, they endear him to all his friends. But when he is acting under their impulse as President, they make of him a sufficiently queer President. He flies from one thing to another with incredible dispatch—throws a somersault and is straightway back again where he was last week. He will then throw some more somersaults and nobody can foretell where he is finally going to land after the series. Each act of his and each opinion expressed, is likely to abolish or controvert some previous act or expressed opinion. This is what is happening to him all the time as President. But every opinion he expresses is certainly his sincere opinion at the moment, and it is as certainly not the opinion which he was carrying around in his sytem three or four weeks earlier, and which was just as sincere and honest as the latest one. No, he can't be accused of insincerity—that is not the trouble. His trouble is that his newest interest is the one that absorbs him; absorbs the whole of him from his head to his feet, and for the time being it annihilates all previous opinions and feelings and convictions. He is the most popular human being that has ever existed in the United States, and that popularity springs from just these enthusiasms of his—these joyous ebullitions of excited sincerity. It makes him so much like the rest of the people. They see themselves reflected in him. They also see that his impulses are not often mean. They are almost always large, fine, generous. He can't stick to one of them long enough to find out what kind of a chick it would hatch if it had a chance, but everybody recognizes the generosity of the intention and admires it and loves him for it.

If Mark Twain caught both the perplexity and popularity that T.R. inspired in the general public in those words, a man as stingy with words as Twain was generous—Henry Clay Frick—more aptly expressed the view of his fellow businessmen in a widely quoted and long-remembered remark to a friend. "We bought the bastard, but he didn't stay bought," he said. On another occasion, Frick exhibited the same attitude when he asked Judge Gary, "What man has Roosevelt ever helped?" But because of T.R.'s mercurial temperament, Frick would be in for a surprise during his most important confrontation with the President.

Amidst all the good things that were happening to the Fricks, there was a sharp reminder of the bad in the spring of 1905 when Alexander Berkman was granted an early release from prison. Frick had refused to take any part at all in the pro and con discussions as to whether the sentence should be commuted for good behavior, and when a detective agency suggested that he might be in need of protection with Berkman at liberty, Frick had a secretary reply on April 14:

> Dear Sir:
> Mr. Frick directs me to say, in reply to yours of the twelfth, that he is not at all interested in Berkman or in any of his class and has no fear whatever. All newspaper reports regarding arrangements made by him to keep track of Berkman, or anyone in connection with him, are unfounded.

Whether this represented the kind of physical courage Frick displayed at the time of Berkman's attack or a kind of arrogance in being part of the unassailable class of the very rich can never be known for sure. It's certain that Frick was operating on a higher level than a man who can be pinned down in an office on a Saturday afternoon. The dues of the club he had joined by moving to New York and becoming one of the nation's celebrated capitalists could be high. In July 1905, for instance, Frick gave $100,000 to the American Academy of Fine Arts in Rome, incorporated earlier that year by an act of Congress. Others who contributed a like amount to the same cause were J. P. Morgan, William K. Vanderbilt, and James Stillman. These gentlemanly gestures of generosity for an institution in one of their favorite foreign watering holes now have to be viewed in the light of the fact that there was no federal tax on their large incomes. In the case of Frick, there was special irony in a story out of Pittsburgh about the "occupational tax" the day before the announcement of his gift. Headlined WEALTHY MEN RATE LOW, the story said that Frick, whose fortune was estimated at $70 million, was assessed on $10,000, the same amount as the Allegheny County Register of Wills, whose annual salary was $5,000 plus fees that could possibly amount to $20,000. Incredibly, this incongruous pair led the list of assessments. As for some of the others, let the story speak for itself:

> President H. C. McEldowney of the Union Trust Co., which has a capital of $20,000,000 is assessed at $500. William Flinn, interested in a dozen large concerns and worth several millions, is assessed at $2000. A.W. Mellon, president of the Mellon National Bank, is assessed at $2000....

Throughout this period, board meetings of the U.S. Steel Corp. were nearly as contentious as those at Equitable. The departure of Schwab did not automatically result in a smoothly functioning executive team because his disciple, Bill Corey, was as dedicated to high living as his mentor. It wasn't gambling or booze that attracted Corey, but the ladies of the theater in New York, where he had settled into a house suitable to the station of a president of U.S. Steel. Corey openly consorted with one Mabelle Gilman while the girl he had married when he was only eighteen—an unpaid mother's helper in his family's Braddock home—stayed in Pittsburgh. Mrs. Corey's true friend was Mrs. Schwab, who had reason to be sympathetic with

the wife of a philandering husband, and Mrs. Schwab accompanied
her to Reno, where she got a divorce and a settlement of $3 million.
None of this went down well with the company's Methodist chairman, Judge Gary, or the Presbyterians of Pittsburgh, and there was
a rump meeting of the directors in December 1905 at the Duquesne
Club in Pittsburgh at which Frick, Morgan, and Rogers were des-
ignated to solve the Corey problem.

Lean and hard as the steel he could make so well, Corey was no
easier to dislodge than Schwab. It took a year and a half of negotiations, and the company ended up paying Corey's stiff price—official
recognition of his wedding to Mabelle Gilman by the presence of
Judge Gary in May 1907. It must have been a distasteful duty for
the Judge since the ceremony, followed by a $6,000 champagne sup-
per, was held at midnight in the Gotham Hotel with police cordon-
ing off crowds of the curious in the streets. Corey was tasteless
enough to inform everybody that he had bought a $200,000 chateau
in France for his bride and set aside $250,000 for their honeymoon.
As part of the payoff, Corey was still President of U.S. Steel during
this garish celebration and the crossing to France. Only after the
couple was settled in the honeymoon chateau was Gary free to announce Corey's resignation.

Although Frick was not guilty of the colorful extravagances of a
Schwab or a Corey, he was nevertheless what might now be called
an "item" for the press from the moment he took up residence on
New York's most splendid avenue. Reporters caught him and quoted
him wherever and whenever they could, and his public and private
transactions were often given front-page play. But once the initial
splash subsided, 1906 turned out to be a lean year for Frick watchers
until its very last month. On December 17, the front pages reported
that Henry Clay Frick had purchased a whole city block between
Seventieth and Seventy-first streets on Fifth Avenue for $2.47 mil-
lion. It was the site of the Lenox Library, then being melded into
the New York Public Library, and the Frick money would report-
edly go toward the purchase of books. *The New York Times* was
inspired to speculate in a whimsical editorial on all the costs Frick
would incur while dwelling in a Vanderbilt mansion and developing
his new property. It ended with a shrug: "They do not seem to cause
any anxiety among the men able to pay $2,400,000 for lots on Fifth
Avenue." A reader, signing the letter D.E.W., couldn't take the spec-

tacle of so much private spending as philosophically: "There are only a few hospitals, colleges and homes for orphaned children requiring as much for annual maintenance as this palace for Mr. Frick."

The editorial was right. Far from displaying any anxiety, Frick continued to make headlines with his spending in 1907—for a summer place he called Eagle Rock at Pride's Crossing, Massachusetts; a $100,000 box at the Metropolitan Opera; and a $200,000 matching gift to the Young Women's Christian Association in Pittsburgh. This sort of largesse was running counter to the mood of the times since a drop in the market in early spring suggested that the economic weather was turning foul. Reporters cornered Frick, the new financial oracle, at the National City Bank, where he was visiting in the office of president James Stillman to get his opinion on the slump. They were kept waiting an hour until a secretary emerged bearing a joint statement that would go down in history as a classic example of the calculated silence so many of the money manipulators practiced:

> The U.S.A. is a great and growing country.
> (Signed) James Stillman
> Henry Clay Frick

> This is confidential and not for publication unless names are omitted.

But as the country slid downward toward what looked like the first serious recession since 1893, Frick found himself obliged to speak out ever more fully. Much of the financial community blamed worsening conditions on President Roosevelt's verbal and legal assaults on business. His suit against Standard Oil Company for accepting rebates, for instance, brought a $29,240,000 fine from Judge Kenesaw Mountain Landis that summer. Although it would later be set aside by a higher court, it was still standing in that time of trouble and on reporters' minds when they questioned Frick as he arrived home from a visit to Europe on the American liner *New York* on August 5. Knowing that Frick had booked passage at the last minute, they suggested that he was making an emergency trip to relieve H. H. Rogers of business burdens brought on by the fine. The usually sober Frick laughed at that, saying, "That's no affair of mine. I've been resting, that's all." When pressed about predictions of a recession, he turned serious and came up with the unconsciously cruel comment of a possessor of money for whom bad times represent opportunity to acquire bargains. "It is possible that there is a business recession before us," Frick admitted. "If so, it will probably have a good effect. It will be a good thing to let up the present intense activity."

On August 21, however, Frick changed his tune when he was interviewed after a directors' meeting of U.S. Steel. On this occasion he tried to deal with the charges that Roosevelt's policies were crippling business. After declining to comment specifically on a Roosevelt speech, he told the *Times:*

> I find nothing in underlying conditions to warrant the apparent great lack of confidence in business generally which seems prevalent. If there is anything to justify that feeling in trade conditions, I do not see it.
>
> I can understand the vague but real unsettlement of sentiment created by current agitation against corporations, but this is in a measure apart from real conditions and is capable of correction. I believe myself and always have in the correction of abuses, whether corporate or individual, but I feel that such care should be exercised in doing this that only the wrong doer should suffer.
>
> Now that the Government is determined to enforce laws hitherto dormant, would it not be well that actions of the past, sanctioned by custom and usage at that time, should not be called into question under the new order of things, but that such action as the Government has shown should be taken as evidence of its intentions as to the future and serve as a fair warning to the management of all corporations?
>
> Of course where corporations are still acting outside of the law, unknowingly, it is to be expected that they should be set right, but I am sure that can be accomplished without harm to anyone, and without the least injury to credit, if the situation is properly and intelligently handled by the Administration.

An astonishing statement! Despite the mushy language, Frick was sending a public message to the White House to pardon all past business transgressions on the grounds of a prevailing disregard of the law ("sanctioned by custom and usage") and deliver only a naughty-naughty slap on the wrist to current transgressors on the grounds of ignorance ("unknowingly") even though ignorance of the law has never been held to be a valid excuse in cases against ordinary citizens. In view of the fact that the corporations then, as now, always employed the highest-priced legal talent available, the conclusion that they indulged in deliberate avoidance of the law is inescapable. Also, there is that note of unsupported and unwarranted optimism that spokesmen for business interests invariably use when confronted with the possibility of panic. Was Frick being deliberately misleading or was he just a poor prophet?

By that fall, the true state of the economy was apparent to everyone. As in 1873, the country went into a money crunch. But unhappily nobody in high places seemed to be any more aware of what was happening than Frick. In October, the nation's chief executive went bear hunting in Louisiana. Equally unconcerned, the uncrowned king of Wall Street, J. P. Morgan, went to Richmond, Virginia, at the same time for an Episcopal convention, taking with him a trainload of bishops whom he would house and entertain royally in a rented mansion with Louis Sherry personally seeing to their needs. Roosevelt was out of touch in the woodlands, where he munched on possum and bear steak, but Morgan, dining in splendor, soon had his digestion disturbed by the telegrams reaching him from New York. Brokerage houses and banks were getting into deep trouble, and on Saturday, October 19, Morgan left Richmond a day early at the insistence of his partners to take command of the financial forces fighting panic in New York.

From then on the centers of action during one of the worst panics in history would be Morgan's downtown office or his magnificent new marble-faced library on Thirty-sixth Street. In either place, the seventy-year-old Morgan would sit smoking, often playing solitaire and mostly keeping his own counsel, while the heads of the nation's leading financial institutions rushed in and out seeking advice and orders. In the words of Herbert Satterlee, Morgan's son-in-law, "the fury of the panic descended on the City of New York and began its destruction" on Tuesday, October 22, with runs on the Knickerbocker Trust Co., the Trust Company of America, the National Bank of North America, and many smaller institutions. Scanning reports of hasty audits by his lieutenants, Morgan quickly decided that the Knickerbocker was beyond saving; it would have to close its doors in the face of frightened and angry depositors lining its lobby and the surrounding sidewalks. As for the others, a plan was needed.

At this point in the panic, it was evident that the trust companies constituted the weakest link in the financial chain. The fundamental problem was an overextension of credit and a shortage of hard cash to cover debts falling due. Because they were exempt from state and federal laws governing other banks dealing in demand deposits, the trust companies had become one of the most effective instruments of speculators. Trust companies did not have to maintain any stipulated cash reserve on deposits, and they were empowered to invest or lend money in real estate and buy and sell stocks without restriction. As revealed in the insurance investigations in 1905, establishing and investing their reserves in trust companies was one way directors of insurance companies got around legal restrictions on certain kinds of speculation. Because they were not prohibited from doing so, trust companies began taking demand deposits from individuals. Their competitive edge over other kinds of banks was the fact that they didn't need to have a reserve. As a result, they could pay a higher rate of interest, and deposits in trust companies in New York grew from $198 million in 1898 to $834 million in 1906. They were all suddenly at risk.

Panic in New York spread across the country almost exactly as Judge Mellon described the last similar occurrence in 1873. In the hindsight of history, the cause has been attributed to the misuse—or, at least, overuse—of financial instruments such as the trust companies by the major money manipulators. Blamed for bringing on the panic and recession by his attempts to make business obey the law, President Roosevelt, who was not known for any interest or expertise in economics, insightfully put the blame on the financial community instead. Realizing some justification for the President's position, where did Morgan place the blame? As silent and stolid through the crisis as a smoke-wreathed Buddha, Morgan created a climate in which every word that he dropped was saved and spread by his disciples like holy writ. In his handwritten notes of those days when the streets were jammed by frantic depositors trying to get their money, Satterlee reported that his father-in-law took the cigar out of his mouth and said, "If people will keep their money in the banks, everything will be all right."

But people felt deceived by their bankers, and the runs went on and on. Although he had no idea of how to end the crisis, Morgan did sense that public confidence had to be restored in the banks and the markets—in the capitalistic system, in fact—as soon as possible. The way to do this was to keep any other major institutions from failing like the Knickerbocker by getting the leaders of all the trust companies and banks together to pool their resources and use them in aid of colleagues in danger, something like drawing water from a common reservoir to hose down outbreaks of California brush fires. The concept was simple but the execution difficult. Many of these bankers had never even met one another, let alone learned to trust one another; all, including and especially those with reserves on hand, were primarily concerned with keeping their own institutions afloat. Only the moral force of Morgan's reputation and personal charisma could persuade them to act in concert. Notes from an unpublished memorandum by Morgan partner George Perkins give the flavor of just two days of deepening crisis:

> —Wednesday, October 23: Run on Trust Company of America. President Oakley Thorne comes to Morgan at noon for help. At 2:15 p.m. a committee from the Trust Company of America arrives to say they have only $180,000 left and will have to close before 3 p.m. A weary Morgan says, "I don't see anything else to do." Perkins gets James Stillman, head of City Bank, and George Baker, head of First National Bank, on the phone and asks them to come over. In consultation with Morgan, they tell Perkins to keep a line open to the Trust Company of America, to ask the Trust Company to send over $500,000 of its best securities and agree to sit there and advance money every few minutes as needed until 3 p.m. One bank stays open for one more day.
>
> Thursday, October 24: Run on Lincoln Trust Company. Also Stock Exchange reports money scarce. Rates on call money up to 100 percent. At 1:45 p.m. Morgan asks that all bank presidents come to talk to him. He tells them that the Stock Exchange needs $25,000,000 in 10 or 12 minutes. Stillman starts the ball rolling with a subscription of $5,000,000, and the rest fall in line. The Exchange stays open another day until the closing bell.

And so it went day after day for two weeks. Working his way north after shooting his bear, President Roosevelt ignored the panic at whistle-stop speeches until he reached Nashville, where he again declined to accept the blame and said, "All I did was turn on the light; I am responsible for that but not for what the light showed." Meanwhile his Secretary of the Treasury, George B. Cortelyou, hurried to New York and checked into the Hotel Manhattan; there the imperial Morgan, who was summoning bank presidents like vassals to his private court, called upon Courtelyou to show his respect for the flag. The secretary returned the respect by saying that although he had already deposited $6 million in Treasury funds in the national banks, he had more that he would put at Morgan's disposal. Unofficially but certainly, J. P. Morgan was in charge of the nation's money supply.

It's to be wondered whether Morgan would have been accorded this confidence and authority if anybody had overheard a private exchange between him and his librarian, Belle da Costa Greene. On one occasion when bankers were gathered in argument and discussion in the vaulted east room while Morgan quietly played solitaire in the west room, Ms. Greene was delegated to take messages back and forth between them. In tired exasperation she finally asked, "Why don't you tell them what to do, Mr. Morgan?" He surprised her by saying, "I don't know what to do myself, but some time, someone will come in with a plan that I know *will* work; and then I will tell them what to do."

Splendid though it was—and is—the Morgan Library was not the setting that any stage designer would conceive for a drama starring practical men of money. In the east room particularly the atmosphere was musty and scholarly. Triple tiers of bookcases were crammed with ancient volumes and manuscripts collected by Morgan in his world travels. Ceiling murals celebrated cultural greats like Dante, Michelangelo, Socrates, Galileo, and Columbus, and above them the signs of the zodiac. If they had time to look at or think about their surroundings, the bankers would have recognized the unintended irony of the huge sixteenth-century tapestry above the mantle entitled "The Triumph of Avarice." Plainer but nevertheless decorated with priceless paintings and artifacts was Morgan's study across the rotunda in the west room. Once when there were more than a hundred men in the building, Morgan surrendered his place by the fire and hid away in Ms. Greene's little office in the middle.

In addition to the bankers Morgan summoned, other members of the financial community came calling of their own accord at the library or his Wall Street offices. One of the first was John D. Rockefeller. Although the two men didn't particularly care for each other, Rockefeller offered to throw $10 million into the rescue fund. Another early visitor was Henry C. Frick, wanting to see how he could help. Frick's chance didn't come until the climactic first weekend in November. After raising and pumping millions of dollars into the system—$40 million into the stock market alone—the Morgan forces thought that the panic was easing off and were beginning to relax when a lawyer named Lewis Cass Ledyard appeared at the library on Friday, November 1, with some of the worse news yet: a prominent brokerage firm, Moore & Schley, would go broke as soon as the market opened on Monday unless they got aid in the neighborhood of $25 million. Morgan didn't have to be told that if Moore & Schley went down, they would take their creditors with them, and on and on in a possibly endless chain reaction.

The problem, according to Ledyard, was that Moore & Schley was stuck with a lot of stock of the Tennessee Coal & Iron Company, which they had used as collateral for loans from banks. In the state of the market, the T. C. & I. stock was virtually worthless and unacceptable to their creditors. To help Moore & Schley, Ledyard's client, Colonel Oliver Payne, had given them good stock in exchange for T. C. & I., but it wasn't enough. He was now in trouble, too. But Ledyard came from Colonel Payne with one of those ideas that Morgan recognized as workable as soon as he heard it. All that had to be done was to persuade U.S. Steel Corp. to buy T. C. & I. by exchanging shares of their good stock for shares of T. C. & I. at its supposed valuation of $100 a share. Since Morgan was considered the creator of U.S. Steel, Payne and Ledyard thought that he could carry out their plan with a snap of the fingers.

But Morgan never worked that way. Once he put someone in charge of an enterprise, he gave them full authority and turned to other things. In any case, U.S. Steel was a publicly owned company controlled by an elected board of directors. The best Morgan could do was to invite Judge Gary and Mr. Frick to a meeting in the library on Saturday morning and pass the Ledyard proposition along to them. It had seemed such a good idea to Morgan that he was surprised when the two men turned him down flat. They had already been approached directly by T. C. & I. and knew from their investigations that acquiring the company, which was located in Alabama despite the name, would be a very bad bargain for U.S. Steel. On

the surface, it would appear to be a steel man's dream of perfection—
a plant right in the middle of inexhaustible fields of coal and iron
ore. But the ore was of poor quality, and it had to be mined instead
of scooped from the surface as in the Mesabi. Although there were
virtually no costs for transporting raw materials, the savings were
more than eaten up by the costs of shipping finished products to
viable markets in the North. Furthermore, the firm had been grossly
mismanaged and wildly financed. One president, for instance, had
kept checks from twenty-seven different banks in the air simultaneously. All in all, T. C. & I. stock wasn't worth more than fifty or
sixty dollars a share even in a good market, according to Gary and
Frick. And wouldn't buying another large steel company open U.S.
Steel to charges of trying to establish a monopoly?

Morgan argued that U.S. Steel's supposedly good stock wouldn't
be worth anything either if Moore & Schley was allowed to fail. "I
do not know whether the United States Steel Corporation can afford
to buy this stock or not," he told Gary and Frick, "but I will say
that, in my opinion, if it does not or unless someone furnishes immediate relief, no man on earth can say what the effect will be on
the financial institutions of the country under these critical conditions."

At this point, Frick said that he would consent to having the steel
company give Moore & Schley an outright loan of $5 million. "Not
enough, not nearly enough," said Morgan, "and there is no time left.
Could you at least call the rest of your finance committee down here
to discuss the matter?"

Gary and Frick agreed to that, and a group of steel men joined
the bankers assembling at the Morgan Library for another weekend
of fund-raising. In addition to the $25 million needed to save Moore
& Schley, another $25 million would be required to keep the doors
of the failing trust companies open, according to Morgan's bank ex-
aminers. By Sunday, November 3, Morgan had three conferences in
progress—representatives of the Clearing House banks in the east
room, representatives of the trust companies in the west room, and
the steel people with him in Ms. Greene's office. Morgan let it be
known that he would arrange for the bail out of Moore & Schley if
the bankers would subscribe the funds for the trust companies. Although he didn't announce the fact, he was determined that not a
man would leave the library until both matters were settled. One
young Morgan associate, thinking his work done, tried to go home

and found that the boss had locked the door and put the key in his pocket. As the gray light of a wet, cold day sank into darkness, the talks went on. Huddled together in shared misery along the sidewalk in front of the brightly lit library, reporters waited to pounce on anyone coming or going for any scrap of news. Monday's dawn would be breaking before they had a chance at a story, and even then they would be bitterly disappointed. Nobody talked, and it would be years before the secret proceedings behind those marble walls were disclosed in Senate hearings on the U.S. Steel Corp. and memoirs of participants.

Having already decided that his own firm would advance the money to Moore & Schley pending purchase by U.S. Steel, Morgan leaned heavily on Gary and Frick to sell the idea to their committee. Overnight his minions had rustled up impressive figures as to the potential of T. C. & I. If properly managed—500 million tons of iron ore, a billion tons of coal, a plant that could make pig iron at two dollars a ton less than competitors. In addition, there was the matter of patriotism. Shouldn't U.S. Steel pay almost any price for T. C. & I. to save the country from disaster? Attorney Ledyard described the breaking point in his Senate testimony:

Mr. Frick came into the room where I was, and he said, "Mr. Ledyard, I want to ask you something. I have known you for years, and I know you very well, and I depend absolutely upon what you say. Have you looked into this situation yourself of Moore & Schley?"

I said, "Mr. Frick, I have looked into it to the extent I have been able. I have not been personally over their books, but I have been over it with their bookkeepers, and I have been over it with Mr. Schley, and I have done what I can to familiarize myself with their affairs and the necessities of their condition."

He said, "Are you of the opinion, from what you have seen and from what information you have gathered—are you frankly of the opinion that nothing less than par will pull these people out and save them?"

I said, "I am, Mr. Frick. I do not think any less than par for the Tennessee stock will pull them out, and I do not know whether that will do it, but I think it will."

He said, "Very good, Mr. Ledyard; if you say so, that is the end of the entire question for me."

It was approximately nine P.M. Sunday night when Frick went back to Morgan and Gary and told them that he was finally persuaded. Gary was still reluctant. He said that he would agree only if he could discuss the matter with the President or the Justice Department. An exasperated Morgan said, "Why? Have they any right to say whether you buy or not?" Gary agreed they didn't, but he didn't want any suits filed against the steel company for making a bad bargain in order to be helpful in a financial crisis. Finally, it was agreed that Frick and Gary would try to see the President and get his reaction before the ten A.M. opening bell of the market the next morning. At ten P.M., Gary located the President's secretary, William Loeb, by phone and was told to come ahead; he could have an appointment first thing in the morning. Frick, a director of the Pennsylvania Railroad, ordered up a one-car special train. Smuggled out a back way to avoid the press, the two steel men climbed into their Pullman in Jersey City at midnight and tried to get some sleep while the car rocked its way along tracks cleared for fast passage.

Back at the library, Morgan lost patience with the trust company people who were still bickering at four A.M. Coming out of Ms. Greene's office trailed by a lawyer with a paper in hand, he went into the west room. He had the lawyer read the paper on which each trust company was listed with the amount it should subscribe to the needed $25 million. Then he put the paper on a table and asked them to step up and sign. When nobody came forward, he put his hand on the shoulder of Edward King, head of the trust company committee, and said, "There's the place, King, and here's a pen." King took the gold pen Morgan handed him, signed, and passed it along to the next man in line. Within a few minutes, it was all over, and Morgan unlocked the doors to let his guests out into the dawn. To Lawyer Ledyard, he said, "You look tired. Go home and get a good night's rest—but be back here at nine o'clock sharp!" Morgan wanted Ledyard on hand to close the Moore & Schley deal when the call came through from Washington.

Gary and Frick went from the train right to the White House, arriving there at eight A.M. Loeb told them that they were first on the President's list, but he would be at breakfast and would meet nobody until ten A.M. Gary hadn't told the secretary the purpose of the meeting, but now he had to confide in him to stress the time element. Loeb departed, and a rather annoyed Roosevelt soon showed up. Since his Attorney General was not available, he sent for Secretary of State Elihu Root, an experienced corporate lawyer, to advise him. Gary and Frick were not completely forthright. Knowing Roosevelt's feelings about Wall Street, they did not name the firm that was in trouble. They did, however, confess to their own doubts about purchasing T. C. & I. and assured the President that its acquisition would bring their control of steel production facilities up to about 60 percent. "You have no legal right to consent to this sale or purchase, but I should think it was a question of policy," Secretary Root advised. Roosevelt agreed and made one of his impulsive decisions; he would not oppose the purchase. Gary went at once to a phone line he had arranged to keep open to Morgan and gave him the good news. It was ten minutes to ten on Monday, November 4, 1907, and it was the real beginning of the end of the panic.

For Theodore Roosevelt, the famed trust buster, it was a political risk, and years later he was still defending himself in his autobiography. He wrote in part:

It was necessary for me to decide on the instant, before the Stock Exchange opened, for the situation in New York was such that any hour might be vital, and failure to act for even an hour might make all subsequent efforts to act utterly useless. From the best information at my disposal, I believe (what was actually the fact) that the addition of the Tennessee Coal and Iron property would only increase the proportion of the Steel Company's holdings by about four percent, making them about sixty-two percent instead of about fifty-eight percent of the total value in the country.... The action was emphatically for the general good. It offered the only chance for arresting the panic, and it did arrest the panic.... But I fully understood and expected that when there was no longer danger, when the fear had been forgotten, attack would be made upon me; and as a matter of fact after a year had elapsed the attack was begun, and has continued at intervals ever since; my ordinary assailant being some politician of rather cheap type.

Frick must have regretted some of his remarks about Roosevelt as he and Gary rode back to New York. As the year of crisis closed, there was an interesting social note in the papers on December 20, 1907, to the effect that Mr. and Mrs. H. C. Frick were "special guests" at a White House dinner.

CHAPTER 18

Life Among the Masterpieces

THE brochure meant to lure paying visitors to The Frick Art &
Historical Center in the Point Breeze section of Pittsburgh claims
that "at Clayton—the Pittsburgh home of industrialist and art collector Henry Clay Frick—the splendor of America's gilded age lives
on." In that an extraordinary amount of time, care, and money has
been devoted to the maintenance and/or restoration of this Victorian
relic, the claim is certainly true. But the emphasis in the literature
and the rote recital of the docent leading a tour is on the hominess
rather than the splendor of the place. It's as if the real purpose of
turning the house into a museum and creating an associated art
gallery is to take the curse off the means by which the splendor was
achieved. It doesn't work. Clayton is a monument to the excesses of
greed and the terrible taste of its prime time, an extraordinary display
of insensitive personal pride.

Clayton exists today because of the passionate and persistent efforts
Frick's adoring daughter, Helen Clay Frick, made to wash the blood
of Homestead from her father's image. For seventeen years, Helen
enjoyed what she recalled as an idyllic childhood at Clayton, and for
the rest of her ninety-six years she used it as a sometime home and
touchstone with her past. By the time of her death in 1984, the other
mansions on what once had been Pittsburgh's millionaires' row had
been dismantled or allowed to sink into decay. Determined that this
would never happen to her "dear old home," Miss Frick created a
foundation that proceeded to devote $5.8 million and four years of
labor by some two hundred artisans to its restoration. The restoration
is uniquely authentic because family possessions down to eyeglasses,
games, toilet articles, and clothes simply stayed put, and there were

detailed records and photographs to serve as guides for any items that had to be refurbished or replaced.

From the outside, Clayton, with its jumble of turrets and dormers and curved corners, looks like a child's stone block creation. Inside, the high-ceilinged rooms are surprisingly small and drearily dark. Walls are wood-paneled or covered with busily patterned fabric; rugs or carpets underfoot are equally busy. The eye reels from trying to take in the often discordant objets d'art resting on every flat surface and the paintings hung museum style against the patterned walls and in every nook and cranny. The detail of special railings installed just below the ceiling moldings testifies to Frick's intent to make of his home a showplace for the art he began to collect the moment he made his first million. Historically, two of the most interesting objects in Clayton are a Tiffany clock and a $265 landscape by a local artist, George Hetzel, that Frick purchased in 1881 for his bachelor apartment in Pittsburgh's Monongahela House. They are the first recorded acquisitions in what would become one of the world's finest private art collections, a prediction that few people who visited Clayton when the Fricks were in residence would have dared to make.

The fact that Clayton could be counterproductive to its purpose became apparent in some of the press reaction when it was first opened to the public almost on the eve of the hundredth anniversary of the deadly Homestead strike. In a column proposing some equal recognition of labor such as preserving part of the abandoned Homestead mill as a park, Mary Pat Flaherty made this insightful comment in the *Pittsburgh Press*:

> There's much hot-tempered history—musty and fresh—tied to labor here that goes a long way toward explaining why Clayton inflames some people. The extreme are vandals who, in the month the Point Breeze home has been open, have scrawled anti-Frick graffiti on a fence and public bathroom.
>
> Clayton, for all its art and archives, remains a showcase of turn-of-the-century life at the top. Down to the woodwork, the mansion drew class distinctions. Two-faced living butted at doors that have burnished mahogany on the side facing the Fricks' rooms, knotty pine on the servants' side.
>
> Coming from a pine-side kind of family, I understand the resentment that generates.

In one sense Clayton does bear out Helen Frick's memories of a family intimacy that may have been unusual for people of their station or for their own subsequent lives in Fifth Avenue palaces and on a Massachusetts estate. Frick's bedroom was just across a small hall from his wife's; Helen's was right next to her mother's; the family sitting room on the second floor contained desks for both parents and toys and games for children; there were high chairs in the breakfast and dining rooms. Behind the knotty pine there were only seven servants awaiting an electronic summons in contrast to a retinue of twenty-five retainers who would accompany them on a later hegira from Eagle Rock for a Christmastime visit to Clayton.

Since Frick left Clayton in large part to protect the more expensive paintings he began to acquire in 1895 from air pollution, it is one of the many ironies associated with his life that the atmosphere surrounding Clayton is now cleaner than that in Manhattan. As at Homestead, where Ms. Flaherty nominated cold blast furnaces as candidates for becoming curiosities in a labor theme park, the smoky mills that gave Frick his millions no longer clank and glow. New York was nevertheless the right place for Frick, who became ever more absorbed by what had started out as a pleasant avocation—art collecting. Then, as still, New York was as much the center of the art market as of securities. Taking a stroll down the avenue between social engagements or board meetings, Frick could browse the galleries or call on dealers like Knoedlers or the Duveens.

By 1908, the crises in the economy, and consequently in the companies in which Frick was invested, calmed down. When portly William Howard Taft, ex-governor of the Philippines, Secretary of War, and Roosevelt's handpicked successor, was elected President, the prospects for a return to normalcy—that is, a government that would let business do what it liked—were bright. Roosevelt announced that he would go on a hunting trip to Africa, and J. P. Morgan used the occasion to express the sentiment of the whole financial community: "I hope the first lion he meets does his duty." For Frick, Taft's ascension meant having friendly golf games with the President, whose "summer White House" was near Eagle Rock. An interesting reflection of the relative status of captains of industry and Presidents of the United States can be seen in the assessment for tax purposes of their properties by the town of Beverly, Massachusetts: $41,175 for Taft; $564,000 for Frick.

Although the very rich were held in respect, and sometimes awe, by the press in those days, reporters seldom overlooked a legitimate opportunity to have some fun with their betters. A contretemps between Frick and his neighbor at Pride's Crossing, Judge William Caleb Loring of the Massachusetts Supreme Court, provided just such an opportunity. The judge declined to let Frick run a pipe across his property to the sea in order to fill Frick's "marble bathing pool," even though Frick said that the doctor had recommended salt water swimming for Mrs. Frick and offered to pay a thousand dollars a foot for the easement. With all this explained, the story in *The New York Times* went on:

> Mr. Frick's million dollar house with paintings said to be worth $3,000,000 has every convenience, but no salt water. Between Mr. Frick and the ocean is a high stone wall—"spite fence" they call it in Beverly—that divides his in shore land from Loring's water front property. From his wide piazza Mr. Frick can hear the waves lapping the Loring sands—in fact, he could throw a stone in the surf and hear it splash, but he can't get any of the water.

This was not the only embarrassing public twitting that Frick had to endure now that he had become a celebrity. There was a memorable headline on a story datelined London that read: FRICK'S $750 UNDERWEAR. The account that followed was quite in line with Frick's reputation as a fastidious dresser. It seemed that a London haberdasher had chosen to display in his window a dozen suits of underwear ordered by the famous Mr. Frick of New York at a total price of $750. This was more than twice the highest price ever paid for underwear at the shop in question and for good reason: "The texture of the garments is heavy woven silk of the sofest, most flexible and glossiest quality manufactured in England. The color is a very light écru. The needlework, binding and button holes are as fine as those of the wedding trousseau of a Princess or the clothes of a royal baby. Each suit consists of only two pieces."

Nobody who kept up with things in those years could have doubted Frick's entitlement to silk underwear. In a *New York Times Sunday Magazine* article in 1910, he was rated as one of the nation's top financiers in an article that said, in part:

Of course, the names of two members of this group would come to your lips if anyone were to ask you if you could guess who comprised the group, and these two are J. Pierpont Morgan and William Rockefeller. But would you guess that the other members of the group are James Stillman, Henry C. Frick, Daniel G. Reed, William H. Moore and George F. Baker. Yet these are the men who constitute a group whose financial power is in excess of the Rothschilds and who have resources at almost instant command that are greater than the national debt of the United States.

Mr. Frick is included in the group for several reasons. First, because he is recognized as one of the greatest constructive business forces the United States ever had. Second, because he is presumed to be the largest owner of the stock of the Pennsylvania Railroad and the Reading Railroad. Third, because he is one of the directors of the U.S. Steel Corp. Fourth, because he is a man of unbounded optimism, having profound faith in the future of his country, and fifth because as an individual he probably possesses as large a measure of capital and credit as any man in the United States, with possibly two exceptions.

Among the avid readers of this kind of story would have been New York's art dealers. Through the next several years, stories of art purchases by Frick began replacing stories about his business activities, often on the front page, and the dealers rejoiced in knowing that Frick's pockets were among the deepest in the land. An early headliner was Frick's purchase of Velázquez's *Philip IV of Spain* for about four hundred thousand dollars, said then to be the highest price ever paid for a masterpiece. But, according to a story attributed to Bernhard Berenson, the famed art appraiser known as B.B., Frick did a little quick calculation in his head when he learned that the king had paid the artist the equivalent of six hundred dollars. At 6 percent interest compounded semiannually, the sum had grown so large between 1645 and 1910 that Frick claimed he had actually bought the painting for nothing.

The gospel of greed was as much of a guide in the art world as the financial world. The raid that America's newly minted millionaires mounted on the artistic treasures of Europe—and to a lesser extent the Orient—has sometimes been likened to Napoleon's sack of Egypt. Some like William Randolph Hearst, the rich heir of a California fortune turned publisher, and J. P. Morgan had an addiction to collecting for collecting's sake as virulent as a craving for drugs. Hearst's wildly eclectic acquisitions overflowed his palace at San Simeon into warehouses where neither he nor anyone else could enjoy them; Morgan stashed the rare manuscripts and first editions he gobbled up in a basement room of his New York home to which he alone held the key. Theorists about the art collecting mania that afflicted—and still afflicts—the very rich have come up with a number of explanations. One is that the commerce from which they extracted their riches was so crass and ethically questionable that they wanted to be associated with uneconomic endeavor and the eternal verities. A more logical and plausible explanation, to which I adhere, is that these men were so imbued with an understanding of the monetary value of everything that they knew a one-of-a-kind valued creation was the best of all investments. Carrying this kind of thinking too far, in my opinion, Stewart H. Holbrook in his study of the moguls, as he called them, concluded that neither Frick, nor his disciple Mellon, really appreciated art.

With respect to Frick certainly, and Mellon probably, Holbrook's surmise is wrong. Frick's interest in "pictures" before he had any money to speak of is well established. It is probable that he had an emotional reaction to visual art as some people do to music or literature. Whether or not it actually did happen, there should have been a eureka moment when Frick realized that his personal enjoyment of art was—or could be—a financial asset as well. Whatever his motivations, Frick approached art collecting with the same clear-headed caution he displayed in business. If it was at all possible, he would "borrow" a work of art and live with it for a while in his own house before agreeing to buy it. He would also insist on authentication by B.B. or some equally qualified expert before plunking down a six-figure payment for a supposed masterpiece. But, again as in business, Frick would not haggle over price once he had satisfied himself as to what he was getting in return.

Frick bought most of his early works through the Knoedler gallery in New York, but he soon became a target of opportunity for the London-based Duveen family. Henry Duveen, brother of the founder, and his aggressive nephew Joseph represented the family in New York and worked mostly with Morgan until Frick began to surface as an even better prospect. The Duveens had a reputation for being able to unearth true treasures for their clients, but the legality and morality of some of their dealings were sometimes questionable. This did not bother the great collectors, who were often the beneficiaries of irregularities in the Duveen bookkeeping and shipping operations.

Duveen clients had an opportunity to prove their loyalty when the great smuggling case broke in 1910. After a disaffected Duveen bookkeeper in New York tipped off U.S. Customs officials to the existence of a double set of books, "Uncle Henry" was arrested on his arrival back from a trip to England and charged with undervaluing imports to the extent of $10 million in the years before antiquities were legally exempt from duty. After lengthy efforts by skillful and expensive lawyers, the sum was whittled down to $1,400,000 plus $10,000 to $15,000 individual fines for four Duveens who agreed to plead guilty. It was at this point according to Joe Duveen's biographer, S. N. Behrman, that J. P. Morgan showed his gratitude for past favors by arranging a loan to cover the settlement with the government. It was shortly after this scandal, which was supposed to have been the ruination of the Duveens, that Joe, who would eventually become head of the house and be knighted, found favor with Frick.

Although Joe started out in life selling furniture for his father's firm, he had long since clothed himself in the manners and dress of an upper-class British businessman or connoisseur. He looked like he belonged among the rich he served, and he understood their thinking. His sales pitch seldom, if ever, concentrated on aesthetics. He stressed the kind of values in his wares that moneymakers could immediately appreciate. He might, for instance, say, "Do you realize that the only thing you can spend a hundred thousand dollars on without incurring an obligation to spend a great deal more for its upkeep is a picture? Once you've bought it, it costs you only a few hundred dollars every fifteen years for cleaning." Or he might argue: "You can always make more money, but if you miss this picture, you'll never get another like it, for it is unique."

Even if Duveen hadn't instinctively shared the value system of his clients, he would have understood it from observation. Frick's calculation as to the cost of the Velázquez was typical. Almost everyone who patronized the dealer occasionally exhibited either guilt or fear of being cheated in expensive deals. When one of the Duveens was visiting the collection of the Philadelphia multimillionaire P.A.B. Widener, he paused in awe before Rembrandt's *Mill,* for which Widener had paid a record hundred thousand pounds. "Yes, I know that I paid too much for this picture," Widener said, "but it has been such an advertisement that everything in my collection has been much increased in value." But paradoxically they would often decline a purchase unless the object was ridiculously expensive. In one instance, Hearst refused the offer of a room for $50,000; when Joe Duveen, testing his sales psychology, proposed purchase of the same room for $200,000, Hearst snapped it up.

In hooking and landing a really rich client, Duveen displayed the sensitivity, patience, and skill of an expert fisherman. Before trying for a strike he would chum the waters, often at great expense and risk to himself, with real bargains of unmistakably high quality. In Frick's case, the clincher was one of the splendors of the Frick Collection in New York, the Fragonard Room. The panels for which this room was specially designed are called *The Progress of Love* and were begun by Jean-Honoré Fragonard as a commission from Madame Du Barry, the mistress of France's King Louis XV. When she rejected the first four, Fragonard installed them in a cousin's house in his home town of Grasse and finished the series with ten more. Acting as agents for J. P. Morgan, the Duveens bought them for Morgan's London home in Prince's Gate. Because of the space available, they had to be folded back and were poorly displayed. Indeed, when King Edward came to the Morgan house for tea (actually iced coffee) and to view the Morgan collection, his only mild criticism had to do with the display of a portrait. "The ceiling is too low in this room for that picture. Why do you hang it here?" the King asked. After his customary period of silence, Morgan finally said, "Because I like it there, sir." Whether Joe Duveen grieved over the waste of the Fragonards or realized instinctively that they were perfect chum for a fish like Frick, he jumped at an offer by the Morgan estate to sell them when the financier died in 1913. The price, $2 million, was a great deal more than Morgan had paid and more than Duveen had ever dared ask Frick to meet. But there was another buyer waiting in the wings, and Duveen decided to gamble his own money and then forego present profit for future riches by offering the panels to Frick at cost. Frick accepted and appreciated the bargain, and a rewarding relationship was established.

The Fragonard deal wasn't the only occasion on which Duveen surprised Frick with his apparently selfless generosity. Before buying any costly work of art, Frick liked to live with it for a while, a desire that the dealers were very willing to accommodate. When Duveen came to call on Frick one morning, he saw two men in the process of carrying a large painting out the door. It was Giovanni Bellini's *St. Francis in Ecstasy,* and it had been sent over by Knoedler's for Frick's inspection. Frick hadn't liked it and had asked that it be removed. Duveen told the men to put the painting down while he had a talk with Mr. Frick. Arguing that he had one of the finest masterpieces of the Venetian Renaissance right there in his house, Duveen told Frick, "You've got to buy it." Frick said, "Very well, but you must get me a letter from Mr. Berenson to that effect." Contacted by Duveen, B.B. was grumpily willing to comply. He was upset only because Frick hadn't approached him directly for an opinion.

B.B. was used to deference from the rich. He was virtually the creation of Mrs. John L. Gardner, of Boston, who plucked him fresh out of Harvard where he was a brilliant art history student and made him her technical adviser on the art she secured for her residence cum museum, which she called Fenway Court. It's likely that Mrs. Gardner's idea of assembling a private collection that could eventually be available to the public was an inspiration to Frick, who was contemplating the same sort of treatment of his Fifth Avenue property at Seventieth Street, but it's more likely, considering his remarkably successful drive to realize youthful dreams, that Frick was motivated by seeing the Wallace collection in Britain on his first trip abroad with Andrew Mellon. In any event, Frick with his lofty plans would have been a godsend to B.B., who needed another patron to allow him to live in luxury in an Italian villa. Although he was known to refer to Frick as "that coke merchant" in the kind of peeve brought on by something like the Bellini incident, he often called him his favorite client. The reason he gave for preferring Frick was not that the man had command of almost unlimited resources but that he had a "beautiful head."

Art had become Frick's consuming interest and major occupation, but life went on in other ways as well. As a result of his studies in Princeton, son Childs had become a hunter of large African mammals with a scientific bent. Those he selectively killed were sent to be stuffed and mounted at Pittsburgh's Carnegie Museum. In 1912, the year that Childs Frick was engaged with the expedition that would lead him to become an honorary curator of mammals at the Carnegie Museum and founder of the Frick Laboratory of Vertebrate

Paleontology at the American Museum of Natural History in New York, congressional hearings on the U.S. Steel Corp. ironically widened the rift between young Frick's father and Carnegie. Responding publicly to testimony by Carnegie that he and Phipps had acted in bad faith in 1899, Frick said:

> These statements, which were false in every particular, were disseminated . . . throughout the country, and, further, were incorporated into the proceedings of the Stanley Committee. The result is that there is now in the public archives a permanent record of charges against Messrs. Frick and Phipps of untruthfulness, chicanery, dishonesty, infidelity to associates, avarice and double-dealing; and these perjured records are backed by the name of a man whose public gifts may hereafter erroneously be supposed to represent his private virtues. This is an intolerable condition and must be relieved.

There was another galling experience for Frick in that year of 1912. His erstwhile leader, Theodore Roosevelt, played Bull Moose to bring down the Republican Party and Frick's golfing partner, Taft. Despite the Princeton connections through Childs, Woodrow Wilson—with what looked like an antibusiness program he called New Freedom—was not a Frick favorite. "President Wilson is admirable personally but not practical enough for the Presidency," he told reporters. In the same interview, he said that the best hope for the country would be a Republican landslide in 1916 that would also give the party control of the Senate. With incredible obtuseness, the man who was creating headlines with his huge payments for paintings condemned extravagance as a threat to the economy and added, "Why take for example the number of automobiles. Fourteen years ago I was the only person in Pittsburgh to get an automobile; now the streets are filled with them." Frick would have been surprised to know that the impractical president also worried about the automobile but for a slightly different reason: He thought that the sight of only the Fricks of the country enjoying them might incite the less privileged classes to riot.

The event of 1913 in the Frick family was the marriage of Childs to Frances Shoemaker Dixon in Old St. Peter's Church in Baltimore. Henry Clay Frick bestowed his blessing on the union in the form of a $12 million settlement on his son. At a postwedding breakfast in the Dixon home, Frick handed the bride a plain envelope containing a check for $2 million. With that kind of start Childs was able to pursue a scholarly career although he did serve for a time in his father's place on the Mellon Bank board. Sister Helen was not neglected. Instead of going off to school as Clay had done, she was tutored at home, and she spent the rest of their lives with her parents. Frick's gifts to his daughter were often in the form of donations for her favorite causes—$500,000, for instance, as a "coming out" party present to buy a plot of ground in Pittsburgh for a park to include a children's playground. In Massachusetts near Eagle Rock, he enabled Helen to establish a summer retreat for working girls on 150 acres called Beverly Farms, which would be, according to the papers, "an Adamless Eden where girls are not allowed to wear 'rats' or 'puff' or unnecessary frills; where flirting and fibbing and gossiping are strictly forbidden."

With Europe plunging into war, Frick kept plunging ever deeper into the international art market. In some respects, he had no other choice. Before anybody knew there would be a war, he had proceeded with construction of his new home, which was completed in 1914 and which by its very nature demanded much more in the way of art and artifacts than he had on hand. Nevertheless, Frick and his family after him were conscious of a possible public backlash from reports of his ever more extravagant self-indulgence while the rest of the world burned. It was particularly ticklish in that most of his acquisitions were coming from a Europe devastated and impoverished by a war that was seemingly without end. An introduction to "Masterpieces of The Frick Collection," which was written by its then director, Harry D. M. Grier, under the supervisory eye of Helen Clay Frick, contains this significant sentence: "In a letter written during the war years, he raised the question whether anyone should at that time invest so much in works of art, but he reasoned that he was justified in doing so because he contemplated leaving his collection as a gift to the public."

That same introduction states that "the role of Joseph Duveen has been exaggerated" in Frick's collecting. Maybe so, but virtually all other sources would indicate otherwise. Duveen is credited with advising Frick on the choice of architects for the house—Carrère and Hastings, who were also architects for the New York Public Library—and with arranging for Sir Charles Allom of White Allom, London, to design the ground-floor interiors. During 1915 to 1916,

Frick went through a frenzy of buying, most of it through Duveen. More than a hundred of a little over two hundred items in the collection at Frick's death were bought in those years. Even Grier concedes that "Duveen's most significant role was in providing some of the furnishings and many objets d'art for this residence, acting as agent for Mr. Frick's purchase of the finest Renaissance bronzes, the Limoges enamels, and the Chinese porcelains from the Morgan collection."

More reflective perhaps of Frick's true regard for Duveen was an incident in the spring of 1913. Frick arrived at the Duveen building at Fifty-sixth Street and Fifth Avenue with two acquaintances in tow. One was easily recognizable to Joe Duveen as Judge Gary, chairman of U.S. Steel, who occasionally bought some art. The other, a younger man, was a stranger, and Frick told Duveen, "This unassuming young man is Andrew Mellon. Some day he will be the greatest collector of us all." It was not only accurate prophecy; making sure that Duveen and his best friend Mellon met each other was a real compliment to the dealer. As he had with Frick, Duveen would go on to aid Mellon in amassing a private collection that would turn into the National Gallery of Art in Washington.

Bringing Duveen into his friend's life may well have been one of Frick's ways of helping Mellon get over the wreck of his marriage. Soon after she tried to settle down in Pittsburgh, Mellon's young and restless bride discovered that he had a mistress far more alluring to a man of his temperament than any woman—money. Business was Mellon's passion, but it bored his wife. When she finally left him, their separation and divorce livened the scandal sheets. At one point, Mellon kidnapped his own children, Ailsa and Paul, as their mother was about to take them aboard a ship and brought them back to Pittsburgh. At another, he tried to ram a special law through the state legislature to keep details of his divorce out of the papers. Now alone again and in need of some form of diversion, Mellon was, as Frick suspected, ready to devote serious time and attention to expanding the very small art collection he had hidden away in the dark halls of his Pittsburgh home.

Being talkative almost to excess was part of Duveen's natural endowment as a supersalesman. This attribute may have been an asset in dealing with such supersilent types as his best clients turned out to be. But he was frequently exasperated by them because he could never tell what they were thinking about any object. It's well Duveen had experience with Morgan and Frick before meeting Mellon. Soon after that first encounter they met again in the Duveen office in Paris. Observing this meeting was Duveen executive Edward Fowles, who wrote: "Joe talked incessantly; Mellon was incommunicative, but observant. Mellon's physical presence was quite unforgettable: tall, thin, with a slight stoop, I always felt that the slightest push would knock him over. In my mind, I can see him standing there to this day: saying nothing, just looking." After that Duveen used to rehearse for talks with Mellon by having his secretary impersonate the banker and try to answer Duveen's questions without saying anything.

Duveen was amply rewarded for suffering silence and periods of uncertainty in his dealings with these men. When they did make a decision, they cheerfully paid the price. Duveen's treasurer particularly enjoyed doing business with Frick. On one occasion he handed Frick an invoice for $7 million. After a quick glance at it, Frick wrote out instructions for his bankers to pay out 50,000 shares of Pennsylvania, 35,000 shares of Atchison, Topeka, and Santa Fe, and $2 million worth of French bonds. It was simply a matter of exchanging one form of Rembrandts for another.

Among the works purchased from Duveen that are now considered showpieces of the collection are panels by François Boucher depicting *The Arts and Sciences,* which were installed in Mrs. Frick's bedroom. Frick's bedroom was adorned with Degas's *Rehearsal,* Manet's *The Bullfight,* El Greco's *Purification,* Carrière's *Motherhood,* and Turner's *Calais Harbor.* Like the clean, rectangular lines of the building's exterior, the rich elegance of the Fricks' bedrooms in their Fifth Avenue mansion stood in sharp contrast to the bedrooms in Clayton which were cluttered with indifferent drawings and family portraits. John Walker, who served a period as director of Mellon's National Gallery wrote of this contrast:

> The two Frick houses, in Pittsburgh and New York, are a remarkable measure of the increase in American sophistication between 1880 and 1914. The earlier house appears to be more original because so much of our Victorian architecture has vanished, but the house on Fifth Avenue has always seemed to me the most beautiful example of domestic architecture and interior decoration produced in the 20th century by our American plutocracy.

Henry Clay Frick had gone a long, long way in the acquisition of both possessions and superior taste in nine short years. Apart from war threatening to involve America and the failure of Republicans to recapture either the White House or the Senate, the living was rich and good for the Fricks and full of promise of more to come as the year 1916 drew to a close.

CHAPTER 19

Getting Rid of It All

IN one of those quick, acerbic asides through which he often revealed himself, Henry Clay Frick asked art dealer Joseph Duveen, "What's the point in Carnegie's giving libraries to all those towns that go busted trying to keep 'em up?" The comment reeks of sour grapes. As Frick's statement about Carnegie's congressional testimony plainly indicated, the reputation the little Scotchman was getting for a form of democratic benevolence galled him. Indeed, Chicago architect Ernest R. Graham, who knew both men, told the business journalist Clarence Barron that "Frick poisoned himself with hatred of Carnegie" to the point of risking illness or death from high blood pressure. In view of this, it is one of the more delicious ironies of these intertwined lives that not only was Childs Frick an honored associate of Carnegie's Pittsburgh museum but that there can be seen on the campus of Princeton University in Princeton, New Jersey, a Lake Carnegie and a Frick Chemical Laboratory.

As in most instances of their rivalry, Carnegie got there first. In carrying out the fund-raising part of his duties as Princeton's president, Woodrow Wilson quite wisely approached the "richest man in America" with high hopes. In addition to building instruments of learning like libraries, Carnegie was endowing institutions for peace, a cause dear to Wilson's heart then and later as President of the United States and a proponent of the League of Nations. It was reasonable to suppose that a grade school dropout with no known college affiliation would be open to—possibly even flattered by—an opportunity to participate in enhancing the educational program of a prestigious university like Princeton. Except for the fact that he had been a coach at one point in his career, Wilson had to have been disappointed when all Carnegie wanted to talk about was athletics. Carnegie deplored football (the sport Wilson had coached) because of its violence and thought that rowing would be a better and more appropriate sport for young scholars; he would be delighted to underwrite creating an artificial lake for this purpose. College presidents don't turn down money for any respectable activity, and for generations of Princeton students Carnegie's unusual vision has provided an enjoyable outlook and outlet.

Mindful no doubt of Childs Frick's good record as an undergraduate and uninhibited by evident political bias, Wilson's successor as Princeton's president, John Grier Hibben, had no qualms about going after one of the heaviest-handed contributors to the Republican Party in the nation. Hibben softened the sell by arranging to have Frick, whose academic credentials were only a hair above those of Carnegie, made a life trustee of the university in 1915. Within a year, the news was out that Frick had given an organ for Procter Hall at the Graduate School in Princeton along with an endowment for maintenance and pay for an organist. Almost as quixotic as Carnegie's gift of a lake, the organ represented another strange affinity between the two men. Carnegie for years had been giving organs to churches, and the organ in Skibo was one of his great sources of pleasure. In the new house on Fifth Avenue, Frick installed a three-hundred-year-old, hundred-thousand-dollar organ imported from France on the landing leading to the second floor. This led to a rather demeaning and oft-repeated word picture of Frick that appeared in its most polished form in Behrman's biography of Joe Duveen:

> It was Frick's custom to have an organist in on Saturday afternoons to fill the gallery of his mansion at Seventieth Street and Fifth Avenue with the majestic strains of "The Rosary" and "Silver Threads Among the Gold" while he himself sat on a Renaissance throne, under a baldachino, and every now and then looked up from his *Saturday Evening Post* to contemplate the works of Van Dyck and Rembrandt, or, when he was enthroned in their special atelier, the more frolicsome improvisations of Fragonard and Boucher. Surely Frick must have felt, as he sat there, that only time separated him from Lorenzo and the other Medicis.

It may have been a feeling that he had arrived at a position in life requiring a certain lordly largesse that accounted for an increase in Frick philanthropies in those years of artistic acquisition. From all indications, Princeton began courting him at exactly the right time, although it would take a few more years before the university's efforts proved really rewarding. There were earlier gifts, of course, such as those he arranged on his daughter's behalf and a few that remained only rumored or unsung. He often insisted on anonymity. In one case, he promised a group of women $5,000 for their cause, a considerable amount in the days when money used to matter, but he asked them not to use his name. When they returned to pick up his check, Frick asked to see the list of donors. Finding his name near the top, he scratched it off, tore up his check, and let them know in no uncertain terms that they could never expect a dime from him since they hadn't kept their part of the agreement.

The man who had his dead daughter's picture imprinted on his checks and her bust on display in his house was more susceptible to appeals on behalf of children than any other cause. This provoked an incident that illuminated his Janus-like nature. One of the men who was not rehired after the Homestead strike managed to get in to see Frick and plead his case. Since the man had been an enthusiastic participant in the strike, Frick said that rehiring him was impossible; it would make a mockery of all of his efforts to reorganize the company on a nonunion basis.

"But I don't want a job for me," the man said. "I need the money to educate my daughters."

"Well, that's a very different matter," Frick said. "Why didn't you say so before? I know what it is to have a little girl and want to take care of her. How many girls have you?"

"Two."

"All right, you select the best school you can find and send them there for the full four-year course and send the bills to me," Frick said.

As the man was mumbling his thanks, Frick came up with a new thought: "And by the way, I know it costs money to get them ready to go, and to keep them there, so here, just take this and buy them something to wear."

As the story goes, Frick then handed the astonished man two hundred-dollar bills. It may be that Dickens invented a more powerful story of the insensitivity of the very rich, but it is doubtful.

Unhappily, nobody followed up on this account of Frick as "a quiet philanthropist," which was given out to the Pittsburgh press when Frick's substantial support of Roosevelt in 1904 was aired. If the worker's daughters ever did go to school and sent the bills to Frick, they went with empty stomachs since Frick sent their father away without a job and shorn of self-respect.

In the light of stories like this, it is hard to credit the unsubstantiated claims that much of Frick's philanthropy was concealed by becoming modesty. The fact is that he never seems to have minded the use of his name on buildings, parks, museums, and other highly visible creations and bequests. It's much more likely that he simply didn't want to create the impression that he was a soft touch, which clearly would have been a false impression. But there was no effort to conceal even his gifts on behalf of children as they grew more imaginative and sophisticated. One that is still functioning effectively today to the benefit of young people is the Henry C. Frick Educational Commission, which enriches the education of teachers through scholarships, lectures, workshops, and the like. The concept for this, according to daughter Helen, was a lunch at Eagle Rock with "a very interesting Russian doctor by the name of Gorodiche." As a proponent of the modesty theory, Miss Frick claimed that it took seven years to persuade her father to lend his name to the program.

The most imaginative and memorable Frick gift—a gift that would echo down through the years and do more than anything else to soften his image—was bestowed during the Christmas season of 1915. Although its formal name was the Pittsburgh Bank for Savings, the solid-looking structure at Fourth and Smithfield streets was informally known as the Dime Savings Bank. It acquired the nickname by accepting as little as a dime, ten cents, to open an account. The bank pushed this small change business aggressively by sending representatives into the schools to persuade children to acquire the habit of saving. In 1915, some forty thousand children had accounts in the Dime Savings Bank, ranging from less than five dollars to a little over a hundred. The children's savings were only a small fraction of the $10 million on deposit when the bank's doors failed to open on December 22, but each account loomed large to each child, and losing it was worse than finding coal in the stocking hung by the hearth for Santa Claus to fill.

When word of the bank failure reached Frick in New York on Christmas Eve, he wired H. C. McEldowney, president of the Union

Trust Co.: "Arrange at once to pay all school accounts in Pittsburgh Bank for Savings, in full, so that the children shall not be deprived of their Christmas funds. Charge to my account." The gesture cost Frick $170,000, but the return on this investment is incalculable. Writing in the *Pittsburgh Press* thirty-seven years later, George Swetnam reported:

> The biggest surprise of all was that the man who played Santa Claus should be Henry Clay Frick. It wouldn't have been too much of a surprise to Pittsburghers if it had been Andrew Carnegie, or Henry C. Phipps, or some of the others who were likely to give something away at any time. But, though many respected Frick, few loved or understood him. Laboring people had hated him cordially ever since the trouble at Homestead. . . . People in general looked on the sixty-six-year-old Frick as an old curmudgeon, with a hunk of iron for a heart, even though several years before he had endowed an educational commission to study school problems in Pittsburgh. . . .
>
> It wasn't the amount that moved Pittsburgh almost to tears. Perhaps in part it was pride in the discovery that another of the city's "iron men" was human, after all. . . . At Trinity Cathedral the crowd almost applauded when Rev. E. D. Travers, speaking on "The Surprise of Christmas," said: "Only those close to the children know the heartache they were enduring. Mr. Frick has done exactly what Christ would have done."

The hardheaded approach that Frick more commonly took toward giving was demonstrated in 1916 when he was first approached by Princeton to fund the building of a chemical laboratory. Frick agreed to underwrite the project until the estimates came in at more than a million dollars. Because he felt that the estimates were based on inflated steel prices, Frick backed off and suggested that construction be postponed until these prices came down. Still a powerful insider at U.S. Steel, Frick knew more than most people how the demands for munitions to feed the continuing war in Europe had artificially raised both prices and profits for industries like steel. After the United States entered the war, this inflation would become so great that Bernard Baruch, chairman of the War Industries Board, would approach Frick personally and plead for him to use his influence to hold steel profits down.

Unhappily for the proponents of peace, war has always been a friend to moneymakers with their consequent political power. In his memoirs, Judge Mellon nearly wrote a hymn to the Civil War:

> It was such a period as seldom occurs, and hardly ever more than once in any one's lifetime. The period between 1863 and 1873 was one in which it was easy to grow rich. There was a steady increase in the value of property and commodities, and an active market all the time. One had only to buy anything and wait, to sell at a profit: sometimes, as in real estate for instance, at a very large profit in a short time.

It will be remembered that making armor plate carried the Carnegie Company through the Homestead strike and the hard times of 1893, and the increased demand during the Spanish-American War contributed to the enormous profit figures that induced Morgan to meet Carnegie's selling price. While noting the high return in profits as a reason for businessmen to find war less than horrible, Thorstein Veblen saw less obvious rewards for business in advocating a military posture in times of so-called peace as well as outright war:

> Business interests urge an aggressive national policy and business men direct it. Such a policy is warlike as well as patriotic. The direct cultural value of a warlike business policy is unequivocal. It makes for a conservative animus on the part of the populace. During war time, and within the military organization at all times, under martial law, civil rights are in abeyance; and the more warfare and armament the more abeyance. Military training is a training in ceremonial precedence, arbitrary command, and unquestioning obedience. A military organization is essentially a servile organization. Insubordination is the deadly sin. The more consistent and the more comprehensive this military training, the more effectually will the members of the community be trained into habits of subordination and away from that growing propensity to make light of personal authority that is the chief infirmity of democracy. This applies first and most decidedly, of course,

to the soldiery, but it applies only in a less degree to the rest of the population. They learn to think in warlike terms of rank, authority, and subordination, and so grow progressively more patient of encroachments upon their civil rights. Witness the change that has latterly been going on in the temper of the German people.

The modern warlike policies are entered upon for the sake of peace, with a view to the orderly pursuit of business. In their initial motive they differ from the warlike dynastic politics of the sixteenth, seventeenth and eighteenth centuries. But the disciplinary effects of warlike pursuits and of warlike preoccupations are much the same whatever may be their initial motive or ulterior aim. The end sought in the one case was warlike mastery and high repute in the matter of ceremonial precedence; in the other, the modern case, it is pecuniary mastery and high repute in the matter of commercial solvency. But in both cases alike the pomp and circumstance of war and armaments, and the sensational appeals to patriotic pride and animosity made by victories, defeats, or comparisons of military and naval strength, act to rehabilitate lost ideals and weakened convictions of the chauvinistic or dynastic order. At the same stroke they direct the popular interest to other, nobler, institutionally less hazardous matters than the unequal distribution of wealth or of creature comforts.

It's hard to believe that Veblen was commenting on the Republican age of McKinley-Roosevelt-Taft instead of the Reagan-Bush era of Star Wars and military adventures, but he was. As the French say, the more things change the more they remain the same. Both a military posture and a wide separation between the rich and the poor are characteristics of ages of greed. Woodrow Wilson, Frick's "impractical" professor in the White House, stood for doing something to change both of these characteristics of society. Indeed, he was reelected in a squeaker on the grounds that "he kept us out of war." Frick, still a Republican bankroller, was a loser in more ways than one in that election. Wilson's opponent, Charles Evans Hughes, was the man whose investigation vindicated Frick's own exposé of the Equitable Life scandal. It is another of the strange and sad ironies of history that Wilson, the apostle of peace, had thrust upon him the task of leading America into the first great World War. Dealing with war and its aftermath necessarily took precedence over the pursuit of social reform, just as Veblen surmised.

When America entered the war, the Frick family displayed commendable patriotism. Helen signed on for the Red Cross and Childs for the budding air service, while Frick himself bought war bonds as if they were railroad stocks. On September 30, 1918, he telegraphed the same McEldowney who played Santa's helper in 1915 to buy $1.5 million worth of Fourth Liberty Loan bonds. It was reported that the order was placed in Pittsburgh as a gesture of gratitude for the place where he got his start. Lest New York feel slighted, he took another million of Fourth Liberty Loan bonds in his new home city. On orders from the Railroad War Board, Frick dismantled his private car, *Westmoreland*.

One sacrifice Frick wasn't willing to make for war was to give up acquiring works of art. According to Behrman, Joe Duveen dined at Frick's home at least once a week when he was in New York. On these occasions, they would discuss in detail the refinements needed to perfect the Frick collection. Gazing at the silverware one evening, Duveen expressed the opinion that it was not of a comparable quality to other things in the house, and he proposed replacing it with pieces crafted by Paul de Lamerie, an eighteenth-century English silversmith, all of whose work was of museum quality. Although it would be difficult, Duveen was willing to undertake the expensive and time-consuming mission of assembling a De Lamerie service. "After some years, he succeeded in making it possible for Frick to invite him to dinner with a feeling of perfect security," Behrman reported.

Nothing, it seems, was beyond Duveen's capacity when it came to pleasing a client like Frick, including trading with the enemy. This bit of interesting intrigue was described by Duveen executive Edward Fowles, who wrote in *Memories of Duveen Brothers:*

> Joe was involved in the negotiations for the purchase by Frick of Vermeer's wonderful portrait of *A Lady with Her Maid* from the collection of James Simon of Berlin, a business which occupied a great deal of time and ingenuity.... Looking at the archives, I was perplexed at first because I could find no trace of the affair in the accounts. I later decided to search through the correspondence files, and found there a "license to trade with the enemy" (dated 25 March 1919)

granted to Scott and Fowles of New York, and a copy of a letter from Joe to Frick in which he explained that negotiations had arrived at the point where no further progress could be made until money for the purchase of the painting had been deposited in a bank at the Hague. Joe stipulated that it should be understood that he, Duveen, was not purchasing the painting nor making any profit on it. He asked Frick, therefore, to confirm that he personally was buying the picture, and to instruct Guaranty Trust Company to deposit the necessary funds with their correspondent at the Hague. Another letter followed in a few days in which Frick pointed out that he held Duveen responsible for the quality and authenticity of the painting. On 20 May 1919, the Guaranty Trust Company reported that the picture had arrived in Holland. Duveen sent Walter Dowdeswell to the Hague to examine the painting on 27 May. On 18 June the necessary funds were paid, and Duveen's representative took delivery.

When I looked up the reference to the picture in the splendid catalogue of the Frick paintings, I noticed that the entry did not mention Scott & Fowles—nor, indeed, Duveen's activities in the negotiations. The house of Knoedler, however, is mentioned: it was probably they who finally hung the picture in the Frick Gallery.

Buying pictures wasn't Frick's only preoccupation in 1919. He was involved in another form of intrigue with what some would still consider disastrous results for the nation and the world. Condemned to fight a war, President Wilson was determined to turn it into a foundation for peace by creating the League of Nations. But a small group of senators under the leadership of Republican Henry Cabot Lodge, known as the Irreconcilables, were equally determined to have the Senate reject the treaty calling for American participation in the League. While the President stumped the country to get public support for the treaty, bringing about his fatal illness in the process, the Irreconcilables mounted a countercampaign. For this, they were in need of money, and one of their number, Senator Philander Knox, suggested that it could come from the deep pockets of Henry Clay Frick and Andrew Mellon, who often acted in concert on political matters.

Knox undertook to put the touch on Mellon himself, but the job of selling Frick on the project went to Colonel George Harvey, a maverick journalist and political figure who would eventually become Frick's biographer. Born in 1864 and named George Brinton McClellan Harvey for the Civil War general, Harvey made his way up through journalism to become managing editor of Joseph Pulitzer's *World*. In that process he was involved in politics. He was appointed a colonel on the New Jersey governor's staff, a title that he used for the rest of his life, and was such an active supporter of Cleveland in 1892 that he was offered the post of consul general in Berlin. Declining, he took a brief leave from journalism to capitalize on a friendship with William C. Whitney and make a modest fortune in public utilities and Wall Street. With this, he purchased the *North American Review* in 1899, and did so well with it that J. P. Morgan, principal creditor of a financially embarrassed Harper & Brothers, asked him to take over as president of that company. Thus he found himself editing both the *Review* and *Harper's Weekly*. Still interested in New Jersey politics, Harvey spotted Princeton professor Woodrow Wilson as a potential president as early as 1901 and supported him through the governership and up to the brink of his nomination. When people in the Wilson camp concluded that Harvey with his Wall Street connections was an embarrassment, both Morgan and Wilson agreed for obviously different reasons, and the subsequent break between the two men drove Harvey into collaboration with the anti-Wilson, anti-Democrat forces. Leaving his Harper posts in 1915, he opposed Wilson in 1916 and started *Harvey's Weekly* with Morgan financial backing to criticize Wilson's conduct of the war and his program for peace. (An early supporter of Republican Warren G. Harding, running on an anti-League platform in 1920 against Cox and Franklin Roosevelt's pro-League stance, Harvey was rewarded with an appointment as ambassador to Great Britain. Of that appointment one of Clarence Barron's informants said that the millionaires supporting Harvey's magazine to the tune of $100,000 a year found it cheaper to have him made an ambassador.)

Such in any case was the senators' emissary who persuaded Frick to put a goodly sum into scuttling the League, which, with American participation, might have prevented World War II. As anticipated, Knox had no trouble in getting Mellon to match his friend's gift. Commenting on this later, Harvey said:

It is an interesting fact, not generally known, that the only two multi-millionaires who supported quietly, but effectively, the successful organized effort to prevent inclusion of the United States in the League of Nations were Messrs. Henry Clay Frick and Andrew Mellon. . . . The desired reservoir had been found and it was both deep and full. All anxiety respecting sinews of war was dispelled. Rejoicing pervaded the camp of the Irreconcilables, efforts were redoubled all along the line and the redoubtable little band pushed on to victory. . . .

One wonders what Andrew Carnegie, who had built a Peace Palace at The Hague and put $10 million into an Endowment for International Peace, would have thought of his former lieutenant's activity had he been aware of it or in any condition to care. Carnegie died at the age of eighty-three that summer in the Massachusetts place he had acquired when wartime travel to Scotland became too difficult. Frick was not among the mourners.

Birth rather than death was on Frick's mind that year. He had already been given two granddaughters by Childs and his wife, and there was an apparent heir on the way. In March, Frick arranged to buy a $550,000, two-hundred-acre estate at Roslyn, Long Island, that had once belonged to William Cullen Bryant to house the growing family. In October a boy to be christened Henry Clay Frick II arrived. A month after that blessed event, the Senate rejected ratification of the Treaty of Versailles, owing in large part to Frick's silent hand in the matter. Despite a bout of ptomaine poisoning on Election Day from which he was having difficulty in recovering, Frick could consider his seventieth year as one of personal pleasure and triumph.

That there would be no ending to that year for Frick was foreshadowed when $2 million worth of paintings he was holding for approval were delivered to Joe Duveen's door late in November. The explanation was that the state of Frick's health would prevent him from arranging financing. It was a total shock to Duveen, whose own financing was predicated on Frick's finally buying those works. Even though giving up on acquiring art was an ominous sign, Frick's family was even more shocked than Duveen when he died suddenly on December 2, seventeen days before his birthday.

Harvey claimed that Frick's death was brought on by risking a journey to Long Island in inclement weather to see his infant namesake. In view of the physical courage and stubbornness he displayed at Homestead, it's believable that he did make this trip. But there is no mention of it in the rather full account of his death in the press. His physician, Dr. Lewis A. Comer, was as surprised by it as anyone. "Mr. Frick for the last month has shown symptoms of an organic affection of the heart, which presumably was the late result of severe attacks of inflammatory rheumatism to which he was subject in earlier life. He died suddenly in the midst of what seemed to be satisfactory improvement in his condition," Dr. Comer told *The New York Times*. In fact, Frick sat up in bed on Monday afternoon, December 1, awoke at five A.M. on Tuesday, rang for his butler, and asked for water. After taking a drink, he said, "I can go to sleep now," closed his eyes and died.

Among those most interested in the news of Frick's death were Emma Goldman and Alexander Berkman, her beloved Sasha. They were awaiting deportation on charges of conspiracy to defeat the draft. In an often quoted version of their reaction, Harvey had Berkman say, "Well, anyhow, he left the country before I did," adding that Berkman and Goldman were deported at a later hour of that same day, December 2, 1919. It made a neat wrap-up to Harvey's account of the assassination attempt, but it creates doubts about other aspects of Harvey's worshipful book. Granted that it is a self-serving platform for propaganda, Goldman's own version rings truer:

> During the farewell dinner given us by our friends in Chicago, on December 2, reporters dashed in with the news of Henry Clay Frick's death. We had not heard of it before, but the newspapermen suspected that the banquet was to celebrate the event. "Mr. Frick has just died," a blustering young reporter addressed Sasha. "What have you got to say?" "Deported by God," Sasha answered dryly. I added that Mr. Frick has collected his debt in full from Alexander Berkman, but he had died without making good his own obligations. "What do you mean?" the reporters demanded. "Just this: Henry Clay Frick was a man of the passing hour. Neither in life nor in death would he have been remembered long. It was Alexander Berkman who made him known, and Frick will live only in connexion with Berkman's name. His entire fortune could not pay for such glory."

The next morning brought a telegram from Harry Wein-

berger informing us that the Federal Department of Labor
had ordered our deportation, and that we must surrender on
December 5.

Frick received better treatment from the press, as in this *New York
Times* editorial on December 3:

> Mr. Frick belonged to a race of creators of industry and
> graspers of industrial opportunity, playing the game as fairly
> as they understood it and as it was played in their time. He
> was one of the founders of the mighty fortunes of which, in
> one form or another, the public is the residuary legatee....
> The very rich are so for others, not for themselves. They have
> but a life tenancy.

On that same day, there was an invitation-only service at five-
thirty P.M. at the Frick residence in New York. It was conducted by
Dr. Leighton Parks, of St. Bartholomew's Church, and the honorary
pallbearers included Judge Gary, U.S. Steel president James Farrel,
Princeton president Dr. John Grier Hibben, Morgan banker George
F. Baker, and Colonel George Harvey. At eleven-thirty that night
the body was put aboard Frick's reactivated private car for an over-
night rail journey to Pittsburgh. There Frick's brother-in-law, Asa
P. Childs, and the Union Trust Company were planning to open
Clayton for a two-hour viewing, but the plans were vetoed by Frick's
son, Childs. Instead, there was another brief service conducted at
Clayton by the Reverend Van Etten, rector of Calvary Episcopal
Church, who read the prayer book service for the dead. A Mrs.
Christine Miller Clemson sang "Lead Kindly Light," and the body
was transported to nearby Homewood Cemetery for burial. Honorary pallbearers in Pittsburgh included Senator Philander C. Knox,
Andrew and R. B. Mellon, and McEldowney, the banker Frick had
once thought too young for his job. Reporting that thousands were
disappointed at not being able to attend the viewing, the press added
sourly, "The same secrecy is being manifested over the will."

If there was an effort at secrecy, it was a spectacular failure. The
Frick will was destined to make headlines for five years. The most
notable news when the first appraisal was released seven months later
was the small amount of U.S. Steel stock in the steel king's portfolio—only 2,101 shares, valued at $214,605.94. He had stuck to his

"Rembrandts" with some 300,000 shares in a dozen railroads. There were bequests of $25 million to the family and the anticipated gift of his New York home and art collection (after Mrs. Frick's life tenure) to the public with a $15 million fund for maintenance. The total of his personal wealth, excluding real estate, was put at $77.5 million. Public interest centered on the "residual" estate—that is, the amount left over after fixed bequests that was designated for charities. Cannily, Frick stipulated that inheritance taxes be paid out of the residual, which would then be divided into equal shares, as follows:

> 10 to the Educational Fund Commission of Pittsburgh
> 1 each to Children's Hospital, Allegheny General Hospital, Home for the Friendless, and Kingsly House Association in Pittsburgh
> 10 to Mercy Hospital (the institution that sent an ambulance to take him home after Berkman's attack)
> 1 each to Pittsburgh Free Dispensary, Pittsburgh Newsboys Home, Western Pennsylvania Hospital, Central YWCA, Uniontown Hospital, Cottage State Hospital, Westmoreland Hospital, Mt. Pleasant Memorial Hospital, Braddock General Hospital, Homestead Hospital
> 30 to Princeton University
> 10 to Harvard University
> 10 to Massachusetts Institute of Technology
> 3 to Society of the Lying-in Hospital in New York
> 13 to Helen Clay Frick for her charities

It's often said that you can't take it with you, but the story of Frick's will is that you can't leave it all, either. The best case in point for this proposition is the Princeton gift, which was calculated at $15 million as soon as the terms of the will became known. Much as he appreciated it, President Hibben was faced with a problem. He was in the midst of a fund drive to raise almost that amount from alumni. In an impassioned speech to alumni in New York on December 15, he said that a Chicago alumnus had suggested that the Frick gift took the heart out of the campaign and insisted that, instead, "it puts the heart into it." With foresight, Hibben argued that the amount might not be that generous when the dust settled. He was right.

What with taxes and a postwar shrinkage in the value of securities, the Frick bequest was only $6 million. In his year-end report for 1920, Hibben wrote, "We set out to raise $14,000,000 and we have so far reached only $8,262,682. Even with the Frick bequest of $6,000,000, the total sum will amount to very little over the $14,000,000." Other recipients of residual shares suffered equally. Princeton at least showed its gratitude by naming the chemical laboratory built in 1929 after him in recognition of his early interest and subsequent gift even though his money had by then been spent on the endowment of faculty salaries. The building did not, of course, go down in price as Frick had assumed but came in at $1,840,000. Frick's interest in Princeton had another result that might have pleased him more. Following in his son's footsteps, his grandson and namesake attended the college, as did his grandson-in-law, J. Fife Symington, Jr.

One revelation from the will was that the spirit of a young man who didn't hesitate to borrow from every conceivable source to work his will was still alive in the elderly man of substance. Frick's outstanding obligations amounted to more than $5 million, about 6 percent of the estate. As listed, they were: $19,000 to the sculptor of a statue of Joseph Choate; $575,000 on the Roslyn property; $1.5 million to Duveen Brothers; $686,101 to C. D. Barney & Co., brokerage; $1.25 million on a First National Bank note of July 27, 1919; $1 million on a First National Bank agreement of October 20, 1919; and $130,150 to Tiffany & Co. for a pearl and diamond clasp. The lesson Frick learned early on in life was that the secret to making money of his own was using other people's money, and he never forgot it.

In another way, too, Frick never changed. He died a dandy, as an inventory of his wardrobe, appraised at five-hundred dollars, showed: seven business suits; two cutaway suits; three golf suits; two suits of evening clothes; two tuxedo suits; two riding suits; three overcoats; nine dozen outing, soft, and dress shirts; three dozen suits of underwear; twelve pairs of shoes; three dozen linen nightshirts; eight dozen handkerchiefs; three dozen socks; two silk hats, one soft hat, and one derby. If the appraisal seems low, it must be kept in mind that these articles were "previously owned," a condition that does more damage to the price of clothing than of hardware like, say, a Rolls-Royce, which Frick also left and can still be seen in the carriage house of his Pittsburgh home.

A block from that carriage house is Frick's final destination, a 4,200-square-foot family plot in Homewood Cemetery. The site is dominated by a forty-seven-ton monument of Westerly pink granite that was designed to Frick's orders in 1892 by Daniel Burnham, architect of the Frick Building. Frick wanted a suitable marker for the graves of his two young children, something that could be easily seen from the windows of their nearby home. When it came time for Frick's own burial, his casket was lowered into a copper-lined vault encased in more than a foot and a half of concrete, an unusual method of burial devised to protect his remains from vandals seeking revenge for Homestead. So far they are physically undisturbed, but there has been no safe resting place for the pecuniary animus that once enlivened those remains.

EPILOGUE

Rewriting History

IT is evident from both their actions and their silences that Frick's family and friends were concerned about his place in history. Although they might not have been aware of Emma Goldman's boastful prediction that her Sasha's *Attentat* would rescue him from obscurity, they were certainly conscious of the fact that Homestead was the central drama of his life. However admired by his peers in business, Frick's stand had made his name anathema to working men and their sympathetic supporters the world over. Frick's only other dramatic act—filing suit against Carnegie—was, however justified, a little like suing Santa Claus in the public eye, for the white-bearded, jolly little Scot had by then scattered organs and libraries far and wide. True, there was all that art in New York that he had willed to the public, but nobody could get in to see it until Mrs. Frick died, and by then it might prove to be a disappointment like the grand gifts to Princeton and other institutions.

In view of this concern, it's not surprising that one of the few people in the publishing world who also moved in Frick's circles—Colonel Harvey—showed up as a guest at Clayton in Pittsburgh in the fall of 1926. Cornered by reporters, Colonel Harvey said, "As Mr. Frick and I were very warm friends, the family has asked me to write a volume about him. During my stay in Pittsburgh, I have had conferences with many persons who knew Mr. Frick intimately. I have gathered a large amount of data concerning him and will write the book as soon as possible. It will not be a biography."

Published in early 1928 shortly after Harvey's own death, the book must have been pleasing to its sponsors. "Writing as a friend of many years and with personal remembrance of the incidents, Colonel Harvey pictures the steel man as a man of steel, yet a kindly, just and far-sighted business man," one reviewer reported. There's no evidence that the book had a wide circulation or a long life. But in 1936 it was reprinted privately, presumably to satisfy curiosity about the man behind the dazzling Frick Collection, which had finally been opened to the public the year before.

However he fared in literature, Frick lived on unseen but possessed of real power in the person of his friend and disciple, Andrew Mellon. Every one of the many biographers of Mellon, including family members, stresses the Frick influence in all aspects of Mellon's life and thinking. It is most apparent, of course, in the Mellon art collection that became the National Gallery of Art in Washington. Less obvious but no less important is the hidden Frick hand behind the policies that Mellon pursued in his long service as Secretary of the Treasury for three Presidents. The close and profitable association between Frick and Mellon in matters of both business and politics over a period of nearly forty years leaves no doubt about the fact that Mellon used his position to implement their joint beliefs.

There is a delicious irony in the fact that a shy and silent Mellon first tried to dodge public service by using his involvement with Frick's Old Overholt distillery as an excuse. Proposed for the Treasury post by Senator Knox, Mellon went out to Marion, Ohio, to tell President-elect Harding that he was not qualified for the post. Reporting the occasion in a memorandum of the visit, Mellon wrote:

> I told him that I did not wish to accept the appointment and felt that I would be a handicap to him by reason of my business and industrial connections, and particularly by my ownership of some stock in the Overholt distillery. Senator Harding waved all that aside, saying that he owned some stock in a brewery himself, that it was perfectly legal to do so, and that he would not take any such excuse from me for not accepting the Treasury post.

It was a feeble excuse in any case since Mellon's nephew claimed that Andrew had already disposed of the Overholt stock he bought for $25,000 for $675,000 years before Prohibition became the law of the land. But a large stock of the product itself remained in Mellon's possession, as did a fine wine cellar. Just as Harding poured whisky at his poker games in the living quarters of the White House, Mellon continued to enjoy wine with his meals despite being the chief enforcer of Prohibition as Secretary of the Treasury. In that era particularly, inconvenient laws were seldom observed by the very rich and the very powerful. The tone for their approach to the law was set for his peers by J. P. Morgan when a lawyer once told him that a plan he wanted to put into motion was illegal. "That is not what I asked you," Morgan said. "I asked you to tell me how it *could* be done legally. Come back tomorrow or the next day and tell me how it can be done." And, of course, a way was found.

Once all of his excuses had been discounted or disposed of by his supporters, Mellon reluctantly went to Washington. There, despite his quiet demeanor, he became the most powerful figure in the cabinets of Harding, Coolidge, and Hoover in succession. With his economic policies given credit for the boom times of the twenties, Mellon was even considered a rival of Hoover, the Secretary of Commerce, for the Presidency in 1928. Basically, what Mellon advocated without coming up with the words for it was "trickle down economics." Most of his efforts went into reducing taxes on the rich that the Democrats had imposed to pay for the war. Although always under fire from liberals in both parties, Mellon's efforts climaxed in the Revenue Act of 1928, which reduced taxes more than $220 million and cut the corporation income tax from 13.5 percent to 12 percent. In 1929, he doled out tax refunds to corporations, including many Mellon organizations. His old friend Frick's U.S. Steel alone got $15 million. Mellon made the rich significantly richer, and a good deal of this wealth went into the speculation that drove the stock market to new heights until it fell over the cliff in 1929, bringing on the Great Depression.

Unlike a similar result from trickle down economics sixty years later, there was no social legislation in place to provide a safety net under freewheeling capitalism. Hoover and Mellon tried to stem the panic by issuing bland statements like Hoover's claim in 1932 that prosperity was "just around the corner." By then Mellon was taking such heavy blame for his policies that Hoover shipped him off to London as the U.S. Ambassador to the Court of St. James's and installed a new secretary. Even with fifty million Americans in want and the banking structure collapsing, Mellon's belief in his economic policies was not shaken. Like his father before him, his friend Frick, his fellow capitalists Carnegie and Rockefeller, Mellon had found that depressions were actually beneficial to the possessors of money, who could pick up bargains and come out of them richer than ever. The thing to do was to sit tight and wait them out; the danger was to use them as an excuse to fool with the system. In an address to the International Chamber of Commerce, the ambassador said, in part:

> I do not believe in any quick or spectacular remedies for the ills from which the world is suffering, nor do I share the belief that there is anything fundamentally wrong with the social system under which we have achieved in this, and other industrialized countries, a degree of economic well-being un-precedented in the history of the world. . . . We shall succeed in time in working out our economic salvation. . . . But it will be done in the future as in the past by individual initiative, and not by the surrendering of business and industry to the Government or to any board or group of men temporarily entrusted with overhead authority. Conditions today are nei-ther so critical nor so unprecedented as to justify a lack of faith in our capacity for dealing with them in our accustomed way.

Given the opportunity, Frick would have said the same thing though in fewer words, as in 1907 when he predicted that a coming recession "will probably have a good effect. It will be a good thing to let up the present intense activity." Fortunately for the survival of the system that Mellon so rightly admired, the American people did not agree with him and opted for Franklin Roosevelt's New Deal. Mellon spent the last four years of his life as a private citizen wran-gling with the government over charges of underpaying his 1931 income tax and operating the Aluminum Company of America as a monopoly in restraint of trade. But he didn't let these disputes, in which he would prevail posthumously, interfere with creating the National Gallery, another acitivity that would have had Frick's en-thusiastic approval.

As staunch a supporter of Frick's Republican principles as Mellon was his daughter Helen. Throughout all of her long life—she died in 1984 at age ninety-six—Helen Clay Frick was generous with her inheritance in supporting Republican candidates. She could be even more generous with her moral support. Never as shy of publicity as her father or the other Frick descendants, Helen Clay Frick took to the press in defense of her causes. After giving $10,000 to the Committee to Re-elect the President during Nixon's 1972 campaign, she followed up with letters to the editors defending him during Watergate. In one letter, she wrote that "the Communists and many liberal individuals who have leanings in that direction hate the president and wish to destroy him"; in another, she claimed that "the honor of the country is at stake if we allow our great president to be impeached by congressmen who cannot offer any proof of his wrongdoing."

Miss Frick also went public in defense of her father's reputation. In collaboration with newspaper reporters, she provided laudatory biographies emphasizing Frick's benign presence as a father, his philanthropies, and his ability as an art collector. In addition, she used her money and influence wherever possible to suppress critical comment about him. In 1964, Random House published a book entitled *Pennsylvania: Birthplace of a Nation,* by a distinguished historian, Dr. Sylvester K. Stevens, who was then executive director of the Pennsylvania Historical and Museum Commission. At Christmastime of that year, Dr. Stevens made the mistake of sending Miss Frick a complimentary copy of the book. She quickly looked up the few index references to her father in an otherwise comprehensive review of the state's history, called her lawyer, and filed a suit in equity to prevent further distribution of the book in Common Pleas Court in Cumberland County, site of Dr. Stevens's home.

In discussing the still astounding industrial development with its offshoot of large individual fortunes in western Pennsylvania in the last years of the nineteenth century, Dr. Stevens mentioned Frick in four passages to which his daughter objected. In one he said that Frick had been a member of a church with an "array of wealth, not all of which had been amassed in exact accord with what many regard as Christian principles and practices." In another, he said that "the power of the union was broken in the bloody and disastrous Homestead strike in 1892 by stern, brusque, autocratic Henry Clay Frick." In two others, he said that Frick had built a monopoly in the coal and coke fields, imported immigrant workers, beat down unionization, lowered wages, and taken advantage of the company store and company houses where workers, often paid in scrip, were overcharged. The case, which went to trial before Judge Clinton R.

Weidner in Carlisle, Pennsylvania, in July 1965, created a stir in publishing and academic circles. Such generally held concepts as that the dead cannot be defamed or that descendants of the defamed dead do not suffer damage were being questioned. Dr. Louis B. Wright, executive secretary of the American Historical Association, said that it would be "disaster for historians" if Miss Frick were to be granted an injunction.

It took two years before all the testimony and the judge's personal study of it were completed. Dr. Stevens agreed to drop the material about the Frick church as a matter of "taste" in any forthcoming editions, but in all other respects Judge Weidner upheld him on the grounds that what he wrote about Frick was true. He dismissed the case. A portion of Judge Weidner's decision in this case demands full quotation here because it stands as a *raison d'être* for this book— and, indeed, for all explorations of history in search of guidance for present and future human conduct:

> Miss Frick asks this court to find that her father was and is a well-known businessman and philanthropist. Further, that she has dedicated her life, her business, and their family fortune to perpetuating his memory. Yet on the other hand she does not want the public to know anything further of her father, particularly his role in the industrial times in which he operated, the manner of his operation, or how he amassed a fortune, which she is now devoting to perpetuating his memory. She disclaims any knowledge of his business, his business operations, or his business character and she does not wish anyone else to know anything about it, write anything about it, or speak anything about it, unless favorable and laudatory. She wants this court, after finding that he was a well-known businessman and philanthropist, to further find that to know the details of her father's business dealings would lower her and her father in the esteem of the community, and further, that for the public to know those facts would cause her emotional distress.
>
> Because Miss Frick has, as Henry Clay Frick had done, put the spotlight on his business reputation, the public is now entitled to know all about the facts, not just those she wishes to reveal and are favorable to him, and debate them.
>
> Further, to enable people to understand and meet the con-

ditions with which they are confronted today, particularly industry, labor, and management, the public is entitled to know
the history of the development of these subjects. They are
important topics today and the development of them is of
importance to the student of history, the student of economy
and the student of labor relations. Industrial conditions and
particularly labor relations are current subjects and problems.
The public is therefore entitled to know the history of their
development in order to understand the history and conditions today in those fields.

Simply, Miss Helen C. Frick seeks to enjoin publication
and distribution of the book, "Pennsylvania: Birthplace of a
Nation," in its present form because she does not believe certain statements about her father, Henry Clay Frick, in his
business dealings, but claims they must be untrue because of
the character of his personal relations with her as his daughter.

By analogy, Miss Frick might as well try to enjoin publication and distribution of the Holy Bible because, being a
descendant of Eve, she does not believe that Eve gave Adam
the forbidden fruit in the Garden of Eden, and that her senses
are offended by such a statement about an ancestor of hers.

After briefly threatening to carry the issue to a higher court, Miss
Frick and her attorneys dropped the suit. Instead, they claimed victory because Dr. Stevens agreed to make some minor changes, as,
for instance, changing a statement that Frick built a coal and coke
monopoly in western Pennsylvania by deleting the word "coal." But
the whole action was quite obviously counterproductive to Miss
Frick's intentions and would not go away. In 1984 when she died,
Russell W. Gibbons, vice president of the Pennsylvania Labor History Society, used the failed suit in support of a passionately critical
piece in the *Pittsburgh Post-Gazette.* It, too, demands rather full quotation because the same sentiments were expressed again in 1992
when the centennial of the Homestead strike evoked the name of
Frick.

Noting the extensive coverage given Henry Clay Frick's death,
Gibbons lamented that our criteria for judging achievement seems
to be the same as in the days of Miss Frick's father, Henry Clay
Frick. The attention paid to Miss Frick's death seemed to reflect

that, as before, "we still celebrate the inheritance of wealth more than efforts toward the just distribution of wealth which work produces."

For Gibbons, the story of "old Henry Frick" is interesting for what it tells us about the role of robber barons in our nation's story, who, while making huge profits for themselves as they helped build our industrial might, cruelly destoryed those who tried to make the workplace more humane. Never shrinking from "his role as our first large-scale union buster," Frick sought out confrontation, and found it. And, while the workers won the battle of July 6, 1892, they lost the war. "Those who went back to Carnegie's mills and their 12-hour days, their wretched housing and the fear instilled by Pinkertons, militia and Coal and Iron Police could thank Frick" for effectively crushing the steel industry's union movement for more than four decades. According to Gibbons:

> Few steel workers of those generations had opportunities to visit the New York collections of the masters or even the Pittsburgh collections which Helen provided "to the inhabitants of my hometown."
>
> Just as Henry could postpone but not prevent eventual democracy in the workplace, daughter Helen could buy art and build museums, but not dictate culture.

Dispite all of Miss Frick's generosity from art collections to parks to museums, she could never erase her father's legacy for thousands of Pittsburgh's working families. For them, "he would always be Frick the strike breaker." As recognized by the judge in the historic trial in which she sought to "ban" a book that labeled her father a union buster, Miss Frick's millions could not rewrite history.

Poignantly, Gibbons painted this picture of Frick and his daughter in contrast to Phillip Murray, another man who played a pivotal role in the lives of Pittsburgh's working class, and Mr. Murray's daughter, Elizabeth Lavery Murray.

> The man who in time led the next generation in the mills out of the jungle that Frick had imposed rarely gets equal billing in the sanctioned histories of Pittsburgh progress. Philip Murray left no monuments or museums, no art collections or mansions. He did, however, help to change the lives

of tens of thousands of workers. . . . When Phil Murray's 90-year-old widow, Elizabeth Lavery Murray, died in her modest Brookline home two years ago, there were no obituaries, just the death notice paid for by her family. Elizabeth Murray, however, had no need to spend her remaining years concerned with how history would judge her husband.

Despite Gibbons's bitter comments, Helen Frick's creative care-taking of her father's legacy in art has been effective in softening his image. The Frick Collection in New York particularly earns nothing but the highest praise from the art world. Much of the credit for this must go to Miss Frick, who personally acquired many fine pieces to fill out the collection and founded the adjacent Frick Art Reference Library, a unique and valuable resource for scholars. Other Frick descendants have kept a remarkably low profile. Helen's brother, Childs, died in 1965 full of honors for his scientific achievements. With a scientific bent like his father, Henry Clay Frick II quietly pursued a medical career in New York until his recent retirement. Dr. Frick's sisters and Henry Clay Frick's numerous great-grandchildren haven't surfaced in public print except for appropriate social notices. Although they have undoubtedly all lived comfortably thanks to their ancestor's skill at making money, the behavior of the descendants may be the best evidence that Helen's assertions about Frick in his role of father and grandfather were as true as Dr. Stevens's critical comments on his business practices.

But the same could be said of Carnegie and his descendants, as well as most of the rest of Frick's fellow followers of the gospel of greed. By their lights, they were good people, nice to their mothers and bankers. Why then Frick's grim prediction as to his and Carnegie's destination? Searching for an answer to that haunting question is the challenge that gave rise to this book. Intrigued as I was, I might yet have let Frick lie secure in his copper-lined vault if the echoes of his business ethics and practices hadn't been too loud in the 1980s to ignore. Certainly and perhaps understandably, his family and retainers now in charge of the Frick legacy were not enthusiastic about my search. Unlike the fiery Helen, they did not threaten suit. They simply dodged, twisted, evaded—all actions that arouse suspicion and evoke determination in the searcher. I only regret their reticence insofar as it may have prevented me from adding corroborating detail to my conclusion that Frick's greatest virtue may have been his honesty, his unwillingness to go along with cant and hypocrisy. I think that Frick, in his oblique way, was trying to answer that question honestly, trying to tell all of us about the end to a life devoted to making money by any means, regardless of philanthropic gestures.

Since Frick was never known for caring about poetry—or any literature, for that matter—it is unlikely that he read the works of William Wetmore Story, a Harvard graduate and son of a Supreme Court Justice whose first book of poems came out shortly after Frick made his first million. But poet Story, who was undoubtedly a sensitive observer of a scene in which society's accolades were being bestowed upon emerging millionaires like Carnegie, Frick & Company, penned lines that seem to capture what Frick was finally trying to say:

> *Speak History! Who are life's victors?*
> *Unroll thy long annals and say;*
> *Are they those whom the world calls victors, who won*
> *the success of the day?*
> *The martyrs or Nero? The Spartans who fell at*
> *Thermopylae's tryst,*
> *Or the Persians and Xerxes? Pilate, or Christ?*

Bibliography

BOOKS

Adams, Charles Francis. *Charles Francis Adams: 1835–1915, An Autobiography*. Boston: Houghton Mifflin, 1916.

Adams, Henry. *The Education of Henry Adams*. Edited by Ernest Samuels. Boston: Houghton Mifflin, 1973.

Allen, Frederick Lewis. *The Lords of Creation*. New York: Harper & Brothers, 1935.

———. *The Great Pierpont Morgan*. New York: Harper & Brothers, 1949.

———. *The Big Change*. New York: Harper & Brothers, 1952.

Barron, Charles W. *They Told Barron: Conversations and Revelations of an American Pepys in Wall Street: The Notes of the Late Charles W. Barron*. Edited and arranged by Arthur Pound and Samuel Taylor Moore. New York: Harper & Brothers, 1930.

Bellamy, Edward. *Looking Backward*. New York: Harper & Brothers, 1959.

Beard, Charles A., and Beard, Mary R. *The Rise of American Civilization*. New York: The Macmillan Company, 1933.

Behrman, S. N. *Duveen*. New York: Random House, 1951.

Berkman, Alexander. *Prison Memoirs of an Anarchist*. New York: Schocken Books, 1970.

Brandeis, Louis D. *Other People's Money and How Bankers Use It*. New York: Frederick A. Stokes Company, 1932.

Bridge, James Howard. *The Inside Story of the Carnegie Steel Company: A Romance of Millions*. New York: The Aldine Book Company, 1903.

Brignano, Mary. *The Frick Art & Historical Center*. Pittsburgh: The Frick Art and Historical Center, 1993.

Burgoyne, Arthur G. *All Sorts of Pittsburgers, Sketched in Prose and Verse.* Pittsburgh: The Leader All Sorts Co., 1892.

————. *The Homestead Strike of 1892,* with an Afterword by David P. Demarest, Jr. Pittsburgh: University of Pittsburgh Press, 1979.

Burr, Anna Robeson. *The Portrait of a Banker: James Stillman, 1850–1918.* New York: Duffield & Company, 1927.

Carnegie, Andrew. *The Gospel of Wealth and Other Timely Essays.* Edited by Edward C. Kirkland. Cambridge: The Belknap Press of Harvard University Press, 1962.

Casson, Herbert N. *The Romance of Steel.* Freeport, N.Y.: Books for Libraries Press, 1907.

Cotter, Arundel. *The Authentic History of the United States Steel Corporation.* New York: The Moody Magazine and Book Company, 1916.

Darwin, Charles. *The Origin of the Species by Means of Natural Selection or the Preservation of Favored Races in the Struggle for Life.* New York: Modern Library, Random House, 1993.

Davidson, Bernice; Munhall, Edgar; and Tscherny, Nada. *Paintings from the Frick Collection.* Introduction by Charles Ryskamp. New York: Harry N. Abrams, in association with The Frick Collection, 1990.

Demarest, David P., Jr., ed. *The River Ran Red: Homestead, 1892.* Pittsburgh: University of Pittsburgh Press, 1992.

Dictionary of American Biography. New York: Charles Scribner's Sons, 1919 ff.

Dunne, Finley Peter. *Observations by Mr. Dooley.* New York: R. H. Russell, 1902.

————. *Mr. Dooley Remembers: The Informal Memoirs of Finley Peter Dunne.* Edited by Philip Dunne. Boston: Atlantic Monthly Press Book, Little Brown and Company, 1963.

Duveen, James Henry. *The Rise of the House of Duveen.* New York: Alfred A. Knopf, 1957.

Encyclopaedia Britannica. Chicago, London, Toronto: Encyclopaedia Britannica, 1956.

Flint, Charles R. *Memoirs of an Active Life.* New York and London: G.P. Putnam's Sons, 1923.

Flynn, John T. *Men of Wealth.* New York: Simon and Schuster, 1941.

Fowles, Edward. *Memories of Duveen Brothers.* New York: Times Books, 1967.

George, Henry. *Progress and Poverty.* Fiftieth Anniversary Edition. New York: Robert Schalkenbach Foundation, 1939.

Goldman, Emma. *Living My Life.* 2 vols. New York: Dover Publications, 1970.

Hacker, Louis M. *The World of Andrew Carnegie: 1865–1901.* Philadelphia and New York: J. B. Lippincott Company, 1968.

Harvey, George. *Henry Clay Frick: the Man.* Privately Printed, 1936.

Hendrick, Burton J. *The Story of Life Insurance.* New York: McClure, Phillips and Company, 1907.

————. *The Age of Big Business.* New Haven: Yale University Press, 1919.

————. *The Life of Andrew Carnegie.* 2 vols. Garden City, N.Y.: Doubleday, Doran & Co., 1932.

Hersh, Burton. *The Mellon Family.* New York: William Morrow & Co., 1978.

Hessen, Robert. *Steel Titan: The Life of Charles M. Schwab.* New York: Oxford University Press, 1975.

Holbrook, Stewart H. *The Age of the Moguls.* Garden City, N.Y.: Doubleday & Company, 1953.

Howells, William Dean. *Selected Writings of William Dean Howells.* Edited by Henry Steele Commager. New York: Random House, 1950.

James, Henry. *The American Scene,* with an Introduction by Irving Howe. New York: Horizon Press, 1967.

Henry James and Edith Wharton Letters: 1910–1915. Edited by Lyall H. Powers. New York: Charles Scribner's Sons, 1990.

Josephson, Matthew. *The Robber Barons: The Great American Capitalists: 1861–1901.* New York: Harcourt, Brace and Company, 1962.

Koskoff, David E. *The Mellons: The Chronicle of America's Richest Family.* New York: Thomas Y. Crowell Company, 1978.

Krause, Paul. *The Battle for Homestead.* Pittsburgh: University of Pittsburgh Press, 1992.

Lawson, Thomas W. *Frenzied Finance.* New York: Greenwood Press, 1968.

Leitch, Alexander. *A Princeton Companion.* Princeton: Princeton University Press, 1978.

Linton, Calvin D., ed. *The Bicentennial Almanac.* Nashville and New York: Thomas Nelson, 1975.

Lorant, Stefan. *Pittsburgh: The Story of an American City.* Garden City, N.Y.: Doubleday & Co., 1964.

Lord, Walter. *The Good Years: From 1900 to the First World War.* New York: Harper & Brothers, 1960.

Martin, Frederick Townsend. *The Passing of the Idle Rich.* New York: Arno Press, New York Times, 1975.

Marx, Karl. *Capital: A Critique of Political Economy.* Edited by Frederick Engels. New York: The Modern Library, 1977.

McAllister, Ward. *Society: As I Have Found It.* New York: Cassell Publishing Company, 1890.

Mellon, Thomas. *Thomas Mellon and His Times.* New York: Kraus Reprint Co., 1969.

Mellon, William Larimer, with Sparkes, Boyden. *Judge Mellon's Sons.* Privately printed, 1948.

Morgan, H. Wayne, ed. *The Gilded Age.* Syracuse: Syracuse University Press, 1939.

Morison, Samuel Eliot, and Commager, Henry Steele. *The Growth of the American Republic.* New York: Oxford University Press, 1937.

Morris, Lloyd. *Postscript to Yesterday.* New York: Random House, 1947.

Munhall, Edgar. *Masterpieces of the Frick Collection.* Introduction by Harry D. M. Grier. New York: The Frick Collection, distributed by Viking Press, 1970.

Myers, Gustavus. *History of the Great American Fortunes.* New York: The Modern Library, 1936.

Noyes, Alexander Dana. *Forty Years of American Finance.* New York: G. P. Putnam's Sons, 1909.

O'Connor, Harvey. *Mellon's Millions.* New York: John Day Company, 1933.

Rockefeller, John D. *Reminiscences of Men and Events.* Privately printed, 1909.

Roosevelt, Theodore. *The Autobiography of Theodore Roosevelt.* Centennial Edition. Edited by Wayne Andrews. New York: Charles Scribner's Sons, 1958.

Satterlee, Herbert L. *J. Pierpont Morgan: An Intimate Portrait.* New York: The Macmillan Company, 1939.

Serrin, William. *Homestead.* New York: Times Books, Random House, 1992.

Shaw, John E. *The Frick Building; Pittsburgh.* Pittsburgh: private monograph, 1902.

Sheppard, Muriel Earley. *Cloud by Day.* Pittsburgh: University of Pittsburgh Press, 1991.

Sinclair, Andrew. *Corsair: The Life of J. Pierpont Morgan.* Boston: Little Brown, 1981.

Spencer, Herbert. *First Principles.* New York and London: D. Appelton and Company, 1916.

Steffens, Lincoln. *The Autobiography of Lincoln Steffens.* New York: Harcourt, Brace, 1931.

Stevens, Sylvester K. *Pennsylvania: Birthplace of a Nation.* New York: Random House, 1964.

Stowell, Myron R. *"Fort Frick" or The Siege of Homestead.* Pittsburgh: Pittsburgh Publishing Co., 1893.

Sullivan, Mark. *Our Times: The United States 1900–1925. Vol. II: America Finding Herself.* New York: Charles Scribner's Sons, 1927.

Tarbell, Ida M. *The Life of Elbert H. Gary.* New York: D. Appelton and Company, 1925.

Tawney, R. H.: *Religion and the Rise of Capitalism.* New York: Harcourt, Brace and Company, 1952.

Trachtenberg, Alan. *The Incorporation of America: Culture and Society in the Gilded Age.* New York: Hill and Wang, 1982.

Twain, Mark. *Mark Twain's Autobiography.* 2 vols. Introduction by Albert Bigelow Paine. New York and London: Harper & Brothers, 1924.

Twain, Mark, and Warner, Charles Dudley. *The Gilded Age,* with an Introduction by Justin D. Kaplan. New York: Trident Press, 1964.

Veblen, Thorstein. *The Theory of the Leisure Class.* New York: The Viking Press, 1967.

———. *The Theory of Business Enterprise,* with a new Introduction by Douglas Dowd. New Brunswick, N.J.: Transaction Books, 1978.

Wall, Joseph Frazier. *Andrew Carnegie.* New York: Oxford University Press, 1970.

Wharton, Edith. *A Backward Glance.* New York: Appleton-Century Company, 1934.

———. *The House of Mirth.* New York: Avenel Books, 1987.

PERIODICALS

Bulletin, December 6, 1919, picture and caption on Frick's death.

Carnegie Magazine, May/June, 1993.

Connors, Jill. "The Fricks at Home." *Americana,* April 1992.

Flaherty, Mary Pat. "Let Frick Keep His Mansion." *The Pittsburgh Press,* October 18, 1990.

Frick, Helen Clay, as told to O'Hara, Mary. "My Father, Henry Clay Frick." *The Pittsburgh Press,* August 3–7, 1959.

———. "Henry Clay Frick." *Pittsburgh Quote,* Summer, 1959.

"Frick: A Man Who Fused Steel and Art." *New York Times Magazine,* December 15, 1935.

"The Frick Family Lot." *The Homewood,* Fall, 1992.

Gibbons, Russell W. "Henry Frick: The First Union Buster." *Pittsburgh Post-Gazette,* November 17, 1984.

Hoerr, John. "Mon Valley Legacy." *Pittsburgh Magazine,* June, 1992.

Hubeny, Lisa A. "Clayton." *Pittsburgh Magazine,* June, 1992.

Neidenberger, Mary. "A Place for Children." *Pittsburgh Post-Gazette,* April 21, 1993.

"Pioneer of Progress." *Carnegie Magazine,* January, 1972.

"Pittsburgh's Great Friend Dead." *The Index,* December 6, 1919.

"Pittsburgh Mansion." *Americana,* April, 1992.

Shedlock, Ben. "Life in Frick's Mines." *Pittsburgh Post-Gazette,* November 17, 1984.

Swetnam, George. "The 'Iron Man' Who Played Santa." *Pittsburgh Press,* December 21, 1952.

Van Atta, Robert B. "Business Career of Henry Clay Frick." *Tribune Review,* Greensburg, Pennsylvania.

Walker, John. Review of *Masterpieces of the Frick Collection. New York Times Book Review,* 1970.

Warren, Kenneth. "The Business Career of Henry Clay Frick." *Pittsburgh History,* Spring, 1990.

Wetzig, Mina. "Work of Frick Honored 100 Years After Birth." *Pittsburgh Sun-Telegraph,* June 18, 1950.

Ziaukus, Tim. "Lockout." *Pittsburgh Magazine,* June, 1992.

NEWSPAPERS

The New York Times, 137 entries from January 27, 1888, to May 21, 1967.

Pitt News, November 2, 1966; May 5, 1967.

Pittsburgh Chronicle-Telegraph, February 2, 1922.

Pittsburgh Gazette Times, December 3, 1919; June 19, 1920; July 11, 1922.

Pittsburgh Leader, December 29, 1910.

Pittsburgh Post, July 25, 1892; May 7, 1893; June 9, 1920.

Pittsburgh Post-Gazette, August 10, 1967.

OTHER SOURCES

Hearings Before the Committee on Investigation of U.S. Steel Corporation (Stanley Committee), House of Representatives, 8 vols. Washington, D.C.: U.S. Government Printing Office, 1912.

Interview and correspondence with DeCourcy E. McIntosh, Executive Director, The Frick Art and Historical Center, Pittsburgh.

Interview and correspondence with Edgar Munhall, Curator, The Frick Collection, New York.

Report of the President, December 31, 1920. Princeton: Official Register of Princeton University, 1920.

The Satterlee File on the Panic of 1907. Archives of the Pierpont Morgan Library, New York.

Telephone conversations and correspondence with Dr. Henry Clay Frick II.

"What Mr. Frick Has Done for Princeton." Address by President John Grier Hibben at gathering of New York City Alumni, December 15, 1919, Princeton University archives.

Weidner, J. Opinion in *Frick* vs. *Stevens,* Court of Common Pleas, Cumberland County, Pennsylvania, May 25, 1967.